My Loving Relationships

MY LOVING RELATIONSHIPS

WILLIAM G. EMENER, PH.D.
AND
WILLIAM A. LAMBOS, PH.D.

Nova Science Publishers, Inc.
New York

For permission to use material from this book please contact us:
Telephone 631-231-7269; Fax 631-231-8175
Web Site: http://www.novapublishers.com

LIBRARY OF CONGRESS CATALOGING-IN-PUBLICATION DATA

My loving relationships / William G. Emener and William A. Lambos.
p. cm.
ISBN 978-1-60692-420-4 (softcover)
1. Self. 2. Love--Psychological aspects. 3. Interpersonal relations. I. Emener, William G. (William George) II. Lambos, William A.
BF697.M89 2009
158.2--dc22 2008041229

Published by Nova Science Publishers, Inc. ✢ New York

Dedication

We dedicate this book to our families.

Individually and collectively, you loved us and taught us how to be who we are – loving individuals.

To each of you, in our pasts and presents – you know who you are.

CONTENTS

LIST OF FIGURES

ACKNOWLEDGEMENTS

First and foremost, we extend a hearty "Thank-you!" to all of our past and current clients, who over the years taught us much wisdom – wisdom that not only greatly assisted us in our professional work but our personal lives as well.

In many ways, the high level veracity and integrity of the content this book enjoys is because of the exceptional field-review editing done on an earlier draft of the book manuscript. Commensurately, we shall forever be grateful to Nicole M. Stratis Kratimenos and Andrea Malas for their timely and diligent attention to detail and real-world issues. In a nutshell – Nicole and Andrea, "We owe ya!"

And just when we thought we had a "perfect book manuscript," we smiled in great appreciation for the exceptional wordsmith skills of Dr. Brian Downing, a professional copyeditor extraordinaire. "Thank you, Brian!"

Our respective families – children, grandchildren and loved ones – have been respectfully caring and compassionate when over the past few months we replied to many of their requests with, "Okay, as soon as I finish editing this chapter." Their unerring love did not go unnoticed and to all of them we extend our sincerest appreciation.

A special and genuine "Thank you" is well deserved by Mr. Frank Columbus, President, and Maya Columbus, Director of Acquisitions, and their staff at Nova Science Publishers. They not only offered numerous words of wisdom along the way and helped us with deadlines while maintaining the highest of standards, but they did it with class and epitomized the essence of first-class professionals in the world of publishing.

Bill and *Bill*

Prologue

I'm awake. I'm not dreaming. And what's that noise? A shutter in the wind. Yeah, that's it. We're at the beach. I feel his heartbeat, not just mine. The lungs of two, breathing separately, together. I smell his fragrance...in his hair, in his skin...and those long brown strands of hair framing his square jaw...It must be early. Daybreak. It's Saturday morning and we're here for the weekend. We got in late last night. He moves slightly. Gently kisses me on the hand and then nestles back to sleep with a worriless sigh. "What are we doing today?" I wonder. "Sailing, diving, swimming? He's so cute, so precious." My ultimate adoration of him is revealed in my ever so gentle yet firm embrace of him. Instantly he squeezes back and in his half-sleep purposefully curls his little toe around my little toe. As the shutter gently squeaks with the wind, I doze back to nirvana with a sheepish grin of peace, tranquility, and serenity.

Wait a minute...I am awake. I'm not dreaming. And what's that smell? Bacon. I'd recognize it anywhere. The sound of lapping waves, the rush of a gentle breeze...and what's that chopping sound? Chop, chop. Chop, chop. We're in a bungalow at the beach. Sun's up. It's nine-thirty already. What's that crazy man of mine doing?

"Good morning, handsome!" I yell out with my just awakened crackling, alto voice. "What are you doing?"

Momentarily, he bolts through the doorway, and with the delicateness of a feather lowers his two-hundred pound, aging yet firm body on top of me and whispers, "I love you."

After a rose petal peck on the lips, he rises up and looks deep into my curious eyes and says, almost in a childlike voice, "I'm chopping peppers, of course! I snuck out early this morning and I walked to the store. Bacon, cheese, onions, mushrooms and peppers. I'm going to make an omelet for you that will knock your socks off!" As he caresses my hand, he reaches for my robe and majestically says, "Pretty Lady, your juice, your coffee and your paper await you on the table." I softly fall back in awe...all aglow – the Queen of Sheba, the Princess of Siam and Miss America all rolled up into one. But is this real? Can I trust all of this? Can I trust him...?

* * * * *

I fall asleep alone and wake up alone. This single life really sucks at times. And my deep feelings of abandonment are really getting to me. I'm still so in love with her. I know our divorce was almost two years ago, but I still can see her running out of the house with that big smile, so happy to see me when I'd come home from work. Why did it all happen anyway? It wasn't fair! I'm still so angry about that. Maybe I didn't try hard enough. Maybe I didn't treat her as nicely as I should have. Maybe it was me? I didn't like her when we divorced – no, I didn't like the woman I divorced. But I still can't get the woman I married out of my mind. But I'm getting better. Every day gets a little better. Sometimes I just feel like my feelings of loneliness are starting to turn to feelings of freedom. And this lady I've been dating lately...well, I just better go slow. I don't want a déjà vu. Especially if it was me.

Sometimes it's like my feelings are on the end of a yo-yo. Up and down, up and down. But enough of that for now. It's time to get out of this bed, get some breakfast, and head off to the beach...she said she'd meet me there around 11:30. It's tough. But it's getting better. Or at least I think it is...

These two kinds of scenarios regarding loving take place every weekend – at St. Pete Beach, in the mountains in Vail, and in apartments in New York City. They also take place in the minds and hearts of millions of adults throughout the world every day. If you are an adult, chances are you have felt these ways regarding someone special in the past, in the present, or you may feel these ways regarding someone special in the future. If not, either you have never been hurt or you live under a rock.

An *a priori* philosophical assumption underlying this book is that human beings want, work for and strive to be in a loving relationship. We also assume that if you are reading this book, you are not living under a rock (or if you are, you are at least peeking out from under it). We have enjoyed the wonderful sight of a loved one running out of the house to greet us, the excitement of looking forward to running on the beach, and walking in the moonlight after dinner. We have awakened to the sound of a shutter in the wind and the smell of bacon, and we have chopped peppers early in the morning. We also know what it's like to live under a rock, and as you may know from your own experiences, the trip from the rock to the beach can be hell. Most times it entails risk, awareness, compromise, forgiveness, commitment, and sometimes the scariest thing of all – change. However, if you have any idea of what we are talking about, you also know that it is worth it. It's what life is all about.

In our hearts and souls, we hope that this book is helpful to you.

A sunset shared is more than a sunset.

About This Book

We have read many books over the course of our lives, and during the past fifteen years our readings and writings have included an increasing number of the popular, self-help types of books. As authors, counselors, psychologists and academicians, we also have gained an enhanced appreciation for a book's prologue. Among other things, a prologue provides a generalized background of a book, a sense of who (not just what) the author or authors are, and a global appreciation for the book's content, organization and overall flavor. Such are the primary purposes of the following.

In many ways, what we bring to this book is an extension of us, Drs. Emener and Lambos, the professionals, *and* Bill Emener and Bill Lambos, the persons, the human beings. On the professional side, we have been professional counselors, rehabilitation counselor educators, university-based researchers and scholars for over thirty-seven years. Between us, we also have been licensed psychologists in three different states for thirty-three years. Each of us has dated, married, divorced, remarried, and each has children whom we lovingly watch grow and experience their own loving relationships. As you shall see, throughout the book we share some relevant aspects of our own, unique experiences and trust that you will enjoy the personal side roads along the way. Importantly, we have been fortunate enough to experience both the knowledge derived through scientific inquiry and scholarly learning, and to see it translates into clinical practice and becomes an integral part of the lore of the professions of counseling and psychotherapy. Sets of "common knowledge" emerge among clinicians. Thus, we would like to suggest that this book, *My Loving Relationships*, is truly an extension of us and of our lives. In addition to a blending of our professional and personal lives, each of our experiences has also been unique in the same way that every loving relationship, like every snowflake, is unique unto itself and will never exist in exactly the same way again. In many ways we simply do not know, nor can we pinpoint, where many of the ideas in this book have come from. Thus, let's just consider this book to be a culmination and sharing of the significant aspects of loving relationships that we two have gleaned during our journeys through life.

We would like to talk with you for a moment about the purposes of this book. It is neither our intention to bore you with research data nor demonstrate how we can meticulously cull and reference academic and professional literature. More than anything else, we want to shine a spotlight on some of the significant and critical issues in loving relationships that we have learned from working with our clients. Our work as licensed psychologists and therapists over these many years has often been focused on working with couples. These include married couples working on marital issues, individuals engaged to be married or in exclusive, "significant-other" relationships, and individuals who were separated, widowed or divorced yet trying to deal with numerous aspects of their love life and their relationships. Each of us has spent months carefully going through all of our experiences from more than three hundred clients with whom we worked over a fifteen-year period as psychologists. It is also important for you to know that while we are sharing with you many of the stories from the lives of these individuals, we have used fictitious names and eliminated any special characteristics that might identify any of them by name or association. As we reviewed our cases, we made very careful notes – what we talked about with clients and what critical aspects of loving relationships were important to them in their lives. As a matter of fact, we find ourselves caught up in the observation that many of the aspects of these loving relationships have been true for the majority of the thousands of individuals with whom we have worked over the past thirty-five years. As you will see, we occasionally talk about our own lives here as well. Collectively, we trust that you will find these experiences to embody a wealth of knowledge that will be helpful to you.

A Companion Book

As denoted by the title of and the 18 chapters herein, *My Loving Relationships* focuses on the individual ("I," "me," and "you") issues pertinent to loving relationships. While writing this book, and using a similar investigation and organizational process, we also wrote another one entitled, *Our Loving Relationship*. As denoted by its title and 17 chapters, the companion book focuses on mutual ("us," "we," and "me and you") issues pertinent to loving relationships. The only overlap is in the last few chapters where both books address important aspects of seeking and receiving professional help with relationship issues. We feel that the two books together offer a complete look at the important aspects of love and relationship management. It is equally important to note, nonetheless, that we designed these two books so that they could stand alone – each volume can be helpful to anyone, individually. Of course, if your goal as a reader is to improve your relationships, you will want to learn the material in both books; becoming a "more loving person" will be best be achieved by reading and digesting both books.

By design, this book and its companion book are reader-friendly and provide easy-to-comprehend and appreciate figures, diagrams and other stimulating materials – for thought, for introspection and for understanding about loving, being loveable and loving relationships. We have found that figures are invaluable in our work with clients. Figures concisely illustrate crucial positions, decisions, and tensions in people's lives that can be readily comprehended and used to work on their lives, especially in relationships. We hope that you also find them helpful in your relationships, unique though of course they are.

We conceptualize loving relationships as representing developmental processes, not events! Your process of reading this book will contribute to, enrich and enhance your developmental process. We urge you, the reader, to remember that as is true of nearly every worthwhile endeavor in life, the journey matters as much as, and at many times is more important than, the destination.

SOME CRITICAL *A PRIORI* PHILOSOPHICAL ASSUMPTIONS

Let us briefly address the question, "Why might you be reading this book?" Two reasons are: First, to increase your knowledge of what loving relationships are about. Secondly, and possibly more importantly, to increase your own personal awareness of yourself, your significant others and your loving relationships. Basically, we are confident that you will grow from reading and personalizing the issues raised in this book.

You may be wondering what we mean by two important words: *loving* and *relationships*. For the purposes of this book we have operationally considered a loving relationship as a dyadic, romantic relationship between two people with a special set of characteristics. For example, such a relationship would involve thoughts regarding longevity, sex, family considerations and a sense of "us." We also suggest that loving relationships involve "life transcendence" considerations. They are not necessarily constrained, for example, by the typical limiting issues associated with parent-child, co-worker, boss-employee, and teacher-student types of relationships. However, while many of the issues in this book may also be relevant to these other types of relationships, the issues addressed in this book are primarily focused on adult, dyadic, romantic, loving relationships.

What do we mean by *loving relationships*? The Greeks talked about the difference between *eros* (a love of self), *philio* (a brotherly/sisterly type of love) and *agape* love (a spiritually bonded type of love). While we truly believe that all loving relationships involve some aspects of *eros*, *philio*, and *agape* types of love, the primary phenomena addressed in this book focuses on "agape intended" relationships of adults. As his name reflects, Bill Lambos is of Greek lineage and grew up in an ethnic family that used these Greek terms as household words while growing up.

From time to time, loving relationships also tend to have special considerations such as status, gender, race, age and culture. In the area of status, it could be suggested that during the courtship, engagement, marriage, separation and/or divorce stages of a loving relationship, there are special characteristics and features. It also has been our experience that the critical issues of heterosexual relationships are also equally vibrant and important in gay relationships. Some theorists also have suggested that there are some differences in "same race" and "interracial" relationships. From the perspective of age, it could be suggested that there are some age-specific issues in loving relationships. We do not argue against any of this. Similarly, we agree that there are some cultural peculiarities pertinent to some loving relationships. (If you saw the film *My Big Fat Greek Wedding*, what you saw was not entirely an exaggeration.) Nonetheless, please remember that we wrote this book with a specific focus on those aspects of loving relationships that tend to transcend issues of status, gender, socio-economics, ethnicity, age and culture.

A BIBLIOTHERAPEUTIC APPROACH

You will notice that this book is written with use of the first person. Thus, when we use the word "you," we are specifically referring to you – the reader; when we use the word "we," we refer to ourselves – Bill Emener and Bill Lambos, the authors. In trying to achieve our specific goal of facilitating an enhanced awakening of your own self-awareness throughout the book, we envision each of us talking with you as if we were sitting on a dock or chatting by a fireplace. Nonetheless, we would like to offer a few suggestions on how to use this book.

As you are reading this book, it is our hope that you would invest yourself so that you would come away from it with a better understanding of your thoughts, feelings and behavior as well as the thoughts, feelings and behavior of others in your life. We also hope that it will challenge your ideas, your thoughts, your conceptualizations and your overall considerations of yourself and your past, present and future relationships. Lastly, we trust that this book will help you to come closer in touch with your own feelings regarding yourself, your loved ones and your relationships with them.

If you currently are in a relationship, furthermore, it might be helpful for you and your loved one to read this book together. Should you choose to do this, we would suggest that you read the book the way Dr. Emener for years has suggested to couples with whom he has worked. For example, last week while talking with George and Betty it was suggested that they read a specific book on relationships. Bill suggested that George get a blue highlighter, Betty a yellow one. "George," said Bill, "I would like you to read chapter one of the book. Read it slowly as if it were talking to you, not like you're studying to take a test on it." George smiled. Bill then continued, "And while you're reading it, when something jumps out at you like

'Exactly, that's me!' take your marker and highlight it. When you have finished reading chapter one, give the book to Betty." Betty was then told, "I would like you to read chapters one and two and highlight in yellow those things that jump out at you. As a matter of fact, you may highlight some of the same things that George already highlighted. There's nothing wrong with that. When you have finished, give the book back to George." Finally, Bill turned and said, "George, you then read chapters two and three the same way that Betty read one and two."

A very important aspect of this *dovetail reading* procedure, also called "integrative reading," is the need to establish a few ground rules. First, while you are reading a given chapter and you notice that either of you has highlighted something and you're curious about it, turn to the other person and point to the highlighted materials and say, "Would you please share with me what you were thinking about when you highlighted this?" The second ground rule to which it is crucial that the two of you agree is: Whatever he or she says to you or you say to him or her, you just listen, and when they have finished you say, "Thank you." Period. The objective of this endeavor is to learn, not to win or prove something. This is not the time to start World War III when you look at the other person and say, "See, for years I've been telling you that your parents have always..."

We also have found that when we discuss this approach with our clients, both members of the couple usually smile and laugh comfortably. We then share with them that just because something is published in a book, does not necessarily mean it is true for everyone who reads it. The contents of a book should not be used exclusively as a verification or validation that one person in a relationship is "right" and the other person "wrong."

Basically, we are suggesting that you *empathize with the issues, the people we describe and especially yourself.* We will be sharing some experiences from the lives of individuals who indeed may have experienced some of the same kinds of things you are going through. Thus, when we say invest yourself, we are suggesting that if you can feel the pain and sorrow of a given individual, do not hesitate to cry;

if you feel a knot in your stomach, do not hesitate to allow yourself to experience that frustration or anger; and if you can truly feel the joy and ecstasy of some of the individuals we will be telling you about, allow yourself to smile and feel the uplift that may naturally come with it. It is our sincere hope that this book will help you get more in touch with your love – *in* life and *of* life.

It may be true that the most beautiful roses are nearest the sharpest thorns. Nonetheless, we submit that loving is an adventure... a beautiful adventure.

* * * * *

I still can't get the man I married out of my mind
But every day gets a little better
Sometimes I feel like my feelings of loneliness
are starting to turn to feelings of freedom

* * * * *

A sunset shared is more than a sunset

THE ROAD AHEAD

We begin our journey through loving relationships by looking at what most of you, our readers, will consider the most important part of every relationship in which you find yourself – *you!* "Wait a minute…" you may protest, "aren't loving relationships about two people, perhaps even more about the *other person* than about me?" Our answer is, "Yes and no." True enough – a loving relationship is between two people. And for some, the noblest aspect of love is the opportunity to place the happiness of your partner above your own needs and desires. So, if these statements are true, how can the most important part of such a relationship be you?

The answer is both illuminating and pragmatic. If you are reading this book, one of the reasons you are likely doing so is because you want to understand more about your own relationships – past, present and future. We further assume that you not only want to better *understand* your relationships, but to discover the means through which to *improve* them as well. This being the case, logic dictates that we focus first on those aspects of our relationships that we can *control* – and that, dear reader, is all about the one part of the romantic dyad over which you have the most influence and control: you. If this answer makes sense but leaves you feeling like the "you" or "my" part is only half the story, recall that this book is one of a companion set of two volumes. The companion book, *Our Loving Relationship*, is all about the "us" or the "we" aspect of loving relationships.

Thus, the truth is, in order to understand our relationships, we must first learn about ourselves. Doing so will lead to understanding the sometimes complex roles we play in them. A relationship offers each partner innumerable choices of thoughts, feelings and behaviors pertinent to and about it. We will see during this part of our journey that we, as individuals, have far more latitude than is normally acknowledged in *choosing* our thoughts, feelings and behaviors. We will discover in this book that the nature of any loving relationship depends more on how it is *perceived* than how it "really is." And one of the more important things we will attempt to convey to our readers that *you can choose* how to perceive many aspects of your relationships.

Unfortunately, making such choices is not as easy as snapping your fingers and deciding to opt for one choice over another. If it were, there would be no reason for a book such as this one. Rather, in order to able to choose one perspective (and its accompanying thoughts, feelings and behaviors) over another, you must first understand the underlying nature of many aspects of daily life that we take for granted as "common sense." As we all have discovered at one time or another – quite frequently, common sense isn't all that common. Moreover, as we shall see, common sense involves thousands of tacit, or unspoken and even unrecognized assumptions that can blind us to the possibilities and choices in front of us. Relationships, as we shall see, are rife with such possibilities. Understanding them and learning how to choose among them, is the major focus of this book. This explains why this volume of the companion set is about *you*. Understanding your own relationships requires rich understanding of (1) how you perceive them, (2) how you think, feel, act and react in them, and (3) how you can choose to do so differently and for the better.

The following eighteen chapters begin with the subjects of *self* and *relationship analysis* and proceed through the roles played by *your past* – a past that accompanies you into every new relationship you enter. We also introduce the subject of *behavior analysis*, allowing you to see, understand and appreciate the causes and consequences of the relationship-oriented actions you take. This leads us to take a look at the old trap of either-or thinking, called *dichotomous thinking*, and the problems that can be avoided by understanding that things in relationships typically come in many shades of gray and how that usually is a *good* thing. This, in turn, allows us to take a look at *feelings and emotions*, which are never all-or-none (though we sometimes mistakenly assume they are). We then examine the inevitable *patterns and trends* in relationships, the cycles over which our thoughts, feelings and choices of behaviors vacillate. We also look at *divorce and separation*, but from the perspective of *you* and how you understand, experience and cope with it. This places us in good stead to look at how a variety of negative emotions can block happiness and interfere with, or even destroy, loving relationships, namely *guilt and shame, fears and phobias, depression,* and *grieving*. We then turn to the roles played by variables arising from the passage of *time* and the importance of *timing* in relationships. Finally, we look toward the rewards of understanding the above intricacies, namely *happiness and joy*. We end the loving-specific chapters with a look at relationships in the 21st century and how they have been impacted by the influence of the Internet, both for better and for worse.

Finally, the last three chapters are about something that every self-help book should take seriously – how to get more help when self-help isn't enough. Some years ago, seeking advice from a marriage counselor or therapist was associated with no small stigma and often was something done privately, even shamefully – if at all. In addition, seeking the services of a family mediator was only done for purposes of dissolving a marriage or relationship. We are happy to report that this has changed for all but a few people, and the need for professional help is no longer considered an admission of personal weakness or relationship failure. In fact, participation in therapy or relationship mediation has come to be considered just one more of the myriad of typical activities of daily living for many members of our complex society. Indeed, the so-called "Baby Boom Generation" (to which your authors belong) and those that have followed, Generations

"X" or "Y," have been collectively referred to as the "therapy society" (is there a "Z" yet?). Anyone who doubts the veracity of this claim need only wander into the self-help section of any bookstore or search for titles in the on-line book sites such as Amazon.com to find that books are available with titles such as *One Nation Under Therapy*, *Pet Loss and Human Bereavement*, *The Mental Health Job Explosion*, *Caught in the Net: How to Recognize the Signs of Internet Addiction*, and *Mediation Therapy: Short-Term Decision Making for Couples and Families in Crisis* (and yes – all of these are real books).

In this section of *our* book, we will neither assist you in overcoming the loss of a pet goldfish nor advise you to seek the services of professional "karmic debt management specialist," but we will endeavor to offer some down to earth advice on what we consider useful information about finding and benefiting from professional help. These three chapters will help you with important matters such as:

When to start seeking professional assistance.
Who or *what type* of professional to look for.
How to go about finding professional assistance that *meets your needs*. And,
When to stop seeing or employing the services of a professional helper.

Bill Lambos often likes to recall the single greatest unresolved question about the practice of counseling and therapy he faced during his clinical training: *Why should simply talking to somebody ever be expected to help anybody?* This may sound tongue-in-cheek, but for someone originally trained as an experimental psychologist with a narrow focus in Pavlovian conditioning and animal learning, it was a valid question. Following four years of clinical retraining, including years of detailed study of the brain and more years yet in his practice as a licensed clinical neuropsychologist, Bill found the answer to his question. Simply stated, every human being constructs his or her own reality based on perceptions. These perceptions are determined by an enormously complicated interplay between genetic inheritance and life experiences, and together they determine not only one's reality but also what one *thinks* about it, how one *feels* about it, and how one *acts* towards it. To wit, every one of us must create our own private, internal narrative or life story, made up as we go along, to deal with the challenges and requirements of daily existence. Sometimes, perhaps even often, our narratives and the perceptions they engender are inefficient, inappropriate or even harmful to ourselves and/or to others, and yet we remain stuck with them. If the narrative is to remain a functional tool for interpreting our perceptions – including, of course, those perceptions of *ourselves* – then in response to the changing demands of daily life, this internal narrative must be flexible and ever-changing.

All too often, unfortunately, our ability to adapt our perceptions and our narrative to our current needs can falter and become stuck in a rut, as it were. In such cases, a professional who is trained and experienced in talk therapy, counseling, family mediation or a related discipline can help us fashion a better narrative, realign our perceptions so as to find meaning where none existed before, and thus create a happier and healthier reality and existence. Bill Lambos knew his "earth-shattering insight" was of great value when, upon explaining all this to his teenage daughter, she looked at him as if he were an idiot and simply said, "Yeah… are there really still people who haven't figured that out, Dad?" More input, which certainly was less caustic and of even greater value, came from sharing this insight with his colleague and coauthor. Bill Emener respectfully listened, then wryly replied, "While I do not disagree with your 'earth-shattering insight,' just remember, my friend – it's not *the* answer… it's *your* answer."

If all this seems like a lot to digest, we agree that it is. Do not expect to read and understand all of this material in one sitting. We suggest that after each chapter or two, you make some notes for yourself, either mental ones or better yet on paper, and go back and revisit them before reading the next chapter. Throughout this book we return to the importance of *processing* new ideas, learning to relate them to existing ideas and incorporating them into your existing knowledge, beliefs, patterns, feelings and emotions. Such processing takes both time and attention. We urge you to give the subjects herein their fair due. We strongly believe that the benefits gained in improving and sustaining your own loving relationships will be well worth the energy spent.

With this map to the road ahead in hand, we are ready to start our journey proper. We turn to the content of the book and trust that you will be better able to provide *your own* answer to the above question, as well as any others you may still have after reading what we have to say therein.

Chapter One

SELF ANALYSIS

In this chapter we will begin our journey by starting with the most important person in a loving relationship – *you*. It repeatedly has been our experience that most people in loving relationships tend to focus on the other person and/or the relationship, and they spend a paucity of time focusing on themselves. The nine subsections of this chapter are designed to help you address some very important questions regarding yourself, such as: (1) *Why is it important for me to pay attention to myself? (2) What is the difference between* what *I am and* who *I am? (3) How does my brain relate to how I feel? (4) Is it possible that I sometimes consider myself too important? (5) What is the role of physical attractiveness in the loving relationship that I am in? (6) Am I a multi-tracker or a uni-tracker? (7) Am I a high-maintenance or low- maintenance type of person? (8) Am I a pursuer or a distancer? (9) To what extent is my ability to trust myself an indication of my ability to trust another person?* Obviously, there are numerous additional questions that could accompany these nine. Nonetheless, this chapter is designed to assist you in developing a clearer, richer and more accurate understanding of yourself – especially as your understanding of yourself relates to your involvement in loving relationships.

THE IMPORTANCE OF ME

It is our contention that there are three things that we pay attention to when we are involved in a loving relationship: (1) ourselves, (2) the other person, and (3) the relationship we create and maintain. We will be discussing these in greater detail later. If you will notice, however, we begin with the importance of paying attention to ourselves. This is critical. We are not suggesting, however, that we should be narcissistically involved in ourselves to the extent that we are unaware of the other person or our relationship with him or her.

When we talk with our clients, we frequently ask them if they have ever been in an airplane. We remind them that what typically occurs is that while the plane is taxiing out to the runway the flight attendant stands up front and gives specific instructions regarding what to do in case of an emergency. The flight attendant says, "Should an unexpected reduction in oxygen occur in the cabin, oxygen masks will come down from the ceiling." The attendant also tells us that if we are traveling with a small child, we are to put our own mask on first. There are many reasons for this – primarily, we must make sure that we are able to take care of the child. In the loving relationships in which we have been involved, we have frequently wondered: If the other person is not able to take care of himself or herself, how could he or she possibly take care of me?

In a loving relationship, the most important thing that you offer to the other person is yourself. We assume that if you love the other person you would want to give him or her things that are good, things that are the best that they could be. Therefore, if the most important thing you offer the other person is yourself, it intuitively would make sense that you would want to be the best that you could be. The bottom line is that when you are in the process of attending to various, important aspects and considerations of a loving relationship, it is important to always be aware of yourself.

What I Am and Who I Am

Throughout our lives, we play many roles and engage in numerous activities that contribute to "what" we are. For example, people frequently tell us that they are a police officer, a school teacher, a mechanic, a receptionist and a variety of other occupational whats. Sociologists have a special term for this, called a person's "master status." We also are mommies and daddies, aunts and uncles, brothers and sisters, golfers, tennis players, friends, and a variety of other non-occupational types of whats – that is, we also hold several other statuses through which we additionally define ourselves. It also is not uncommon to hear people describe their loved ones with "what" pronouns. For example, "I am married to an accountant." "My fiancé is a librarian." And, "My boyfriend (or girlfriend) is an excellent tennis player." The famous psychologist Albert Ellis has stated as a central part of his theory (called "Rational Emotive Behavior Therapy") that it is a mistake to define oneself in these ways. According to Dr. Ellis, we mistakenly equate one or more of these statuses (instead of how we act, especially toward other people) with what we are. It is more accurate to define ourselves less upon the basis of our various statuses and more on the basis of how we behave. This is simply a different way of stating that frequently we do not accurately attend to the "who" we are or the "who" other people are.

While recently addressing these phenomena with the members of a counseling group he was running, Bill Emener said, "Okay Jerry, we clearly know **what** you are. Nonetheless, **who** are you?" Jerry paused, stared out the window, turned and replied, "You mean since my divorce last year?" Bill said, "Yes." Jerry looked down at the floor then back out the window, and with a sullen voice said, "I think what is contributing so much to my depression is that *I am a family man without a family*." In a similar fashion, Bill remembers Linda recently saying to him, "Yes Dr. Emener, I know **what** I am. I am a very, very successful **what**! What is sad for me, however, is that *I am a loving woman with no one to love*."

Similarly, a client of Bill Lambos, Anna, recently asked him if she should divorce Phil, her husband of 25 years. She then added emphatically, "Dr. Lambos, Phil isn't the same man I married. He used to be motivated and energetic, but now he just lies around and watches television every night. That's not the type of person I want to spend the rest of my life with." Again, Anna was focusing on her husband's habits of recent years and defining **what** Phil had become rather than how and why he was behaving as he had been.

You may know the words in a country song, *There's Nothing more Beautiful than a Woman in Love.* We would like to suggest that this is not a gender-specific aspect of life. We would add, "There's Nothing more Beautiful than a Man in Love." While recently talking with one of our clients about a difficulty she was having at work with her new supervisor, she concluded the session by saying, "The suggestions that you offered me and the new ideas I have with regard to how to improve my relationship with my new supervisor are very helpful. I thank you. But you know, Dr. Emener, things right now are going so well with Ed and me, that to some extent this really doesn't matter that much. I guess that when you are loving, when you have someone to love and when you feel as incredibly loved as I do, the eight-to-five and the Monday-to-Friday kinds of things are relatively easy to take care of." When we hear clients say this, we often cannot help but smile in appreciation.

Physiological and Emotional Considerations

Today, neuroscientists and psychologists know an enormous amount about how the human brain and body interact to create the felt experience of emotion. Perhaps more importantly, scientists have learned that the human experience cannot be understood without appreciating the role feelings and emotions play in our ability to navigate even the simplest tasks of daily living. We are going to take a short detour to look at this topic. Don't worry – this is interesting stuff, and won't be too scientific or dull. Read on and be surprised!

A popular idea offered in many science fiction shows and novels (e.g., the *Star Trek* series comes to mind) is that people-like entities, e.g., "Mr. Spock" or the cybernetic "Mr. Data," can be just like humans, except devoid of emotion. Although this makes for some interesting entertainment, the fact is such beings could not exist at all and behave as they do. It is now well understood that emotions play a central role in every human decision and behavior, no matter how trivial. There is simply no such thing as behavior or thoughts that do not contain an emotional component.

As we said, this is a book about relationships and not the neuroscience that underlies the human condition. Therefore, our focus on the role played by physiology in relationships, will be somewhat superficial – just enough, we hope, to inform you how what is known about the subject guides us in understanding relationships from a non-technical and human-level perspective.

The best way of appreciating this is to learn just enough about the brain to see why emotion and physiology are so central to the human experience. Despite being the most complex structure in the known universe, with its billions of nerve cells and trillions of connections among them, the brain is *functionally* divided into a much smaller subset of parts. As depicted in Figure 1.1, looking at the head from the side (i.e. looking at the ear), there are three main parts. These are not the same as the "lobes" you may have heard of. Roughly speaking, the back half of the head is specialized to recognize the outside world. Think of this area as the "world parser" or "world identifier." The front of the head is charged with making decisions that meet our needs, including the need to maintain successful relationships and terminate bad ones. This "executive" part of the brain constantly receives information about what is happening outside (from the back part), and then has the job of acting on that information or just ignoring it.

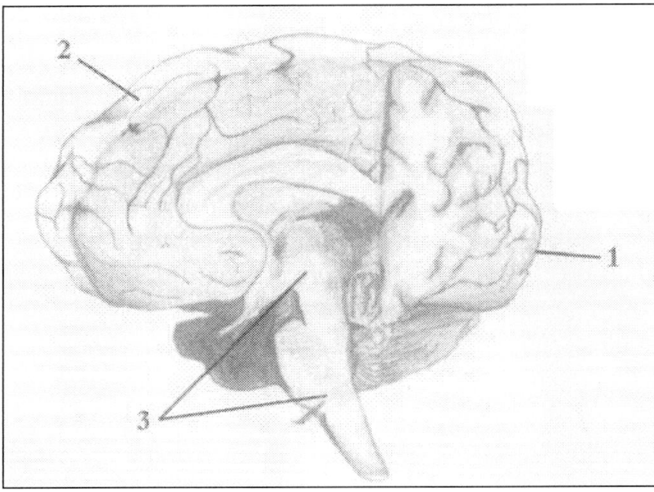

Figure 1.1. A View of the Human Brain from the Side.

Finally, between the back and front halves and below the ear lie the centers of emotion – the so-called limbic system. This part of the brain assigns "values" such as "good or bad," or "I want it!" or "Ugh! Get away!" to what the back of the brain detects in the world. The front of the brain uses these values in every step of the decision-making process. The limbic system also controls our level of arousal, from deep sleep to hyper-focus and concentration. The "values" assigned to what we sense in the world determine in large part how aroused we need to be in order to properly react to it. When the limbic system senses something dangerous "out there" (e.g., a poisonous spider), we become very physiologically aroused and take immediate steps to get away from it (or perhaps to freeze in place so it might not see us). When the limbic system determines that the thing out there is desirable (i.e. that gorgeous single-looking guy at the bar), we similarly become aroused and take steps to approach it ("Hi there, handsome!").

In both cases, as well as the vast majority of instances in between the really bad and really good, we cannot make even the simplest decision whether to freeze/avoid, approach, or ignore what we sense in the world without this limbic value processing. Thus, there could never truly be a Mr. Spock or a Mr. Data – such a being could never decide how to react to the world using logic alone. Living organisms simply cannot make sense of their environment without assigning values to it. And in the human experience, those values constitute emotions.

Now you, our reader, may be ready to ask, "Okay, so how does this help me understand myself and my loving relationships with other people?" Good question! The answer is that some combination of our genes and our lifetime of experiences determine how we value every aspect of both ourselves and the people with whom we relate. This in turn determines our level of arousal. Both the "good versus bad value" and the "level of arousal we feel" are central in determining the decisions we make in responding to other people and their actions.

Think for a moment about other people you know who are particularly adept at interacting successfully with others – the "people persons." Whether they are really good at the bar scene or highly effective leaders in business or politics, what they have in common is that they have learned how to sense what others want or need of them, *and* how to appropriately respond to get what they are looking for. They do this well because they have learned to regulate their level of arousal so that it is always appropriate for the situation, and they have a great deal of knowledge about both themselves and the others they relate to. It sounds simple, but as most of us know, relating successfully with other people is truly more art than science. And a big part of the art comes from self-knowledge and the ability to control one's own arousal and emotions.

So much for the science lesson. The main point of this section is that for readers who want to understand *why* they feel a certain way when they do, this offers a simple yet intuitive explanation. And what about controlling these emotions? Well, that's what much of the rest of this book will help you do.

SELF-INFLATION

Our self-concept, self-esteem, and overall sense of self-worth are very important aspects of our lives. It is also important, nonetheless, that we temper our self-concept and sense of self-worth with some reality. When Bill Emener was talking with Julia and she was sharing some aspects of her relationship with Frank, her fiancé, she frequently was using the expressions, "When I did this, he did that. And I know he did that because I did this. And if I could only do this, then he would do that." After hearing a number of these types of scenarios, Bill chose to use some paradoxical intention and humor in his response to her. He said, "I have the feeling that everything Frank does, in fact everything that everyone around you does, is a function of you. That makes sense. What the hell – you're the center of the universe!" Being a very intelligent and quick-witted young woman, she instantaneously looked at him and said, "Of course, Dr. Emener, that's the effect of your modeling!" They both enjoyed a hearty laugh.

In our attempt to understand ourselves better, our significant others and our relationships, it is important that we be careful of those times when we fall into the trap of believing that everything other people around us do is a function of us. On the contrary, it is typically the case that people around us do things totally independent of us. Our brief digression into emotion reminds us that people are motivated primarily to meet their own needs. Knowing that difference – that others do not base their realities on us – is probably the most important difference of them all. As Julia was leaving his office, she asked Bill if there was anything else he would suggest she do. Bill looked at Julia, smiled and tongue-in-cheek quipped, "Sign up for a course in astronomy." "What?" Julia asked with a furrowed brow. After a pause, however, she smiled and through a laugh replied, "The sun really is the center isn't it?"

PHYSICAL ATTRIBUTES AND ATTRACTIVENESS

We have known many individuals who felt that if they had strong feelings with regard to any preferred or "necessary" physical attributes of a current or future "significant other" then they were a shallow individual. "Why is this being shallow?" we ask. In the ideal world, when you love another individual, you love the whole person – not just one part of them. Nonetheless, it has also been our observation that prior to the development of a loving relationship between two individuals, in most cases they tend to find each other physically attractive. During a therapy session, one of our clients prepared a chart similar to the one in Figure 1.2. She was suggesting that there are some men whom she dislikes or finds distasteful, in

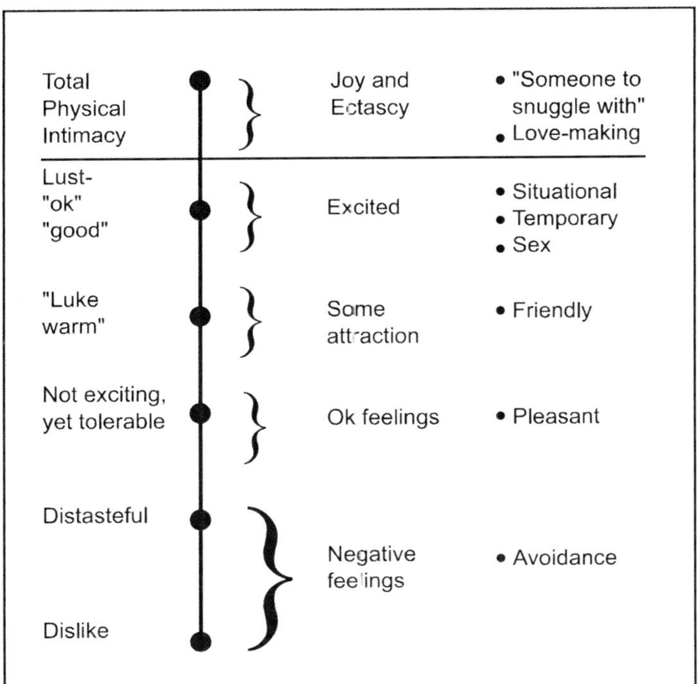

Figure 1.2. Physical Attributes and Attractiveness Issues.

terms of their physical attributes and appearance. She tends to have negative feelings toward them and avoids them. Moving up her continuum, it can be seen that at the other extreme there is total physical intimacy, where she would feel joy and ecstasy. She also said that this describes someone with whom she would enjoy snuggling and someone with whom she would enjoy making love. It is interesting to note how she separated love-making from sex. We specifically chose this area, physical attributes and attractiveness, as an important consideration for two reasons: (1) it is important for a person to be clearly aware of how they feel about the physical attributes and physical attractiveness of another person with whom they may be contemplating having a loving relationship; and (2) it is also important to be realistic in terms of the extent to which we may want or expect a person to modify or to change their physical attributes and appearance. For example, it may be unrealistic to expect a fifty-year-old woman, even with cosmetic surgery, to look like a thirty year-old, or for a longtime couch potato to look like a marathon runner, even if he jogs regularly. This consideration surfaced during a group discussion in which Joan said, “In terms of his physical attributes, I can tell you very quickly that I love everything about Mark. There is nothing about him that I do not love and cherish. Simply said, in terms of this discussion, I love his body the way it is.” Vince, in his typical wry and humorous way, turned to Joan and quipped, “Joan, that’s great. I am very happy for you. But since Mark is six-foot-eight, I really hope that you like tall men!”

Multi-trackers and Uni-trackers

As we have suggested earlier in this chapter, some people are tall and some people are short, some people have black hair and some people have brown hair, and some people tend to be heavy set and some people tend to be slender. People are different. Likewise, some people tend to be multi-trackers and some people tend to be uni-trackers. Multi-trackers have the ability to handle multiple tasks simultaneously, while uni-trackers can only handle one at a time. Scientists know that these differences are due to how our brains are wired, typically from birth, and they also play a large role in certain conditions such as ADD/HD and obsessive-compulsive disorder. From the viewpoint of the brain, they reflect tendencies or preferences toward what is called *sustained* versus *divided* attention styles.

As displayed in Figure 1.3, and with the following scenario regarding Jane, an attorney who came to see Bill Emener because she was extremely frustrated with her husband Alex, the concepts of uni-tracker and multi-tracker and of sustained versus divided styles of attending to the world should become clear to you. "On almost a daily basis, Dr. Emener, I simultaneously pay attention to my job, my three

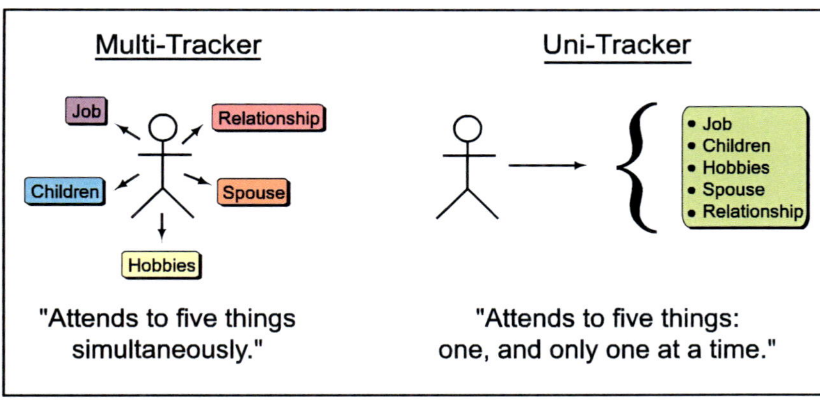

Figure 1.3. Uni-Trackers and Multi-Trackers.

beautiful children, and my hobby, which is playing tennis. My husband Alex and I also pay attention to our relationship. I can attend to all five of these things simultaneously. For example, while driving the children to little league practice, I can also be thinking about my job, and on the way back, I can think of stopping at a store to pick up a special treat for Alex. Alex, on the other hand, drives me crazy. Whatever he does, he does it incredibly well. The only problem is that he can only do one thing at a time. For example, if he is trying to negotiate a new contract at work, where he is a construction supervisor, it seems like that's the only thing he can do until the contract has been finalized. If the children or I talk to him, or if I want to go to dinner with him, he is preoccupied. It's like he's somewhere else, out in space." Bill quickly suggested to Jane that she and Alex might want to talk about this at their earliest opportunity. His sense was that Jane was continuing to become more and more frustrated with Alex, she was interpreting his uni-tracking lifestyle as an indication that he did not care about her or the children, and that she was feeling alone with an increased sense of responsibility to take care of everything.

In a subsequent session, Jane and Alex discussed this and it was very helpful to them. For example, Jane committed herself to trying to be more patient and understanding of Alex, and Alex committed himself to trying to be more multi-tracking in his lifestyle.

In a general sense, we are suggesting that it is important for you to be aware of the extent to which you and your loved one may be a multi-tracker or a uni-tracker. Furthermore, try your best to be aware of the extent to which any differences between you and your loved one might have an impact on your relationship. For example, Alex shared with Jane that to him her multi-tracking lifestyle appeared to be very chaotic, shallow and at times out of control. "Sometimes it seems that you just focus on getting things done rather than on getting things done right or with any attention to quality. Sometimes this really frustrates me," Alex added. In the final analysis, it was helpful for both Jane and Alex to understand each other's lifestyles and how their differences impacted each of them and their relationship. Neither style is necessarily better than the other, but understanding one's partner's style and that it may differ from one's own, can help greatly to reduce relationship problems.

High-Maintenance and Low-Maintenance People

We use the terms *high-maintenance people* and *low-maintenance people* to represent the extent to which a person needs attention from, or needs to be in contact with, their loved one. A couple Bill Lambos recently saw, Peter and Anita, were in trouble and Peter was ready to call off their engagement. He knew that if he did not call Anita every day, two or three days would go by without him hearing from her. To Peter, this was a sign that Anita was not committed to the relationship. Anita was stunned when she heard this. Her response was, "Peter, I think about you all the time, but I just assume you'll call me if you need something until our next scheduled time together."

In a similar example, Victor and Carla came to see Bill Emener because they were beginning to get very frustrated with each other. And since their wedding date was set for only seven months away, they felt that this was a good time for them to figure out what was going wrong. Victor said to Bill, "I don't understand Carla at all. Sometimes we can go for two or three days without having any contact with each other. She doesn't leave messages for me on my answering machine, she won't give me a call at work just to say hello. And even though I know that sometimes she works late into the evening, she will not return my phone messages until the following afternoon." Bill said to Victor, "It sounds like sometimes you wonder if she really loves you. You almost sound as if you are feeling abandoned." Victor replied, "That's exactly it. Sometimes I feel lost and lonely without contact from her." Carla, on the other hand, said, "I don't know what's wrong with Victor. He has to realize that I work two jobs. I have a day job and then I do some typing in the evenings. I'm also caught up in the arrangements for our wedding and I try to work out at the gym three nights a week. It seems like if I don't see him or talk to him everyday, he goes ballistic!" Bill looked at Carla and said, "Carla, it sounds like sometimes you feel smothered by Victor. Maybe you also are wondering if he is just a little insecure about your relationship when he acts this way." "Sometimes it's just too much!" she quickly replied.

Later, with some clearer understanding of each other as well as the establishment of some boundaries and limits, they agreed that before ending a telephone conversation or departing from seeing each other that they would always try to indicate to each other when they would call or see each other again. Basically, the two of them were able to identify a more comfortable relationship lifestyle. As indicated in Figure 1.4, Victor was able to lower his maintenance needs and Carla was able to increase her maintenance responses. Thus, they were able to identify a comfort zone for themselves.

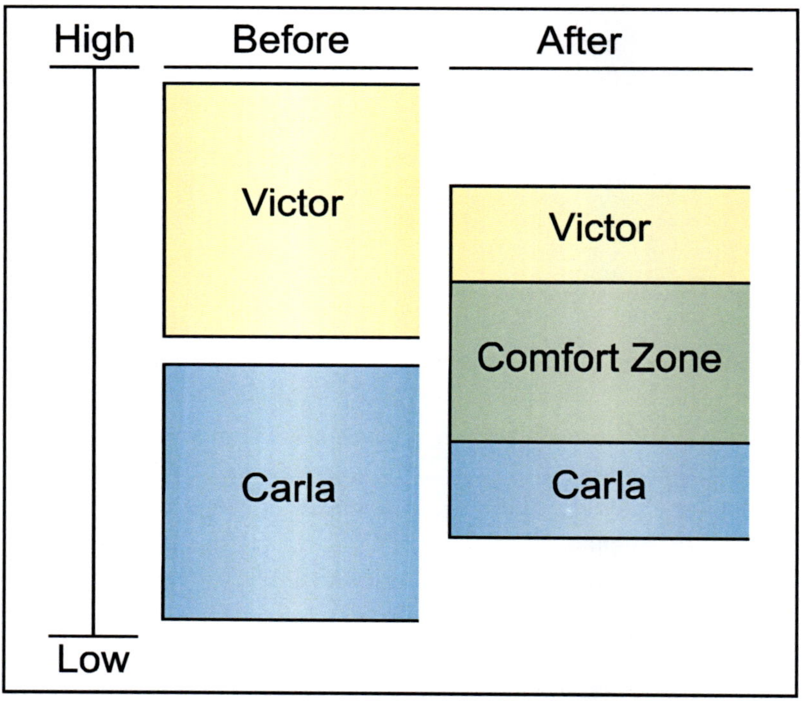

Figure 1.4. High-Maintenance and Low-Maintenance People.

It is important for us to be cognizant of our maintenance needs, the maintenance needs of our loved ones, and the extent to which our relationships attend to our needs, desires and wants in these areas. As Carla and Victor experienced, by talking about it and working out arrangements so that your relationship can get into a comfort zone, bigger troubles can be avoided.

PURSUERS AND DISTANCERS

A *pursuer*, also known as a chaser, is a person who in a relationship tends to be the one always making things happen, initiating contact with the other person, and assuming responsibility for making plans for everything they may or may not be doing. On the other hand, a *distancer*, also known as a runner, is a person who tends to sit back and wait for the other person to make things happen, to wait for the other person to contact him or her, and to wait for the other person to suggest plans for what they may or may not do. Basically, it is important for you to remain aware of the extent to which you are a pursuer or a distancer and the extent to which your loved one is a pursuer or a distancer. Furthermore, it is critical for you to be aware of the "interaction effect" of your two individual styles. For example, if George is a pursuer and Mary is a distancer and they both feel comfortable with that, chances are that they will not experience any difficulties in this area of their relationship. However, if they are both pursuers, they may be tripping over each other all the time, and if they are both distancers they may eventually not have a relationship because neither of them will contact each other frequently enough. Sometimes it is very helpful for couples to talk openly about their pursuing and distancing. For example, a pursuer can easily feel hurt and ignored by a distancer, and a distancer can easily feel smothered and trapped by a pursuer. When discussing this phenomenon with one of our colleagues, she suggested an interesting little phrase, "Don't lunge after a gerbil." Basically, she was suggesting that if you have ever tried to catch a gerbil you quickly discovered that the more you chase it the more it runs away. Sometimes the best way to catch a gerbil is to sit down quietly and turn your thoughts to other things, and eventually the gerbil will find you.

ME AND YOU – SELF AND YOU

In your process of self-analysis, you may be wondering, "Why am I paying so much attention to me?" We often find it helpful to suggest to clients that their ability to trust their significant other is ultimately an indication of the extent to which they can trust themselves. The further we discuss this, the clearer it normally becomes that this is true. As a continuance of this perspective, we also have wondered, *Is my ability to love you an indication of the extent to which I can love myself?* If this were carried further, other postulates also could be considered: *Is my ability to understand you an indication of my ability to understand myself? Is my ability to take care of you an indication of the extent to which I take care of myself?* Each of these questions may not necessarily be valid questions for all people. Overall, however, we strongly suggest that whenever we ask ourselves any questions regarding what we can or cannot do with, for, or on behalf of a loved one, it might be important for us to ask ourselves to what extent are we able to do such things with, for and/or on behalf of ourselves.

* * * * * *

Sigmund Freud theorized that two-thirds of our lives reside in our subconscious. Without the functionality of our defense mechanisms, such as repression and denial, most of us couldn't make it through the day. Nonetheless, a major challenge in life, à la Socrates, is to "know thyself." Pertinent to loving relationships, it very well may be that *my ability to understand you and our relationship is highly contingent upon my ability to understand myself.* The philosophy underlying this critical interface between one's self and one's significant other is poignantly illustrated in Shakespeare's compelling tragedy, *Hamlet*, where (Act 1, Scene 3) Polonius says to Laertes:

This above all: to thine own self be true,
And it must follow, as the night the day,
Thou canst not be false to any man.

Chapter Two

RELATIONSHIP ANALYSIS

As couples counselors, when we agree to take on new clients, we explain that neither person alone is considered our client. Rather, our client is the two individuals *and* their relationship. Although this may sound unusual, we have found it to be the most effective approach to helping couples.

Why does this approach work? Even though there are many angles to the issue, the simplest answer is that when two people decide to come together as a couple, they must do so in the context of a set of shared assumptions and rules (often tacit, implicit and even unrecognized) that define their relationship. When they seek relationship counseling (or "couples counseling" or "marriage counseling"), they are looking for professional help in fixing or improving their relationship. If either person felt that the relationship did not need help and/or that they had an individual issue that needed to be addressed, they would not have come as a couple. Thus by the very fact that they have come for assistance together, the counselor knows that the issue is likely to be with their relationship.

Treating the relationship as "the identified client" (to use counseling terminology) has many benefits and cuts to the core of the matter. It also helps counselors from being viewed as biased toward one or the other of the two individuals. On the other hand, if "the identified client" is the *relationship*, then the counselor better have a solid understanding of relationships, including when, how and why they work effectively or become dysfunctional. He or she also must have goal-specific strategies and techniques, or *interventions*, for making them healthier. Helping you understand what constitutes both healthy and unhealthy or poorly functioning relationships, is the primary goal of this chapter.

A House Built on One Stilt or Many Stilts

Chuck and Nancy had been married for almost a year and were living in a very nice apartment not far from Chuck's family in Tampa. Nancy's family was in Minneapolis. She had moved to Tampa shortly before their wedding. When they first came to see Bill Emener, it was clear that Nancy was incredibly frustrated with Chuck. It was her contention that Chuck did not value her or their relationship as much as he should. Indeed there were numerous aspects of Nancy and Chuck's relationship that were addressed in their sessions. However, an early breakthrough occurred when she said, "If he would only pay half as much attention to our marriage as I do, everything would be okay." Bill asked them to tell him about their individual lives over the past year, and especially over the past three months. He specifically asked them to share their typical activities on a daily and weekly basis. After listening to each of them, Bill suggested that it was clear that they loved each other very much, even though their individual lifestyles were discernibly different. He then drew for them the little sketch that is in Figure 2.1. "Nancy," said Dr. Emener, "You are devoting almost one-hundred percent of your energy to your relationship with Chuck. You are enjoying your opportunity to stay at home during the day, exercise on a regular basis, and prepare some of the most scrumptious meals any man could hope for. There is nothing wrong with your life, except for the fact that you are practically living in a house that is built on one stilt – your relationship with Chuck. When you were in Minneapolis, you had numerous friends who you went out with, your family was nearby, you had a job with several co-workers whom you enjoyed, and yet you paid attention to your relationship with Chuck even though it was long distance. But look at what you have now."

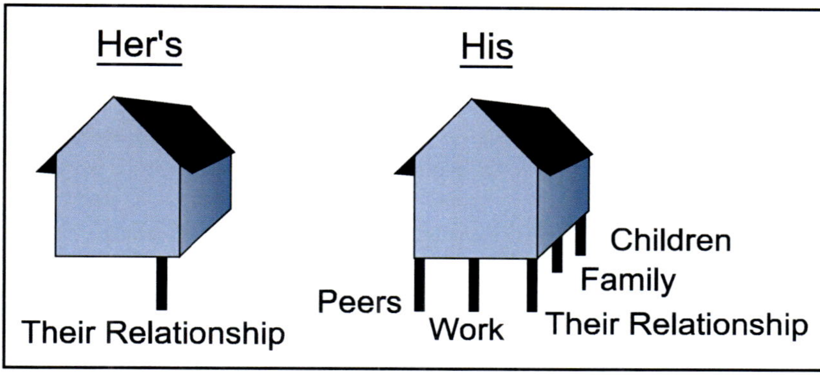

Figure 2.1. A "House" Built on One Stilt
Compared to a "House" Built on Many Stilts.

Nancy looked at the diagram, and through a smile said, "Yes, I see what you mean." Bill then pointed to "Chuck's house," and said, "Chuck, if I understand your life, it appears that you have a house built on five stilts. You have your peers, your fellow attorneys with whom you enjoy spending time, you enjoy your work and its various job tasks, you obviously pay a lot of attention to your relationship with Nancy, you spend a lot of time with your mom, dad, and two brothers, and you also attend to your two children from your first marriage. You basically have a variety of things to which you devote not only physical time, but psychological time." Chuck also smiled and said, "I understand. Yes, that's the way it is for me."

Further in the conversation, Nancy related that it was true that she was paying so much attention to their relationship that she had forgotten about other important aspects of her life. Chuck volunteered that he frequently felt pressure and "a tremendous amount of responsibility for Nancy." He had sensed that she was devoting too much energy to their relationship. In terms of the "house built on one stilt" phenomenon, it was clear that when Chuck and Nancy would have a minor argument, Nancy would immediately get scared, go into a tailspin and become very upset. In a very insightful way, Nancy offered, "Yes, I can understand that. When something seems to be going wrong with Chuck and me, I flip-out. I go crazy. It seems that what I might need to do is to develop some friendships, look for a job so I can go back to work and broaden my interests." Chuck looked at her lovingly and said, "Nancy, I would really like to encourage you to do that. Not only would that be more helpful for us and our relationship, but it would be so much better for you. I want you to be happy. I love you, Nancy."

It is important that we take time to see to what extent our house is built on one stilt or many stilts.

DEPENDENCE AND INDEPENDENCE

It repeatedly has been clear to us that partners can be confused in terms of what is an act of *dependence* and what is an act of *independence*. For example, Bill Emener was counseling a couple, Beverly and Nate, in which Beverly offered numerous instances in which the two of them did what Nate wanted them to do, and she was upset because she felt that she was constantly complying with what he wanted to do. Furthermore, Nate shared a number of instances in which one of them would purposely go just the opposite way. For example, when he looked at Beverly and asked, "The other night when we were watching television, did you put that movie on because you wanted to watch the movie, or did you put the movie on simply because you knew I wanted to watch the basketball game?" She said, "I wanted to watch *that* movie." He turned away with frustration and grimaced in disbelief.

Bill then drew for them a diagram similar to the one in Figure 2.2 and explained, "When we comply with another person or anti-comply with another person, it is still an act of dependency because our decision to comply or anti-comply is still dependent upon what the other person wanted, said or did. At the other end of the continuum is independence, where we do what we do because that's what we want

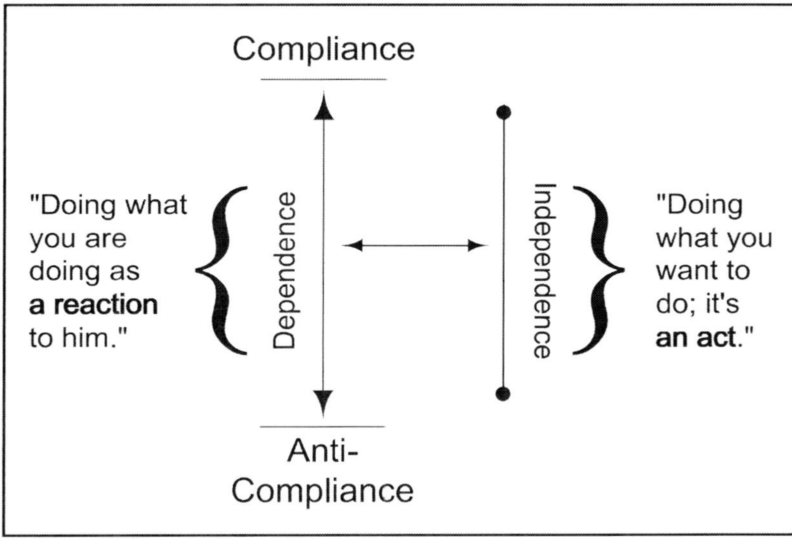

Figure 2.2. Relationships among Compliance and Anti- Compliance, and Dependence and Independence.

to do, not as a compliant or anti-compliant reaction to the other person." At the end of their conversation, it was clear to Bill that they understood what he was sharing with them. They did ask, however, if Bill could comment on the differences among doing things for me, doing things for you, and doing things for our relationship. Depending upon an individual's motivations, intentions and verbalizations, the differences among these three can be obvious. Using Nate as an example, Bill offered the three following illustrations:

When Doing Things for Me: "Beverly, if it's alright with you, tomorrow I am going to call a travel agent and see if we can get a weekend special at the beach somewhere down south. We can leave here Friday night and come back Sunday night. As you know, I have had to work the last two weekends and at least two or three nights each week. I really feel worn-out. I need to get away. If it's alright with you, it would be great if we could do this. I simply need to get a break. As I said, I need to get away."

When Doing Things for You: "Beverly, I know that for the last two weeks you have been taking care of your mom almost every evening and spending most of the weekends with her. I think you need an opportunity to get away. If it's alright with you, I'm going to call a travel agent tomorrow to see if we can get a weekend special at the beach down south. I think you just need to get out of town for a few days."

When Doing Things for Our Relationship: "Beverly, I know for the past couple of weeks the two of us have been running hectically almost twenty-four hours a day. Given my work, your work and your mother's illness, you and I have been like two ships passing in the night. If it's alright with you, I am going to make reservations for us to go to the beach for the weekend somewhere down south. I feel like the two of us just need the opportunity to get reconnected and back together again."

Both Beverly and Nate were able to understand Bill's illustrations, even embellishing them by suggesting it is not only important for people to understand their motivations and intentions but also that they honestly, openly and clearly articulate not only *what* they want to do, but also *why* they want to do it and *when*.

My Need for Someone in My Life

In the process of your self-analysis, it might be important for you to glean some estimation of your need to have someone in your life. For example, Bill Emener vividly remembers Jack, a man who had been divorced three years prior to his seeing him, and who recently had ended a six-month relationship with a woman with whom he was very much in love. Bill very quickly realized that Jack was the type of person who felt much better about life when he had someone with whom to share it. Bill sketched a diagram similar to the one in Figure 2.3. Jack clearly was able to see what parts of his life were devoted to

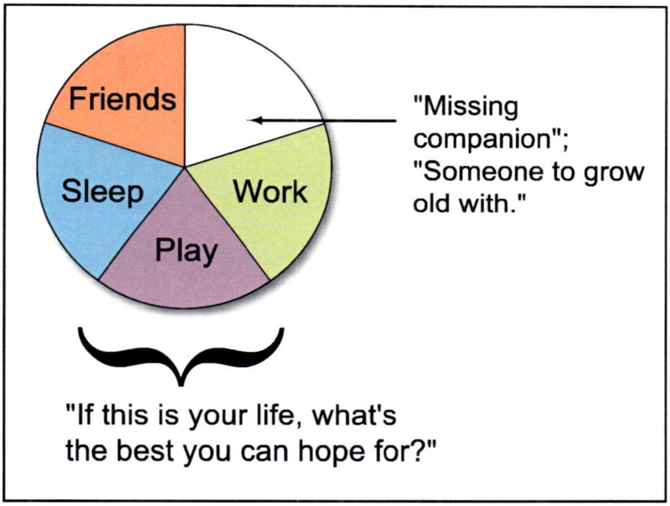

Figure 2.3. Living an Unbalanced Life without a Special Someone.

his friends, to sleep, to play, and to work,and that there was a "missing piece of pie" that he referred to as "a missing companion." Jack also shared with Bill that the one thing he was hoping for at the age of fifty-five was "someone special to grow old with." This realization was somewhat comforting for Jack. To wit, he said to Bill, "If this is my life, one in which I would simply desire to have someone to share it with, then at least I know what the best is that I can hope for... that is, a life without someone special to grow old with."

If in view of your philosophy of life you find your life much more meaningful when you have someone to share it with, then in the absence of such an individual you may occasionally feel a little off balance, unfulfilled and incomplete. There is nothing necessarily wrong with this. However, we think Jack offered a good suggestion when in such a situation: "If that's the way it is, then I better make sure that all of the other pieces of my life are the best that they can be. If all I have are lemons, then I better do all I can do to make the best lemonade I can." Unfortunately, many people don't follow Jack's advice. Instead, they imagine that whenever they are unable to get what they are looking for *right now*, it defines a catastrophe. The results of such *irrational beliefs* typically are some combination of anxiety or depression, which then causes them even more problems in managing relationships.

PUBLIC SPACE AND PRIVATE SPACE

It is very important for people in loving relationships to remain cognizant of their need for, desire for, or preference for spending time in what we refer to as *public space*, *private space*, and *together space*. As depicted in Figure 2.4, public space is representative of where (and when) we are doing things with other people. Private space is

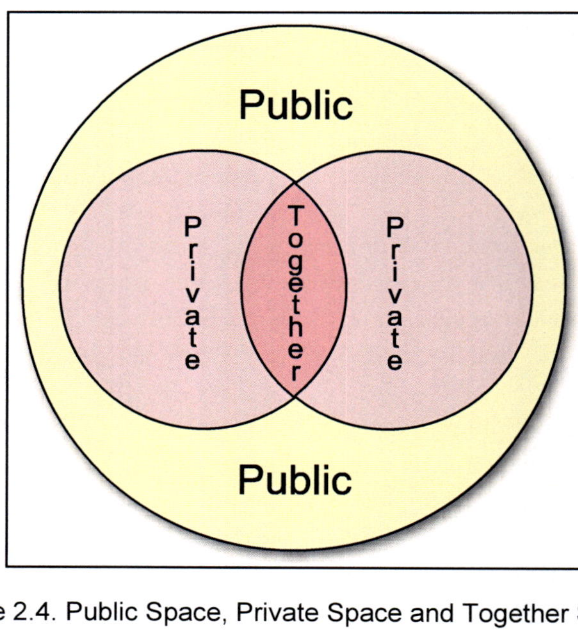

Figure 2.4. Public Space, Private Space and Together Space.

where (and when) we are doing things alone, by ourselves, and usually by choice. Togetherness space is where (and when) we are doing things exclusively with the person with whom we are having a loving relationship. When the *amount of time*, the *percentage of time*, and the *when of the time* we spend in these spaces (e.g., on a daily basis, weekly basis, monthly basis, etc.) are commensurate with our needs, preferences and desires, then we tend to be happy (or at least happier). Difficulties occur when the *way*, *how*, *when*, *where* and *with whom* we spend our time are less consistent with what we prefer, need or want. For example, consider the following illustrative statements that we occasionally hear people make:

- "Sometimes I just wish that Alice and I could spend more time doing things with other people. I would enjoy going to concerts, picnics and dinners with other people."
- "I really love John very much, but sometimes I just like to have some private time for myself. I wish he could understand that!"
- "Monica and I really get along well. We give each other time to have privacy and spend some time alone, and we also spend time with other people. However, it really would be helpful if sometimes we could do things, just the two of us. The truth is that sometimes I just need to have Monica all to myself."
- "Alex and I seem to have everything worked out pretty neat. We have a lot of good friends with whom we spend time. We give each other time for ourselves, like sometimes when I just enjoy curling up on the couch to read a book by myself or like when he enjoys going to the driving range to hit golf balls by himself. And yet, we also make time to do things together, just the two of us – we have fun together and stay connected."

From an overall perspective, it is important for each person: (1) to be aware of his or her own needs, desires and preferences for public space, private space and together space; (2) to be aware of their loved one's needs, desires and preferences in these three areas; (3) to remember that from time to time our needs, desires and preferences in these three areas may change (or have to change due to external causes); and (4) to actively assure that their relationship sufficiently accommodates each of them.

My Need to Be Fought For

Over the years, we have observed that some people have a high need to feel fought for. To some extent, in a loving relationship this is an indication for validation of their loved ones feelings for them and their own perceived sense of worth. This became vividly clear to Dr. Emener when he was talking with Henry, a forty-five-year-old car salesman who was grieving over his recent divorce. Henry had been married for twenty-three years to Beth, a forty-four-year-old bank teller. When Bill asked Henry to tell him about his pain, he shared the following:

"For the past ten years, I felt that she had shut down with me. I didn't feel genuine affection from her – she gave it all to the children. I felt emotionally abandoned. I also felt that she didn't value our relationship or me. She enjoyed the big house, the fancy cars and the nice vacations my money provided. Okay, it's true that I was the one who filed for divorce. But I actually felt that she had emotionally divorced me ten years prior. If I ignored her, she would act hurt and the kids would feel sorry for her. I had affairs, which I honestly felt she knew about, but again she just acted hurt, and the kids felt sorry for her. When I told her I wanted a divorce, she said, 'If that's what you want, Henry, there's nothing I can do about it.' I figured that she didn't care enough about me and our relationship to do anything about it."

Bill asked Henry, "What were you hoping she would do?" Staring out the window and painfully fighting back tearful eyes, he said, "I was sitting in the hallway of the courthouse waiting to be called by the judge. I kept looking down the hall. Even my attorney asked, 'Who are you looking for?' My fantasy was that Beth would come running down the hall, like Dustin Hoffman in the movie *The Graduate*, saying, 'Henry if you think I'm giving you up this easily, you're crazy! Whatever it takes, I'm not giving you up. I love you too much. I need you… No, I don't need you – I want you! Where's that judge? I'll just tell him. Let's work it out Henry. I'm going to fight for us. Not for your money or anything else. I'm going to fight you for you'."

Bill never met Beth, yet he was sure that she had her side of the story. However, Bill did suggest to Henry that she may have wanted the divorce more than he did. Based on our experiences as couples counselors, it is not uncommon to find that the person who files for a divorce isn't always the one who wants the divorce more.

The one thing that Henry recognized, nonetheless, was his need and strong desire to be occasionally fought for. In the absence of overriding psychopathological issues, such as a serious psychological disturbance or mental health problem, there is nothing wrong with a need or desire to be fought for. It might be helpful to remember, however, that if your need or desire to be fought for is relatively high, then it may be a good idea to select a partner who is a fighter and that he or she considers you worth fighting for. The most important thing is for you to be aware of your need or desire in this area and how it impacts your relationships with those you love.

Don't Give Up You

Successful and enduring relationships are those in which each person's needs, wants and desires are more or less balanced with those of the partner. In our experience, many relationships have failed because one of the two partners decided that maintaining the relationship was more important than continuing to be the person they were when the relationship started. For example, Catherine and Jim, a couple who came to see Bill Lambos to discuss whether or not they should split up, were asked to explain the pros and cons of each choice. Catherine was clear and forceful, and spoke first. "Dr. Lambos," she said, "when I met Jim, he was so independent I wondered if he even liked me very much. But he always kept in touch and kept asking me out, and so we got involved – and I was thrilled! But after about three months, he started to act as if he was afraid to do anything without my input and approval. When I told him to just make a decision and do what he wanted, he looked hurt and told me he wondered whether I cared about him anymore. This, from a guy who played it so cool for so long!"

Jim then spoke. "After I got comfortable with Cathy, I realized how empty my life had been. It was like I was only happy if I knew she was happy – with everything! Yet the more I try to please her, the more irritated she seems to get with me. What am I doing wrong?"

Bill asked the couple to do some role playing, in fact to reverse their roles and pretend each was the other person for a few minutes and have a conversation about going out that evening. Cathy was quite the actress when playing Jim's role, and for a while Bill was afraid her sarcasm would hurt Jim's feelings deeply. To Bill's surprise, Jim was just as up to the game and did a shrewd imitation of Cathy sounding like she was sick of his doting on her. After about ten minutes, both Jim and Cathy looked at one another and started laughing. Jim said, "Boy, I must really sound like some kind of weasel half the time – I had no idea!" Cathy quickly replied, "Jim, listening to you imitate me – I'm lucky you didn't dump me a month ago. I can be really insensitive."

Bill subsequently told them both that what had happened was that Jim lost himself and stopped being Jim, because the relationship became so important to him. However, by giving up his identity for the sake of the relationship, he was actually putting it at risk! Bill also told them that if they wanted to stay together, and it seemed they did, Jim had to agree not to give up who he was, and Cathy had to gently remind him if he started doing so again.

Six months later, Bill received a note from Jim and Cathy thanking him for the single session and letting him know that they were still happy and engaged to be married. We sometimes joke that we would make more money by being less effective and making sure relationships took longer to fix! In truth, of course, it matters little; in reality, few relationships are so easily repaired.

Relationship Pros and Cons

If you are thinking about the topics we have covered in this chapter, you are probably thinking about how they apply to your own relationship (if you are in one). We would like to end the chapter with an exercise that may help you learn more about it.

Figure 2.5 includes a chart we have asked many of our clients to fill out. The exercise consists of making three lists of three to six

Things About My Partner...		
I Like, Love and Cherish	I Wish Were Different and It (or They) Okay	I Wish Were Different and It (or They) Need Fixing

Figure 2.5. Three Lists to Assess My Relationship Pros and Cons.

items each. The first is a list of those things you love about your partner and wouldn't want to change. The middle column is for listing things you wish were different about your partner, yet you can live with them. The rightmost column asks you to write down those things about your partner you wish were different, but these are things that need to be fixed for the relationship to continue. You may have nothing to list in this last column, but many couples who seek the help of a professional counselor typically have at least one item in that area.

Once you have filled in the chart, you may want to look it over and weigh the pros, so-sos and cons about your relationship. The more items cluster to the left side, the healthier your relationship probably is, at least from your point of view. The more that the chart is skewed to the right, the higher the chances that your relationship has serious issues that should probably be addressed.

Of course, your chart gives only half of the story. Your partner will have his or her own lists in each column; to get the full picture of the relationship, both you and your partner need to fill in the worksheet. Then, with the understanding that the exchange of information is intended to strengthen the relationship, the two of you should gently compare notes and discuss how each of you can make the other person happier.

Two truisms are often said: (1) "Everything important you needed to know in life, you were taught in kindergarten;" and, (2) "It's not *what* you say, but *how* you say it." As professional couples counselors, we could not agree more with these statements. As you will see in the next few chapters, blaming your partner for the problems in your relationship is a surefire way to guarantee you will damage it. On the other hand, by calmly discussing the issues in your charts and each of you accepting responsibility for your part in the problem areas, a loving relationship can be strengthened immeasurably.

* * * * * *

Socrates said,

"The unexamined life is not worth living."

Emener and Lambos say,

"The unexamined relationship is not worth being in."

Chapter Three

My Past

Both of us have many years of experience counseling clients who sought help for problems with alcohol and/or other substances. Later in this book, we will have more to say about the subject of how relationships can be deeply stressed or destroyed when one or both partners have drug and/or alcohol abuse issues. In the meantime, the subject serves as a good way to introduce the subject of this chapter: how a person's past experiences can influence a current relationship.

Some years ago, Bill Emener accompanied a friend of his to an AA (Alcoholics Anonymous) meeting. It was an "open meeting." During the discussion part of the meeting, one of the gentlemen in said something significant. He humorously yet poignantly said, "If you live your life with one foot in the past and one foot in the future, the best you can hope for is to piss on the present." We understand and agree with this philosophical position; it is important for people to be able to stay in the present. It is important for people to be in the here and now – not only physically but also psychologically and spiritually. Nonetheless, our *past*, as well as our hopes, dreams and aspirations regarding our *future*, affect our present. Indeed, they affect what we are and who we are in the present. Thus, while it is important for us to be in the here and now – to be in the present and to be here in this moment in time – it also is important that we not ignore our past, especially as it is affecting us in the present. When Bill shared some of these propositions with the group, another member said, "My recovery is not contingent upon my ability to forget my past, it is contingent upon my ability to remember and forgive."

In the prologue of this book, when discussing how and why we planned to focus on *adult* loving relationships, we stated that we operationally defined an adult as "anyone over twenty years of age." Our reasons were threefold: (1) individuals over the age of twenty tend to have had sufficient experiences in living such that they now enjoy some sense of independence; (2) they have had some experiences with relationships (personally as well as by observation); and (3) any adult loving relationship that one enters into also includes some leftover baggage from previous relationships. We trust that the meaning and importance of this last assumption regarding leftover baggage will be clearer to you by the end of this chapter. This chapter will describe and discuss some of the critical ways by which *our past loving relationships*, *our past observations* of other peoples' loving relationships, and *our present conceptualizations* of loving relationships (which are highly affected by our past) can significantly affect our present and future loving relationships.

Mom and Dads – Our Primary Teachers

Our parents have taught us, and continue to teach us, directly and indirectly, many important aspects of loving relationships. Possibly because we believe this so much, it is not uncommon for us to say the following to our clients, students and friends:

> Daddies teach their little girls how to deal with men – they teach them many things about loving a member of the opposite sex. Daddies also teach their little boys how to deal with men – they teach them about male bonding.
>
> Mommies teach their little boys how to deal with women – they teach them many things about loving a member of the opposite sex. Mommies also teach their little girls how to deal with women – they teach them about female bonding.

> Together, Mommiess and Daddies teach their children how to deal with loving relationships – they teach them many things about how two members of the opposite sex can love each other, be in love with each other, and be loving toward each other.

In terms of what we know about loving relationships, we consider mothers and fathers to be our primary teachers. Typically, our parents were the ones from whom we first learned our beliefs, attitudes, values and behaviors regarding what it means to be loving, what it means to be loved, what it means to be loveable, and what it means to be in a loving relationship.

Jonathan, a thirty-year-old welder who told Bill Emener that he was "totally confused about many aspects of his relationships with women," came to see him because he "could not figure out why [he] was having so much trouble developing and maintaining meaningful relationships with women." During their first session, they briefly discussed Jonathan's childhood, his relationship with his mom and dad, and what it was like when he was younger and living at home. Their conversation ended with a mutual agreement that it would be helpful for them to spend some time focusing on Jonathan's relationships with his parents and the modeling effect of his parents' relationship on him. Bill suggested a homework assignment to Jonathan. He asked him to give some serious thought to, and write out his answers to, the three following questions:

1. What did you learn about loving relationships from your father?
2. What did you learn about loving relationships from your mother?

and,

3. What did you learn about loving relationships from observing your parents' relationship?

His experience of thinking seriously about these three questions and writing out his answers to them was extremely helpful to Jonathan.

We suggest that you, the reader, also may want to give some thoughts to these three questions. The process of doing so can be very enlightening and helpful. Should you choose to do this, however, please remember that you are doing it to discover more about yourself. That is, you are seeking to understand yourself better. Please do not consider this to be a fault-finding mission! We truly believe that whatever parents do (and don't do) with, for, and on behalf of their children, at the time they are doing what they are doing, (1) they are doing the best they can, and (2) they are not necessarily doing it with any intent of malice. Holding your parents responsible for you and/or blaming them for what and who you are is *not* the purpose of inquiry such as this. In fact, doing so will in all likelihood cause you more problems than any you perceive to be the "fault" of your parents. We trust that you understand and appreciate that it is healthier and much more productive to remember that **you are responsible for you**. As the AA member shared with us at the beginning of this chapter, "My recovery is not contingent upon my ability to forget (my past), it is upon my ability to remember and forgive." If we believe that our parents were our primary teachers, then it also is important for us to remember that if or when we have children of our own, then we also become primary teachers. As parents and grandparents, we suggest that you keep these things in mind as you address these three questions.

LEARNED INTERPERSONAL NEEDS

Ginger, a co-owner of a dry cleaning business, told Bill Emener that she had been "married twice, divorced twice, and currently was fed up with her boyfriend, Jack, whom she had to take care of all the time." During their first session, Bill asked Ginger to tell him about the men in her life. In response to his question, Ginger said, "Hank, my first husband, was an alcoholic and after two years of putting up with his crap I just couldn't take it anymore. I married him right after high school. Maybe I just needed to get away from home… My second husband, Russ, was a real mommy's boy. He thought he was the center of the universe. He was so in love with himself. There was no room in his life to be loving toward anyone else. I was like a slave to him. Took care of him, probably better than his mother did. He used to say to me, 'You're just lucky that I married you.' Can you believe that? Then along came Jack about three years ago. He's the one I'm dumping. Jack's a workaholic. He devotes all of his time to his business – works day and night. But when he's not working, he just expects me to wait on him hand and foot. He also expects me to be emotionally responsive to him all the time. When he comes home, the first thing I have to do is to see what kind of mood he's in. Then I know how I can be and how I can deal with him. But I've had it. I told him I want him out of my house by the end of the week!" Ginger was controlling her anger very well, and without a doubt beneath her anger was a lot of sadness and sorrow. Bill said to her, "Ginger, it surely does seem that the men in your life were emotionally expensive." She began to cry. "What about the other man in your life?" Bill asked her, handing her a tissue, "Your Daddy?"

"I loved my Daddy," she said. "He drank too. Probably that's what killed him. He died about six years ago." As they continued their discussion, Bill asked Ginger to tell him about her relationship with her father. "All in all," she replied, "I had a real good relationship with my Dad. I even think that he felt closer to me than he felt toward my mother. She used to holler at him all the time, especially when he was drinking or mad about something. I just would attend to him. When he didn't feel good, she'd yell at him; I would fix something for him to eat or tell him to lie down on the couch and take a rest." In addition to suggesting some reading materials to her, at the end of the session Bill asked Ginger to continue to think about her relationships with the men in her life.

At the start of their next session, Ginger exclaimed "Between reading this book on codependency and talking with my sister about what you and I were talking about, I think I figured out why I have continued to pick losers! What I learned from Daddy was that if I wanted a man to be nice to me and love me, I had to take care of him. Simple, isn't it. I even became good at finding men who were looking for someone to take care of them – like Hank, Russ and Jack." Subsequently, Ginger and Dr. Emener talked at length about her learned needs and her feeling *responsible*, especially *emotionally responsible*, for the men in her life. "Looking back on all of this, one of the best things I did to help myself," she told him at another session, "was when I wrote that letter to my Dad which you asked me to write. It sounded silly at first when you asked me to write him a letter and mail it to you. He's dead. But my writing that letter allowed me to remember my loving thoughts about him, to no longer feel guilty about how I acted in order to get his love, *and* to choose not to be that way with men any longer. Like I told you when we reviewed the letter, I never want a man, or anyone for that matter, to be dependent on me. Nor do I want to be dependent on him. I want an interdependent relationship with a man."

The last time Bill spoke with Ginger, she was doing very well. She told him she "was dating a man who was so different. He's healthy!" she added with a smile.

Ginger's experiences helped us to truly appreciate how people's relationships with their parents can subconsciously set the stage for how they deal with other people throughout their lives. Fortunately for Ginger, she was able to grow beyond the "bondage" (as she called it) that she learned when she was a child.

PAST PEOPLE, CHARACTERISTICS, AND RELATIONSHIPS

More often than we realize, people will replicate the kinds of loving relationships they have had earlier throughout their lives. Moreover, when such replications occur, people may tend to attract, be attracted to, and have relationships with, similar kinds of people.

As we saw in the case of Ginger, this does not mean people are doomed to recreate their relationships from early life, only that people tend to do so, and will benefit from being aware of the tendency. Family therapists and relationship counselors such as ourselves have a phrase we use to describe this tendency: "the impact of family of origin issues." Let's look at some examples of this based on our counseling sessions.

Bill Lambos was seeing a couple, Jackie-Ann and Patrick, who generally got along but occasionally would come to quarrel so vehemently that one or the other would threaten to end their relationship. In retrospect, they told Bill, the issues were not major ones, but the problem kept recurring because both of them would get to a point where they would "dig their heels in and *insist* on getting their way." After a threat of breaking-it-off was made (sometimes by Phillip, sometimes by Jackie-Ann), one would back down and the issue would be settled… until the next time. Said Jackie-Ann, "Dr. Lambos, what's so frustrating about these arguments is that they tend to be about things that aren't all that important to us. We just get this idea that *we have to get our way*, and then come the explosions."

Dr. Lambos then asked each of them about their relationships with their parents when they were children. Phillip explained that he was from a British family and that whenever family decisions were discussed, his father had the final say – and that was the end of the discussion. Jackie-Ann related that she was reared by a strong woman who was the ruler of the roost. When it came to matters at home, her mother made the final decisions. It occurred to Bill that each of them was carrying the expectations learned from their family of origin into their current relationship. Phillip unconsciously expected that final decisions should be his to make, and Jackie-Ann felt they were hers. When Bill pointed this out, it was an "Aha" moment for them. Once they could see the reasons for their expectations, a plan was hatched. Dr. Lambos, helped the two to divide the areas of their home and affairs into two groups – his domain and her domain. Each ceded final say of one of the two areas and agreed not to challenge the other's final decision in their respective domains. The negotiations were tense at times, but a breakthrough occurred when Phillip allowed Jackie-Ann to have final say in matters of home décor, in exchange for Phillip having final say on the use of frequent flyer miles for vacation planning. To Bill's knowledge, this couple is still together and doing quite well, having been able to change the expectations they had learned from their families of origin.

Then there was Robert, a client who was seen by Dr. Emener. "When I was sixteen years old," Robert said, "I fell in love with Julie and went steady with her for over two years. When I got to college, only about two months after breaking up with Julie, I met and eventually married Barbara. Last May, Barbara and I were divorced, and since last June I have been going with Sherry. But now that relationship seems to be going sour. I don't know, but there's got to be something wrong with me. The same thing seems to happen over and over." To some extent, Robert was right. Dr. Emener suggested to him: "Robert, rather than assuming that there is something wrong with you, I prefer that we assume that based on your life's experiences and what you have learned as a result of living, you are the way you are. And being the way you are and living your life the way you do, it just doesn't seem to work out the way you would like it to. So instead of fixing something that is *broken* or *wrong*, let's just agree that we are going to try to understand how you deal with people in your life and see if there are any changes that you would like to make." Robert agreed with this approach (and seemed to like it better too).

Toward the end of their session, Bill drew a diagram for Robert similar to the one in Figure 3.1. As we looked at the diagram, Dr. Emener said to him, "Based on what you have been telling me, there seems to have been a pattern in your life. When you were sixteen, you felt alone in the world and felt scared of being alone and by yourself. Then came Julie for the next two years. When you got to college, you again felt alone and scared. Then came Barbara. When you were twenty-three, you got your divorce from Barbara and then you again felt scared and alone. Then came Sherry. Now this one is going sour.

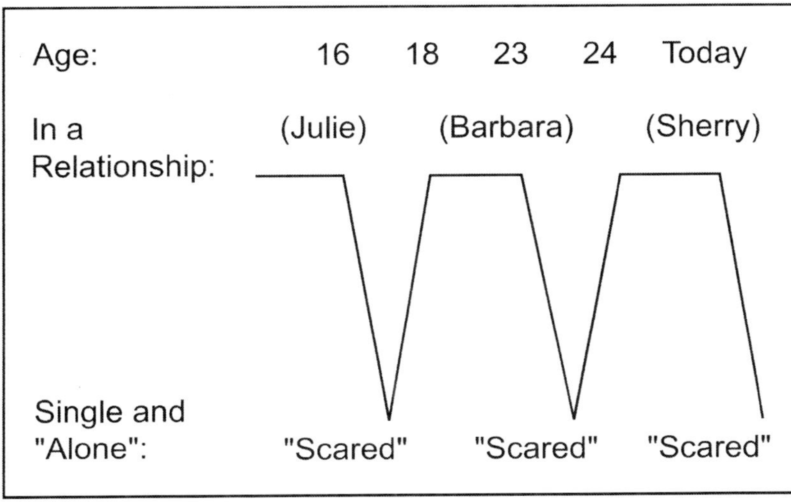

Figure 3.1. In a Relationship for Fear of Being Alone.

How were you feeling toward the end of your relationships with Julie and Barbara, and how are you feeling now that you seem to be toward the end of this relationship with Sherry?" Robert pondered these questions for a few minutes and then said, "Angry… I feel angry and trapped. I also feel lost. I don't know who I am anymore. And I sort of had the same feelings with Julie and Barbara." Then he added, "But if I end this relationship with Sherry, then I know I'll probably just feel scared and alone again. I can't win!"

Bill invited Robert to work with him and try to work through his fears of being alone in the world. For years, his strategy of dealing with his aloneness was to run into another relationship. Fortunately for him, Robert said, "Okay, let's give it a try. I can't just keep doing this for the rest of my life."

A few months and a few sessions later, Robert shared, "I now see how my old pattern used to work. I would establish a relationship. I would enjoy the relationship, possibly even more than the person, but I was enjoying the relationship, not necessarily because the relationship was so great but because it was better than feeling scared and alone. Then I would feel like I was losing me, feeling lost and like I was going nowhere! I would sabotage or actively end the relationship, feel scared and alone again, and find someone else to start the cycle with all over again. However, now that I have been reading some of these books, attending an Adult Adjustment Group and working with you, I recognize my fear of abandonment issues from my past. For the first time in years I can feel good about me, good about being in the world as me. Most important, I don't have to have someone in my life to be able to feel good about me. That, in and of itself, simply feels wonderful!" Robert later added, "And the next time I am in a relationship, it will be because I *want to*, not because I *have to*!"

By analyzing himself and the people as well as relationships in his past, Robert was able to identify and understand his "self-defeating relationship pattern." And from that monumental first step, along with feeling much better about himself as a person, he was able to explore and find new ways of establishing and maintaining more meaningful interpersonal relationships. Occasionally taking time to process similar types of phenomena in our own lives can be extremely enlightening and helpful.

SECRETS

We understand and respect the philosophical position of many people who assume that secrets in loving relationships are bad. They tend to believe that "there is no place for secrets in a loving relationship." However, we prefer an alternative conceptualization – that is, not to consider secrets as being either good or bad. Our experience tells us that it is preferable to allow individuals to decide for themselves what place their secrets have in their lives and relationships. Thus, rather than asking yourself whether your having a secret is good or bad, we suggest that you ask yourself the following six questions:

1. What kind of secret is it?
2. Why do I feel a need to keep it a secret?
3. How do I feel about keeping it a secret?
4. From whom am I keeping it a secret?
5. What effect is my secret having on my loving relationship?
6. What would happen if I no longer kept my secret?

Please do not expect this book to tell you what to do with your secrets. Your life is your life – it's your decision. Your answers to questions such as these six, nonetheless, will be helpful to you in making your decision.

In loving relationships, there are different kinds of secrets: (1) *secret-secrets*; and (2) *not-so-secret secrets.* A secret-secret is a piece of information (for example, a fact, a feeling, or an idea) that is known to you, not known to your loved one, and you consciously keep him or her from knowing it. Sometimes it translates into *lying by omission* (i.e. by not telling something) or *lying by commission* (i.e. by denying it or telling a falsehood). A not-so-secret secret is a piece of information that both individuals know (or think they know) but do not recognize their knowledge of it or talk about it (i.e. we both know something, we both know or strongly suspect that we both know what it is, but we never openly recognize it or talk about it). Again, what you do or do not do with your secret-secrets and your not-so-secret secrets is up to you. However, at times these two types of secrets can have different functional outcomes in a loving relationship. And as you answer questions five and six you may want to consider what kind of secret your secret is. The following are illustrative examples of functional differences between a secret-secret and a not-so-secret secret, as well as how different people handled their secrets.

Donna was terribly troubled by an important aspect of her marriage to Arnie. "There is something about my life that I have never shared with Arnie. It scares me to think about it!" she said. Donna and Arnie had been married for twelve years, they had one child, and "all things considered, we have a good marriage," she added. "However, we always have prided ourselves on our honesty.

We have an open and honest relationship. With one exception. Last year I went to a four-day conference in Chicago. One of my old co-workers who was transferred two years ago to Houston was at the conference. We had a great time going out to eat with the group, dancing at a nearby club and attending the meetings all day. However, I spent the last two nights at the conference in his room. Basically, we had a two-day affair. I feel so bad about having done that! And even though I have worked through my guilt about what I did, I have never done anything like it again, never will, and I feel just as in love with Arnie as I ever did. Possibly even more. What is tearing me apart, however, is that I just can't look Arnie straight in the face. Continuing to keep this a secret from him is killing me!"

In addition to offering some suggestions to Donna, Dr. Emener asked her to think about and write out her answers to the six questions listed above. At their next session, Donna shared her answers to the six questions. It obviously had become clear for Donna: "For me to continue to live with this secret would be worse than what Arnie might say or ever do if I were to tell him." Thus, she decided to tell him. It was very difficult for Donna. It was very difficult for Arnie. The important thing, however, is that Donna had decided what was best for her. Moreover, she determined that what she did also was best for their relationship. "Arnie told me that he thought there was something wrong for a long time, but figured I would eventually tell him." Donna further added, "I told Arnie that the best way of showing my love for him was by not keeping the secret from him any longer. Importantly, he felt my love for him."

For a personal, illustrative example of a not-so-secret secret, we will share with you what occurred with Bill Emener's maternal grandparents. For Easter vacation in 1966, he went home for a visit with his family, especially to spend some time with his Grandma and Grandpa. They lived next door. Unfortunately, however, it turned out to be a very difficult visit. When his grandfather had been in the hospital, the doctors told him that his cancer was spreading uncontrollably throughout his body. They basically sent him home to die. By the time Bill got home to see him, he was bedridden. Grandpa was more than just an avid baseball fan; he probably was the biggest fan the Brooklyn Dodgers ever had. As soon as Bill got home, he went next door to see Grandma and Grandpa. Big smiles and big hugs, as usual. However, when Grandpa and Bill were talking alone, he said, "Willie, promise me you'll take me to Ebbets Field this summer. I want to see the Dodgers play." With a sad face, not only because he knew the Dodgers had moved to Los Angeles in 1958, Bill said, "But Grandpa, you're not well and you're not going to get any better because..." At that moment Grandma came running into the room, pulled Bill aside, and with tears in her eyes whispered, "Please go along with it. Don't tell him. It would break his heart." "Okay," Bill replied. He then turned to his Grandpa and said, "I'll take you to Ebbets Field, Grandpa." Instantly, he smiled and said, "Thanks Willie, we'll have a good time!"

That evening, Bill walked back over to talk with Grandpa. Bill's stomach was in knots. Finally, he couldn't help himself. "Grandpa," he said, "I was talking with my Mom and she said..." At that moment, as Grandma was walking into the room, Grandpa held his finger up to his mouth and said softly, "Shush. We're going to Ebbets Field and that's that. You hear me? And what ever you do, don't tell her. It would break her heart." The truth was that Grandpa knew the Dodgers weren't in Brooklyn anymore and he was dying. Grandma knew it too. But because they loved each other so much, they did not want to see each other hurt. Out of their love for each other, they kept a not-so-secret secret from each other. Bill realized that it was not his place to interfere with that! Bill never went to Ebbets Field that summer. Every day, however, Grandpa and he talked about going. On July 9, 1966, Grandpa died. And for the next eight years, Grandma lived on with a warm glow and the comforting thought that in Grandpa's final hours she loved him with all her heart, by keeping a secret. Importantly, he felt her love.

ONLY-CHILD ISSUES

We have suggested many times that in a multi-child family, as soon as the second child is born the battle begins: the first child fights for what he or she has lost – to be the one and only; and the second child fights for what he or she will never have – to be the one and only. In a multi-child family, the children not only have to learn how to develop and maintain relationships with mom and dad, but with sisters and/or brothers as well. In a one-child family, another consideration may also exist. "Since I am the only game in town (the only kid mom and dad have), it's me or nothing. So if I don't get what I want, I can withhold my attention and affection from them, they'll feel bad, have no one else to turn to, and I'll eventually get my way." We have explored this type of subconscious thinking with a number of our clients, and many of them have sheepishly smiled and said, "Makes sense, doesn't it." We are not suggesting that this is true for all only-child people. Please do not hear that. Parent-child relationships and the types of interpersonal-relationship learning that takes place in one-child families, however, many times tend to be different from multi-child families.

A very famous early psychologist named Alfred Adler, a student and later a colleague of Sigmund Freud, built a theory of personality development around the importance of the being an only child versus having siblings. In the latter case, Dr. Adler also examined how birth order and one's position contributed to one's sense of identity. This, Adler claimed, is especially true regarding how one interacts with other people as an adult. It also has consequences for one's own feelings of inferiority versus superiority. Although for many years Adler's ideas were almost forgotten, today they are witnessing a major resurgence. Neither of us is surprised by this. The following case of Dr. Emener's is an excellent example of why this is so.

When they first met, Gus told Bill that he was fearful that his marriage was slowly falling apart. Gus and Loraine had been married for slightly less than nine years. They had three children. Gus said, "Loraine keeps telling me that I always want to get my own way. And when I don't get my own way, I emotionally shut her out and give all of my affection to our children. She said that for years it was just easier to let me get my own way because she didn't like being shut out. But the other night she said, 'I've finally come to the point where I just can't take anymore of your self-centered, get-my-own-way bullshit.' Basically, I think that she's right. I guess I never realized how I was manipulating her, by withholding affection from her, to get my own way." When Loraine came to one of their sessions, she identified numerous situations in their marriage when Gus would do this. Fortunately, some of her frustration and anger had subsided by that time, she was more understanding of Gus, and even though it was not easy for her to be as understanding as she was, she offered to help in any way she could. It was helpful for Loraine to understand that for Gus it was a matter of a learned behavior pattern: "If I don't get what I want, I pout, I withhold affection, and eventually I get what I want." Her complying with his manipulative behavior for nine years also reinforced his learning. It was not easy for either of them. With some additional counseling, however, Gus was able to better understand the only-child, manipulative way of life that he had learned to use successfully with his parents (as well as with others in his life). Loraine also realized that some of his withholding of affection was not necessarily an indication of how much he loved or didn't love her. It was a learned behavior pattern. She also was learning some effective strategies for dealing with Gus when he wouldn't get what he wanted. The last time they spoke, Gus told Bill that he and Loraine were even starting to humorously refer to his having been an only child as a gentle way of keeping things in perspective. Gus has made excellent progress in his "challenge of growing up," as he called it, and he and Loraine have made excellent progress in improving their relationship.

Not every adult who was an only child has learned to manipulate people as Gus had. If you were an only child or your adult loved one was an only child, however, you simply may want to remain sensitive to the possibility that there may have been some unique aspects of your or your loved one's childhood that may be influencing your relationship.

* * * * * *

Understanding: (1) what I learned about loving relationships from each of my parents; (2) what I learned from my own loving relationships; (3) what I learned from observing other loving relationships in my past (such as my parents'); and (4) how all of this may be affecting me as a person, collectively influence and affect my current and future loving relationships.

Watch your charts and keep an eye on your bow –
make sure you know where you are going.
Look over the stern occasionally too,
appreciate your wake –
it can tell you a lot about you and your boat.

Chapter Four

Behavior Analysis

"You talk the talk, but can you walk the walk?" It is amazing how often we hear people make that statement, and it is frequently expressed with emotion. What is essentially being communicated is a request or urging for another person to quit talking a good game or saying what they will or will not do, and simply translating what they are saying into behavior. "When I see it I'll believe it!" is another typically emotionally-laden verbalization of this phenomenon. One of our clients recently said that she bought a shirt that she wears around the house on Saturday mornings when she and her husband typically do their weekly house chores. It reads in big bold letters, "**JUST DO IT!**" In this chapter we will embark on another leg of our analytical journey and look closely at the importance of consistent behavior, how perception relates to behavior, the difference between avoidance and escape behavior, and different modalities of compensatory behavior.

Importance of Consistency

It is very helpful if our behavior (i.e. what we do as well as what we don't do) is consistent. In loving relationships, especially if the behavior is desired, preferred and important to the other person, the consistency of behavior tends to be, among other things, very comforting to the other individual. When we consider the importance of consistency of behavior in relationships, we are referring to two different types of behavior: actions and expressed intentions. The latter type of "behavior" is what we usually refer to as language, but it is behavior nonetheless (in fact, the famous behavioral psychologist B.F. Skinner referred to all human language as "verbal behavior," and wrote a book named just that). Thus, as we look at the importance of consistency in loving relationships, we shall purposefully address both types of consistency: (1) that people *act* towards each other in a consistent fashion across different times and situations, and (2) that people will act as they claim they will act, and "walk the walk" as well as "talk the talk."

The primary reason that consistency is so important is that it is pivotal to a relationship as being *predictable*. The importance of the ability to predict the actions of others cannot be overstated. When we accurately can predict and anticipate what a person will and will not do, we tend to be less nervous, less anxious and more at ease. For example, a client recently said, "I don't necessarily like everything that Ralph does and I wish that he would actually do some things differently. Nonetheless, he is very predictable! And I have to admit to you that it is somewhat comforting for me because I can always accurately predict Ralph's behavior. I know where he is and what he is doing." On the other hand, when a person's behavior is inconsistent, we tend to find ourselves occasionally walking around on eggshells. The bottom line is that in loving relationships it is comforting and much less anxiety-producing when we can accurately predict what another person will do or will not do, simply because their behavior is consistent.

There is yet another type of consistency: *message consistency*. As noted above, people communicate their feelings and intentions toward one another through actions and language. Message consistency refers to the ongoing degree to which behaviors (actions) and language messages (verbal statements) are consistent with one another. When action and language messages do not communicate the same thing, people become suspicious of one another, and trust breaks down. In such cases of so-called mixed messages, relationships become unstable and partners feel confused or worse.

Recently, Dr. Lambos counseled an attractive couple in their mid-forties whose marriage of twenty-five years with three children was close to ending. (She was seventeen and he nineteen when they married.) There were a number of reasons for their presenting problems, but it became clear within the first half of the session that they were suffering from what is sometimes called the "empty nest" syndrome: their youngest child was preparing to go off to college and the parents had very different ideas as to how their lives should proceed. This is not an uncommon situation for couples counselors, and Dr. Lambos was not overly concerned until he watched the two interact as the session continued. Sitting together on a loveseat, Gary spent much of the session affectionately stroking Sherry's arm and hair. Sherry seemed to like this very much and smiled frequently with each caress. At the same time, however, they spoke of each other with disdain and without regard to the other's feelings. For example, Gary said, "Dr. Lambos, she is shallow and dresses provocatively at best, and like a whore at worst. At the gym she parades around like some kind of spandex exercise-bunny, flirting and flaunting herself at any guy there. It's embarrassing!" All the while he was saying this he continued to stroke her hair and look at her lovingly. Sherry responded, "Gary is like a ball and chain – I have friends, he has none. I work at my massage therapy business and make as much or more as he does, and then come home and clean and cook before he gets home. He waltzes in, eats, doesn't help with the dishes or laundry, and promptly lies down on the couch with his only friend, the remote control, and that's it for the night until bedtime. If I ask him to come out with me and meet some friends at a local hangout, he is uninterested and won't go. But if I change into my after-work clothes and go out by myself, he tells me I dress like a slut and am probably having an affair. I really want to leave him, but I know he loves me and it's very hard to do it." Meanwhile, she was holding his hand throughout this description of their daily interaction, gladly accepting Gary's caresses.

This was perhaps the largest discrepancy between verbal and nonverbal behavior Dr. Lambos had ever witnessed. The level of message inconsistency was hard to reconcile even for an experienced counselor. Dr. Lambos expects to be seeing this couple for quite some time, and although he believes they love one another and that the marriage can be saved, their communication patterns have to be addressed before any of their other issues can.

Bill Emener recalls a couple that struggled with a different kind of inconsistency, yet equally as troubling to a relationship. When Roberto and Marta first came to see him, they appeared to be incredibly frustrated with each other. Marta was especially frustrated and very angry with her husband Roberto. For example, in the first session she said to him, “Roberto, you drive me crazy! You tell me that you’ll do something and then you never do it. And when you tell me you’re not going to do something, most of the time you wind up doing it anyway. For instance, for the last month you kept telling me that you would take me to the movies so that I could see that movie I wanted to see, yet you never did. For the last two months, you told me

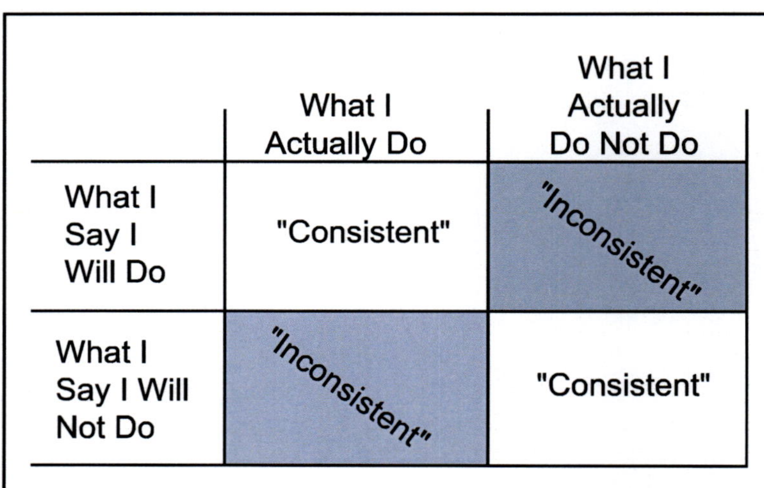

Figure 4.1. Relationships among What I “Say” and “Don’t Say,” and What I “Do” and “Don’t Do.”

that you would stop going by the pool room so often and that you would come right home instead. But there you go, Roberto, you say you're not gonna to do it but you continue do it anyway!" As illustrated in Figure 4.1 that Dr. Emener diagramed for them during the session, it was clear that Marta was saying to Roberto that she would prefer him to be more consistent in what he says he will or will not do and what he actually does or doesn't do.

Issues of predictability, comfort, and trust tend to be highly associated with *consistency*. Generally speaking, our experiences suggest six recommendations:

1. Think about, and give careful consideration to, the extent to which your loved one believes you, trusts you, and is invested in you and what you say when you tell him or her what you will and will not do;
2. Be sensitive to when you say you "will do" something versus when you say you "will try to do" something;
3. Remain appreciative to the extent to which your loved one becomes emotionally invested in your commitments and statements of what you will do and what you will not do;
4. Anchor your commitments and statements with specificity. For example, if you truly plan to take someone to the movies and you know that he or she will be genuinely excited and looking forward to it, if at all possible do not say "I will take you to the movies next week," but rather "I will take you to the movies next Saturday night"; and,
5. Be consistent at the *micro level.* That is, do what you say you're going to do and don't do what you say you will not do. At the *macro level*, try your best to keep your behavior consistent throughout your relationship.
6. Be conscious of the nonverbal messages you are sending, and try to ensure that your body language is consistent with your verbal messages. If you are frowning while saying "everything's fine," you are inviting confusion and doubt (and may even be accused of being deceitful or lying).

As Marta shouted at Roberto, "You sure can talk the talk, but someday I would like to see you walk the walk!"

BEHAVIOR AND PERCEPTION

One principle of human behavior that is pertinent to loving relationships that our experiences have shown to be true, is:

> *People tend to behave in ways consistent with their perception of other people's expectations of them.*

This principle became vividly clear when Dr. Emener was talking with Paula. During one of their sessions, Paula was sharing that even though her husband, Leonard, would repeatedly say to her things such as, "I'll be back in an hour – trust me," "I won't do that anymore – trust me," and, "I'll stop by the store and get that for you someday this week – trust me," she continued to feel the need to always check up on him, remind him and "pester him." She felt that she could not trust Leonard. Bill said to her, "Paula, I wonder if it is possible that he behaves in untrustworthy ways because he figures that you won't trust him anyway?" She calmly asked, "What are you trying to tell me, Dr. Emener?" "What I am suggesting to you, Paula," Dr. Emener replied, "is that maybe if you want Leonard to behave in more trustworthy ways, it would be helpful if you could begin to act toward him in more trustworthy kinds of ways."

Paula pondered Bill's thought and said that quite frequently when she would talk with Leonard, he would say to her, "It really doesn't matter what I do, Paula, you never trust me anyway." It was very difficult for Paula to begin to treat Leonard as if he were trustworthy. We are happy to share with you that the two of them are doing much better in this area. In a recent session, Leonard declared, "Of course I'm being more trustworthy and responsible to Paula. I have consciously tried to change my ways. However, I also know that she is beginning to trust me and believe me, and that feels good to me. I don't want to spoil it!"

PERCEPTIONS OF DIFFICULTIES

When it comes to predicting and planning our behavior and its outcomes, it also is important for us to keep our goals and expectations realistic. For example, when we anticipate the amount of time it will take to do something, it is important that our perceptions and expectations be based on some realistic considerations. Bill Emener has frequently and kiddingly referred to what his graduate students affectionately call "The Emener Formula." In his lecture, he says, "When I am planning to do something and I try to estimate how long it will take me to do it, I multiply my expected time by 2.75." Befittingly, Dr. Emener once shared with Leonard, "I would suggest that before you tell Paula that you will have her rock garden finished by next Sunday afternoon, make sure that is a realistic expectation and that you actually could have it finished by then." He smiled, looked at her and said, "I will have most of it finished by next Sunday afternoon." Paula looked at Leonard and smiled, saying, "Leonard, you're beautiful!"

Sometimes when we are doing things with, on behalf of or for a loved one, it is helpful to temper our perceptions of setbacks with some reality as well. For example, Norman was getting very upset because he had promised his wife that he would finish painting the house by Sunday evening, and when he ran out of paint with only one wall to go, he panicked. Nonetheless, once he realized that is wasn't the end of the world and that he could pick up some more paint on his way home from work the next day, he felt much less frantic and was able to feel good about what he had accomplished. As Bill Emener processed this with him, he remembered Norman saying, "There's a difference between a pothole and a bridge washout." With a smile and a touch of laughter, he continued, "It's one thing to run out of paint with one wall to go, it's another thing if you realize that you used the wrong kind of paint and have to redo the entire house!" It is amazing how many times people will encounter a pothole and perceive it to be a bridge wash-out, and immediately go into a panicky stop.

Avoidant and Escape Behavior

Larry and Pat had been married for about ten years, and it appeared that for the majority of their marriage, especially over the last three to four years, Larry would somehow avoid any confrontational conversations with Pat. "Whenever we have something heavy or messy to discuss, Larry never seems to have time to talk about it," she once said. A very important consideration that emerged in subsequent sessions was that Larry was reared in a dysfunctional family. Any form of confrontation in the family was extremely painful for him. "It seems," he said, "that now whenever I anticipate having a confrontational conversation with Pat, I simply do anything and everything to avoid it." Pat was very frustrated regarding this. To help the two of them understand what Larry had *learned* from his childhood, Dr. Emener drew two little figures similar to the ones in Figure 4.2 and offered them the following: "One of the very interesting pieces of research on behavior conducted in the

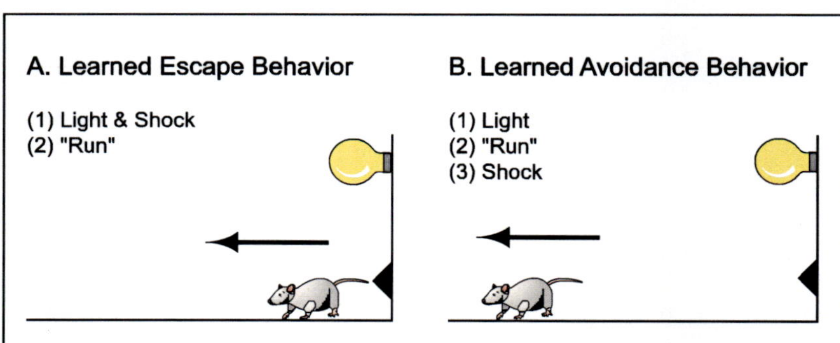

Figure 4.2. Learned Escape Behavior and Learned Avoidant Behavior.

field of psychology was related to how we could teach rats how not to get shocked. In Experiment A, when the rat was in the box eating some food, a light would come on and simultaneously a shock would come on. Immediately, the rat would run away. After some learning, at which time the rat associated the light with a shock, all we had to do was turn the light on and the rat would run. Eventually, however, when we changed the experiment and by continuing to turn the light on *without the shock*, the rat soon learned, 'Hey, now they're just turning the light on without the shock. I can stay here and eat even when the light's on.' Thus, it was demonstrated that the rat could not only learn to run away when the light and the shock came on simultaneously, and learn to run away even when just the light came on, but the rat also could eventually learn that when the shock was *not* associated with the light, it could stay there and eat. This process is referred to by learning psychologists as, "extinction of behavior in the absence of reinforcement." In Experiment B, however, the light would come on and the shock would not come on until ten seconds later. The rat soon learned that when the light would come on it could stay there and continue to eat for eight or nine seconds, and then it could run away and not get shocked. Once the rat had learned this, we reversed the experiment so that the light would come on but the shock would never come on. Basically, we changed it as we did in Experiment A. In Experiment B, however, no matter how many times we would have the light come without the shock, in eight or nine seconds the rat would always run away – it never learned that the shock wouldn't come on as the rat eventually learned in Experiment A. In Experiment A the rat learned *escape behavior* – that is, how to get away from the shock after it received the shock. In Experiment B, however, the rat learned how to avoid the shock – a*voidant behavior*. The important thing to note from these two experiments is that learned escape behavior can be extinguished, or unlearned, whereas learned avoidant behavior cannot be extinguished or it is extremely difficult to unlearn. What Larry learned as a child was *learned avoidant behavior*. What he learned was: I don't have to participate in confrontational conversations with loved ones as long as I can figure out some way of avoiding them. Dr. Emener explained, “Pat, it’s not that he doesn’t love you or that he doesn’t want to talk with you, maybe he is just doing what he has learned to do – avoid confrontation.” As time went on, and with some therapeutic intervention during subsequent sessions dealing solely with Larry, he eventually learned how to overcome his learned avoidant behavior with Pat. And now that the two of them can participate in confrontational types of conversations, a multitude of other types of difficulties are avoided and their relationship is so much more pleasant and meaningful. At the end of a session one day, Larry said to Dr. Emener, “I never thought that our relationship would be improved if I only knew how to fight better – verbally that is!” Pat grabbed Larry by the arm, pulled him close and said, “Now that we know how to argue better, we are loving so much better!” Needless to say, we are happy with and for them.

Negative and Positive Compensatory Behavior

It is not uncommon for people to compensate for their inadequacies and inabilities with alternative behaviors. The important thing is that the compensatory behavior be positive – not negative. For example, Robert was separated from his fiancée for six months because his company sent him to Florida to work on a special project. About every three weeks he would fly back to Dallas to spend a long weekend with Billie. When he came to see Dr. Emener, he said, “About three nights a week, when I am really feeling down and missing her, I go out and eat a big dinner. Then I go to a sports bar and drink a lot of beer. Look at me. I’ve gained almost 40 pounds in the last six weeks!” Among Dr. Emener’s responses, he said, “Robert, that’s a negative compensation. Is there anything you could do on those three nights a week, or possibly on a regularly scheduled basis, that would help you feel less lonely, feel better about yourself, and not have a negative outcome?” Subsequently, Robert joined a local gymnasium. Three nights a week he goes there to work out, and then he goes to a different sports bar where he eats a big salad and drinks low calorie soda. The last time Bill spoke with him, Robert told him that he had already lost eighteen pounds, was not missing Billie as much as he had been, and was feeling much better about himself. He also added that when Billie would see him next, he expected that she also would be pleased with his new way of dealing with missing her.

There is nothing wrong with compensatory behavior; the important thing is that we continue to remain aware of how our compensatory behavior is affecting us, our loved one and our relationship. One thing we can tell you for sure is that Robert and Billie are joyously happy with Robert's new compensatory behavior!

* * * * * *

For some people, the idea of analyzing their individual behavior and their relationship-related behavior is a noxious thought. "It's not very romantic... that's not love," Ben said to Dr. Emener.

"Do you love her? Does she love you? Do you love each other?" Bill asked Ben and his wife. "Yes," was their answer to all three questions. Bill then asked them to consider the following:

- If you love her and she loves you, how do you know it?
- And if you know you are loved by each other by what you think, feel and *do*, then doesn't it make sense to *pay attention to what you do*?

"I know that in your mind, I'm your number one," Lana said. "I know how you feel about me – you love me with all your heart. You tell me you love me every day. But those flowers you had sent to my office for no special reason – wow, that blew me away!"

* * * * * *

It is important for you to think, feel and talk like you love me;
it is important for you to act like you love me too.

Chapter Five

DICHOTOMOUS THINKING

"During Christmas break, we were together every day. It was wonderful. If we can't have it that way all the time, I don't want a relationship with him at all."

"If I can't spend every day of every week with her, it just seems never to be enough for her. It's either all or nothing. Forget it!"

"There's no way that I'm going to meet him for coffee. If I do, I know what will happen – we'll wind up in bed. No way!"

How many times have we heard someone make statements like these? How many times have we said something like this to ourselves? These kinds of thoughts and verbalizations are indicative of *dichotomous thinking* and indeed deserving of primary consideration in trying to understand and enhance our loving relationships.

DICHOTOMOUS THINKING AND EMOTIONS

"Dichotomous thinking" is representative of a cognitive process by which we mistakenly conceptualize aspects of life that typically vary along a range or a continuum as being binary, or all-or-none, in nature. For a dichotomous thinker, there are no midpoints. Quite frequently, we also tend to have equally extreme feelings associated with the phenomena at the extremes of continuums. Dichotomous thinking is a type of what the well-known psychologist Aaron Beck (who, with Albert Ellis, led the Cognitive Behavioral Psychology movement), calls a "cognitive distortion." It is a way of looking at a world made up of shades of gray and distorting it so that we see it only as being all black or all white at any given time.

For example, when Terry and Arlene came to see Bill Emener because they "were trying to rekindle, renew and work on their relationship," it became very clear that both of them were engaged in dichotomous thinking. At one point, Bill drew a sketch for them similar to the one in Figure 5.1 and said, "It appears to me, Terry, that

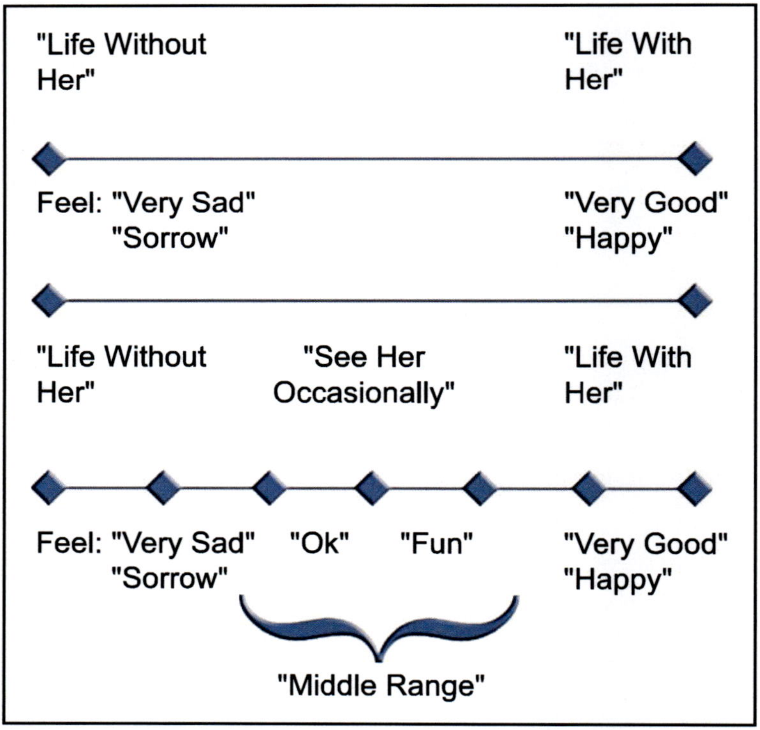

Figure 5.1. Dichotomous Thinking and the Development of a "Middle Range."

you see life either with Arlene or without Arlene. You tend to vacillate between these two extremes. You are either with her all the time and you feel very good and happy, or you are without her and you feel very sad and sorrowful." Bill then looked at Arlene, and said, "Arlene, you tend to be the same way." With a sigh, she replied, "Yes, Dr. Emener, that's true." Turning back to Terry, Dr. Emener continued, "Might it be possible that rather than either being with her all the time and feeling very good and very happy, *or* being without her and not seeing her all the time and feeling very sad and sorrowful, that there might be some mid-range alternatives that we could talk about? For example, Terry, could you see her occasionally – for example, maybe once or twice during the week when the two of you are very busy with your work and other personal activities?" Both of them, looking at each other and then looking at Bill said, "Yes, that's possible. It makes sense too. Let's try to see if we can work something out." Subsequent sessions revealed that both Arlene and Terry also had been individually struggling with other critical aspects of themselves as well as their relationship (e.g., abandonment, feeling smothered, etc.). Importantly, however, the two of them were able to identify some middle-range kinds of activities, interactions and ways "to be with each other" without having to have an all-or-nothing relationship and experiencing either horrendous sadness or incredible joy.

It is not only people in loving relationships who fall into the tendency to make this error. Some of the brightest minds in science, politics and business have made the same mistake. In science, we refer to this as "binary" thinking: someone is either an alcoholic or not, a success or failure in their career, a Republican or a Democrat or, in the words of a politician, "with us or against us." The truth of such assertions, however, is rarely so simple. Nature and human experience are typically more accurately described as varying along ranges of values rather than oscillating between the end points of these ranges. Of course, there are exceptions (for example, pregnancy comes to mind – you either are or you aren't), but for the most part, dichotomous thinking is an error in judgment and sometimes a costly oversimplification.

How We Spend Our Time

Bill Lambos was counseling a couple, Sally and David, for whom Sally's career was becoming more and more of a "deal killer" for David. Having never finished college, Sally took a job at an advertising agency as an assistant to an account executive. The executive soon realized that Sally's talents went beyond clerical and filing tasks, however, and after eighteen months arranged a promotion and raise for her to the position of junior account manager. Sally was thrilled that someone else valued her abilities and she threw herself into the job with gusto. At first David was happy; it meant more income and new things for them. However, David, a foreman at a warehouse, soon became dissatisfied: "Dr. Lambos, Sal has to realize that she's either my wife or she isn't – she can't have it both ways," he exclaimed with authority. Dr. Lambos asked them to describe their normal work week. Each put in about nine hours a day, including commute-time, except that Sally stayed late on the average of two nights a week to finalize a proposal or finish a project. On many of those nights, she would make sure David's dinner was in the refrigerator before she left the house in the morning and always called David if she had to stay late. Nonetheless, David was not satisfied; he felt if she could not get home every night by six, she "was not there for him anymore." Even after calculating the number of hours per week that Sally worked late and showing David that it amounted to less than ten percent of their total time together before the promotion, it did not change David's outlook. David had fallen into the trap of dichotomous thinking and would not budge. Sadly, they divorced within six months. David still blames Sally "for choosing her job over him," and Sally has moved on and is seeing someone else. When people are unable or unwilling to give up their "all or none" outlook on their relationships, those relationships often end.

Bill Emener recalls a similar case with a better outcome. Susan and Nelson had been living together for approximately six months, were planning to eventually get married, but as they said, they "were living in an extremely hectic and frustrating life together." Susan was working part-time in a restaurant. She also was a full-time law student at a nearby law school. Nelson was working part-time as a real estate agent and attending advanced real estate classes in night school. During two weeks of the Christmas holiday season, when both of them were on Christmas break and not in school, their relationship was exceptionally good. They felt "very together" and "very happy." After both of them went back to school and to work, however, they both began feeling down, lonely and abandoned. Both of them were constantly wondering, "Why can't he (why can't she) find time to spend time with me?" The verbalizations that really got Dr. Emener's attention were: "If he really loved me, he would find more time for me during the week," and "I know she's busy, but sometimes I hardly ever see her during the week, and if she really loved me she'd make time for me!" While they looked at a figure that Bill drew for them, like the one in Figure 5.2, he suggested that their relationship could be thought of as a bell-shaped, or normal distribution curve, in which over a year's period of time there were limited instances – like when both of them were on Christmas break and could spend a large amount of time together; or at the other extreme instances when both of them were studying for exams and hardly had time to breathe, much less find time for each other. What they quickly realized was that the two weeks during Christmas break and the two weeks of exam time were not typical of their relationship time. Bill suggested to them that if the normal curve distribution were representative of their relationship, as they were describing it, approximately sixty-eight percent of their time was somewhere other than these two extremes. Then he said to them, while pointing to Figure 5.2, "What can you do during this sixty-eight percent of the time?"

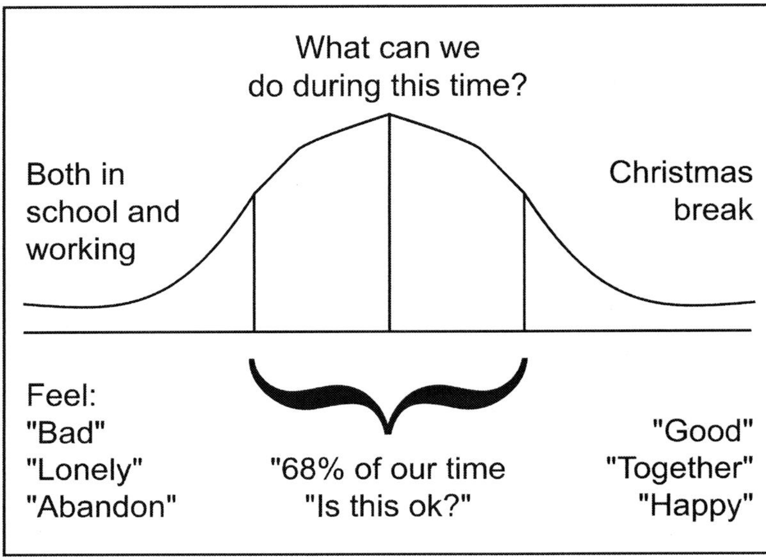

Figure 5.2. How We Spend Our Time.

With some modifications in their class and work schedules, they were able to identify one night a week when the two of them could go out to dinner and two evenings during the week at which time they could devote some time specifically to themselves and their relationship. Bill is happy to share that when they came back for their last session, Susan told him, “We have come to realize a number of things. While the two of us are in school and working, it is not very easy. The two weeks of exam time are typically the pits around our house! At the other extreme we certainly enjoy our Christmas breaks and are looking forward to our week together during Spring break. However, during this middle-range time we now are enjoying those precious opportunities when we can spend time together, realizing that the relatively small amount of time that we have together is by choice. It has nothing to do with our love for each other; it has to do with our career developments.” Terry looked at Bill, smiled and added, “It seemed that once we were able to stop ourselves from blaming each other for our scheduling constraints and stop seeing the limitations of our time together as indications of our love for each other, we were able to take control of our schedules and ultimately take control of our lives. Now we are truly enjoying each other so much more." Needless to say, we are very happy for and with them.

BOUNDARY SETTING AND EXPECTATIONS

When Carrie first came to see Dr. Emener, one of the things bothering her so much was, "I'm only twenty-four years old and I'm attractive and good-looking, but for the last couple of years whenever a man invites me out to do anything, I just seem to freeze and say 'No thank you,' and then spend the next several days wondering what's wrong with me." In subsequent counseling sessions, Carrie's story unfolded. It appeared that as a result of having had some very painful and discomforting relationships as a teenager, Carrie developed a dichotomous-thinking attitude toward men. For example, she had an irrational belief that if a man would invite her to go for coffee, to go to dinner or to do anything, the only thing he wanted to do was to have sex with her, and she had no choice and could do nothing about it. One of the first things Dr. Emener did was to challenge the irrationality of her belief system. Eventually, she said to him, "Okay, I now believe it is possible that just because a man invites me for coffee that... well you know." After a few minutes of silence and with a wry smile on her face, she looked at Dr. Emener and asked, "But now what can I do about it?"

Bill shared with Carrie that it indeed appeared to him that she was looking at her interactions with men as only having three points on a continuum, similar to the continuum in Figure 5.3. He said to her, "Carrie, at this one extreme you simply avoid all contact with men. You even shy away from talking to men on the telephone. In your mind, you believe that if you took a risk and joined a man for a cup of coffee it would automatically lead to sex. That thought was very fearful to you, and if you would have contact with a man you simply

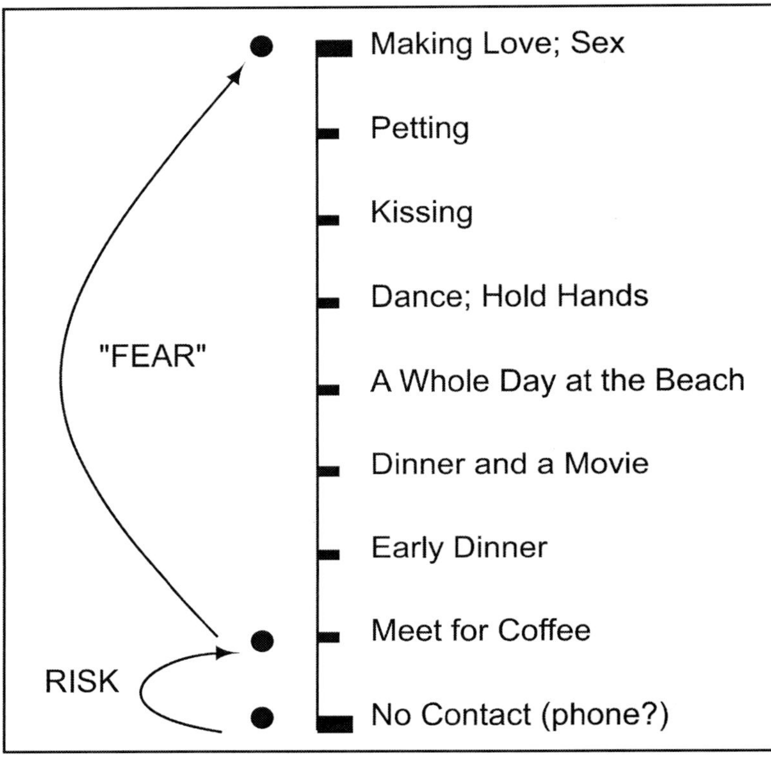

Figure 5.3. Setting Boundaries and Expectations.

would avoid any future contact with him whatsoever." She nodded in agreement. Together, Carrie and Dr. Emener fleshed out 5.3, and in doing so anchored the nine points along the continuum with each point being slightly more involved, more emotion-laden, and more risky and threatening. For example, the scale goes from no contact at all, to meeting for coffee, to an early dinner, to dinner and a movie, to a whole day at the beach, to dancing together or holding hands, to kissing, to petting, and then to making love. Bill also suggested to Carrie that if she were able to talk with a man and set some very specific boundaries with him, she then could have more finite expectations of (and control of) what would and would not happen. She tried out the strategy and at a subsequent therapy session she shared the following: "Two weeks ago, John, a very nice young man from work, asked me if I would like to go for coffee after work. I told him that I would like to do that, but I just needed to think about it. Later that afternoon, I went by his desk and told him that I would like to meet for a cup of coffee, maybe later on that evening at a nearby restaurant. I also told him, however, that I might not have much time because I was working on some reports for work. We met, had a wonderful conversation and I really enjoyed myself. Last week he asked me if I would like to go out to dinner with him. I immediately said, 'Yes.' I also told him that I was getting up early Saturday morning to go to visit my sister and that after dinner I would have to get back so that I could go to bed early. He understood. We had a lovely dinner and he had me back home by ten o'clock. It was a lovely evening. Now that I am learning to set some boundaries to stay in control of situations, I now can more accurately know what to expect. I am able to go out – at least I've done it twice now – and I am enjoying myself." With a smile and a tremendous sense of self-pride, she sat back in the chair and grinned at Dr. Emener. He then looked at her and said, "Carrie, I have a feeling there's more to the story."

"This Saturday night, he's picking me up a seven o'clock so that we can go to dinner before catching the nine-thirty movie." "What movie are you planning to see?" Bill inquired. "It really doesn't matter, does it?" Bill replied, "Of course not. Maybe it's the smile on your face, the sense of control that you are exercising over your life and what you do and don't do, and the fact that you now know that you can enjoy yourself on a date with a man... and you're feeling very good about yourself... that's what's important."

People Are either "Good" or "Bad"

In addition to having "lived through a stormy lifestyle for the past fifteen years," Kate, a thirty-eight-year-old single parent with two children, also told Dr. Emener in their first session that she "wanted to be able to sustain a meaningful, loving relationship for a change." Kate, who was from a rather typical dysfunctional family, also said, "Over the past fifteen years I have been in a number of relationships with men, most of whom were good, decent human beings. But after about six months, when we would really start to get to know each other, the relationship would get very rocky and turbulent. Then within two weeks of arguing daily, we would separate and poof, the relationship would be over. Maybe there's something about me that brings this 'here-we-go-again outcome' all the time? How can I stop this pattern?" After confirming what she specifically wanted to change about herself and her life, they clarified Kate's therapy goals. In addition to reading some pertinent self-help books, Kate also began journaling (writing down perceptions, thoughts and feelings on a daily basis).

During a subsequent session, Dr. Emener drew a diagram for Kate similar to the one in Figure 5.4 as he was explaining to her what he saw as being a critical component of her difficulties in relationships with men. "By and large, Kate," he suggested, "most of us learn to conceptualize people as being Good and Bad. That would mean that if I saw you as Good and Bad, I (1) would see you as being one person, and (2) would accept you and love you for both your good qualities, which I liked, and your bad qualities, which I didn't like. If we were in a loving relationship, I hopefully would work toward minimizing those qualities about myself that you didn't like, and you hopefully would try to be tolerant and accepting of my qualities that you didn't like. Unfortunately for you, Kate, you see men as being Good *or* Bad. And that would mean, for example, that (1) you would see men as being two people, and (2) you would accept them and 'love them dearly with all you've got when they were good' and 'run like hell when they were bad'." As tears streamed down her face, Kate said, "Yes, that's exactly how it is for me. When Joe was Good, I talked to him every day and spent evenings and weekends at his house. But when he was Bad, I would go to my apartment, not talk with him and simply avoid him for four or five days. Finally, he just got fed up with the craziness."

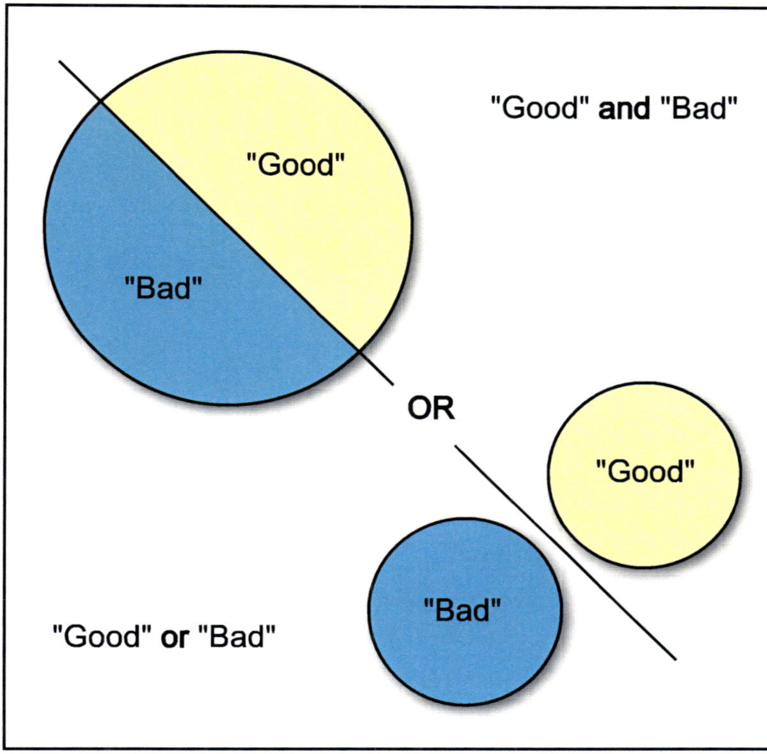

Figure 5.4. People Are either "Good" or "Bad".

Over the next ten months, Kate continued to journal, selectively read self-help books and worked on her "conceptualizations of men and how she dealt with them." About six months after their last session, Bill by chance saw Kate in a shopping mall. As they briefly chatted, he felt a warm closeness for her when she said, "I was lucky, Dr. Emener, Joe was understanding and willing to try to work things out. And even though he really pisses me off sometimes and it's hard for me to hang in there and work through my negative feelings with him, I do love him dearly. *Both of him*!"

ALL OR NOTHING RELATIONSHIPS

The following two stories are instructive of another type of binary, or dichotomous thinking – the All or Nothing relationship fallacy. The first is an example from Dr. Lambos's current marriage, and although it is not our goal in this book to talk about ourselves, this is one of those situations where an exception is warranted (after all, the propriety of self-disclosure in counseling is not a dichotomous choice either).

Bill and his wife Diane spent many years living together and working together in their consulting business. Although they worked in separate departments of the company, they still were together nearly all the time, and both became quite comfortable with the arrangement. In part, it worked because they agreed to boundary conditions, both during and after work. At work, Bill handled the technical aspects of the accounts and assigned the appropriate staff to handle them; Diane ran the accounting department and managed the financial end. At the end of each day, another boundary kicked in: No shop talk at home. Years later, when their consulting company was approached by a buyer with an offer they couldn't refuse, they sold it for a considerable sum and decided to give retirement a try. Unfortunately, both being very much Type A, take-control types, this turned out to be a bad option for them. Bill and Diane subsequently chose new careers and began attending post-graduate courses and working separately (Dr. Lambos joined a private practice and Diane earned her Masters degree in special education and became a teacher for profoundly retarded children). Those interim years were hectic and challenging; they went from sharing their lives day and night to barely seeing one another. After about a year and a half, both realized it was time for a sit-down. "Diane," Bill said, "we have gone from *always* together to *never* together, and I can't say I'm happy about it." Diane quickly replied, "Bill, weren't you the one who said Dr. Ellis taught you that you don't have needs, only preferences?" (She was referring to Bill's training at the Albert Ellis Institute in New York.) "Well then," said Bill, "I would damn well *prefer* we start spending some time together, and the sooner the better!" After both enjoyed a good laugh, they realized what both already knew – *relationships aren't all or nothing unless we let them become so*. "We now make time-together a priority while still pursuing our new careers," Bill recently beamed, "and we are both still very much in love and happy."

From Dr. Emener's files comes a similar story: "Ever since Norman got out of the Army and we became engaged, our relationship is either everything or nothing." That was the way Betty described her relationship with Norman when the two of them came to see Bill. It appeared that for weeks at a time they would spend almost all of their time together, except when they were at work, *or* they wouldn't see each other at all for a three or four day period. He sketched a diagram for them similar to the one in Figure 5.5 and suggested that their relationship was extremely dichotomous: "It is either an *all relationship*, or it is a *nothing relationship.*" Since Norman mustered out of the Army, the only thing he did was take a job, move into a new apartment and spend time with Betty. Likewise, Betty would go to work every day, be home alone in her apartment, *or* do something with Norman. Pointing to the middle of the diagram in Figure 5.5, Bill said to them, "We already have identified the midpoint where the two of you enjoy time together. This is the shaded area. However Norman, you could renew your enjoyment of some wind surfing on the weekends and maybe some softball in the evenings during the week; and Betty, you could get back to playing tennis and spending more time with your sisters who you said live nearby." What Norman and Betty needed to do was to take some time to develop a relationship that did not have the characteristics of either extreme: All or Nothing.

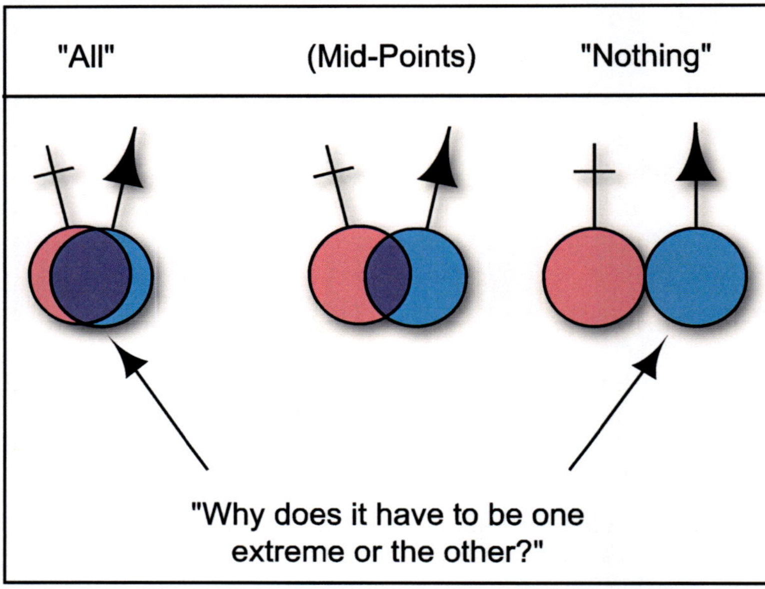

Figure 5.5. All or Nothing Relationships.

In the process of identifying a midpoint for their relationship, Betty was able to realize that she could go out for an evening with her sisters or play tennis on a Saturday afternoon and not be any less in love with Norman. Nor would Norman feel any less loved by her. Similarly, Norman could spend the better part of a Saturday wind surfing with some of his old buddies or playing in a softball game during the week and neither feel any less loving toward Betty nor worry that she was feeling any less loved by him. Once the two of them were able to realize the dichotomous nature of their relationship and appreciate the benefits of their midpoint, they were able to exercise some control, use their creativity and imagination, and develop a relationship lifestyle that was less dichotomous. Furthermore, their "new relationship" was more enjoyable to them, more manageable, and more characteristic and supportive of the kind of overall life that the two of them wanted to live – individually as well as collectively.

One Saturday morning while Bill was coming out of the post office, he saw Betty. She excitedly shared with him that she had just finished playing tennis and was heading out to the beach because she wanted to watch Norman do some wind surfing before they would go home, take a nap and then go to a movie. Bill said to her as they were parting, "Please say hello to Norman for me." As she was getting into her car, she said, "I sure will, and we'll send you a picture of the two of us – me with the tennis racket and Norman with his surfboard." It was with a smile on his face and a warm feeling in his heart that he watched her pull out of the parking lot.

* * * * * *

Sometimes the extreme highs in life are what we wait for and live for. Sometimes the extreme lows are what we detest and try our best to avoid. *Without the lows, however, the highs lose their richness and full meaning, and without a myriad of midpoints in between, we don't have a context for the extremes.*

Chapter Six

FEELINGS AND EMOTIONS

"I know that we love each other, and I know that we have a good relationship.

But sometimes, and I don't know why, I just don't feel good about us."

Hundreds of people have said that to us. You may have said something like it to yourself. We have said it to ourselves. And on such occasions, we think, "There's a message here. Could this be a signal to take some action?"

Action that can be very helpful, as well as preventative, is to address some important questions such as: How do I feel about us? How do I feel about me in this relationship? How are my feelings related to my actions? I know that I occasionally get angry, but is my anger related to any other feelings? What do I do with my feelings? Where do my anxiety and jealousy come from? Why do I sometimes just not feel anything? How can I get some resolution to my feelings and have a sense of serenity with this relationship? This chapter is specifically designed to assist you in addressing questions such as these, especially in terms of how they may relate to you and your loving relationship.

Emotional Intelligence

The role of emotions in understanding human behavior has a long and diverse history. Various schools of thought have taken very different positions on the role that emotions play in determining human behavior. Such approaches have varied from placing emotions at the epicenter of the self and as the root determinant of all other behavior (e.g., the phenomenological approach of Carl Rogers), to the opposite extreme of denying the role of emotion as a proper subject of study of human psychology (e.g., radical behaviorism à la B.F. Skinner). Common sense tells us, however, that whenever an issue seems to have only two sides, in reality a continuum of values exists about the subject, and truth is typically somewhere in the middle. Remember what we learned in the last chapter about dichotomous thinking? The subject of emotion is no exception.

Since the 1980s and the emergence of the Cognitive Behavioral Movement, the debate over the importance of emotion versus cognition in guiding one's life had been leaning toward the role of *thoughts* as the primary determinants of behavior. Eminent psychologists such as Albert Ellis and Aaron Beck stated loudly and with near certainty, that our emotions are the result of our cognitions and our beliefs, rather than the other way around. But just when it looked like the brain was about to assume prominence over the heart forever, the debate was rekindled dramatically. In 1995, a now equally famous psychologist named Daniel Goleman published the best-selling book *Emotional Intelligence: How it Can Matter More than IQ*. Since then, nonetheless, the heart has made a strong comeback and psychologists have relearned the importance, if not the primacy, of emotion.

As described in Chapter One, it is now recognized that there can be no such thing as pure intellect in the absence of emotion. Emotion and intellect are bound at the hip and will forever be so intertwined. Shortly we will describe in detail how emotions impact loving relationships and the importance of emotional management in healthy couples. But as long as we are on this short detour, let's reexamine why this is so from the point of view of 21st-century neuroscience. It won't take long, and we feel our readers may avoid falling into several of the common pitfalls of emotional mismanagement if they understand why the heart and the mind must always walk side by side.

Consider the following two questions: (1) What is the capital of France? and (2) Where should I go on vacation this summer? What is the most important difference between these two questions? After a little thought, you will probably figure out that the first question can be answered definitively: Paris is the capital of France, and no other answer is correct. On the other hand, where you should spend your summer vacation has no right or wrong answer: it depends on your values, what you want, and what pleases you (and perhaps your partner and family). As we also noted in Chapter One, the brain is divided into different areas to deal with these two aspects of reality: knowledge about the world, and knowledge about our needs and wants. The latter issues, which are called *Issues of Agency*, turn out to be just as important as the former, and perhaps even more so. In the last fifteen years, psychologists and neuroscientists have learned that a sense of agency – seeing the world as emotionally pleasing or not – is inseparable not only from intelligence, but from consciousness itself. The bottom line is that emotions determine how we see the world and how we react to every aspect of it. Anyone who tells you differently is simply wrong (and, in all likelihood, is emotionally attached to their belief). So if you wish to learn how to intelligently manage your relationships, you had better start by learning how to intelligently manage (or at least meaningfully influence) your emotions.

Analyze and Target Your Feelings and Actions

When Bill Emener walked into the waiting room and met Tori for the first time, he immediately had the feeling that he was about to meet a troubled woman. Her beautiful long, light-brown hair, perfect white teeth and overall air of class could not mask the worry and deep concern coming through her watery eyes, her apologetic downward look and her stooping shoulders. As Tori began to share with him what was troubling her, she reached for the tissue box and said, "I'm so scared. Roger and I got engaged at Christmas and it seems like ever since that time I'm feeling more and more uncomfortable... more and more distanced... I don't know what's going to happen." Since completing her bachelor's degree in business, Tori had been working in the regional office of a large company and recently promoted to a supervisory position. She loved her job and was apparently very successful in her work. She added, "Even Wally, my cat, was proud of me when I got this promotion two months ago!" Nonetheless, Tori was very concerned about the way her relationship with Roger was

	When I am...	
How I...	Around Him	Not Around Him
Feel?	A.	C.
Act?	B.	D.
?		

e.g. think?

Figure 6.1. Analyze and Target Your Feelings and Actions.

developing, especially since their engagement. Bill asked her to talk about her "feeling more and more distanced." As their session progressed, he drew a chart similar to the one in Figure 6.1. The boxes marked A, B, C and D represented the interactions between "How I feel and act..." and "When I am around him and not around him." As Dr. Emener pointed to each of the respective boxes, he asked Tori to think about the following questions:

1. How do you FEEL when you are AROUND Roger (i.e., when you are together)?
2. How do you ACT when you are AROUND Roger (i.e., when you are together)?
3. How do you FEEL when you are NOT AROUND Roger?

and,

4. How do you ACT when you are NOT AROUND Roger?

As they discussed her responses to these questions, Tori began to see differences between her feelings and actions, depending upon whether she was around Roger or whether she was not around Roger. For example, she said, "There seems to be a pattern. When I am not around Roger, like at work or at the tennis club, I feel confident and proud of myself... basically I feel good about myself... I feel happy. And I seem to act that way too. But for some reason, when I am around Roger I feel insecure and almost a little scared... I can't say I feel happy. And it's funny… I seem to act that way too." As Tori processed her feelings and her behaviors associated with them, she suggested that it also might be helpful for her to consider her "thoughts" – when she was around and not around Roger.

Bill never met Roger, who according to Tori was a very successful junior executive at a large bank in the area. As time went on, however, Tori also began to describe Roger as an arrogant, self-centered young man who always appeared to be good at whatever he did. Moreover, she said, "He always seems to be subtly putting me down, like I always have to take a back seat to everything. He never can just give me credit for what I do and what I can do. And no matter what I think, his ideas are always better." Tori eventually asked Roger to hold on to her engagement ring for her. She told him that she "needed a little space... just for a few days so I can think about some things before getting on with wedding plans." That had been six months previous.

Two weeks later Tori called Dr. Emener to tell him about her recent trip to Los Angeles to visit her sister. While she was there, she met John, who worked with her sister. She also said that she was planning to go back to visit her sister again very soon, adding, "Only to see my sister of course!" Bill chidingly replied, "Tori, remember who you're talking to here... sounds like it may be more than that." She laughed with a genuine heartiness that was very refreshing to hear. And when Bill asked her, "How about Roger, do you ever talk to him or see him?" she replied, "Once in a while I see him... he's in love." Bill asked, "Oh really?" "Of course, he sees himself in the mirror every morning!"

As you will see throughout this book, a basic principle that we hold near and dear is: *The best indication of the nature of your relationship is how you feel about yourself in his or her presence.* And for Tori, her awareness of how she *felt*, *acted* and *thought* about herself when she was around Roger was very revealing for her. Importantly, Tori was able to understand more clearly the nature of her relationship with Roger and make what she labeled as "some very insightful, good and timely decisions for herself."

My Feelings about Us

Kristin and Jerry were going through the final phases of being approved so that they could adopt a baby. Kristin had known since her automobile accident when she was a teenager that she would never be able to bear children. That was not a significant issue for her and Jerry. Five years prior to coming to see Dr. Emener, they had decided that when they got married they wanted a family and that eventually they would adopt one or two children. During their approval process, however, they had had numerous opportunities to seriously discuss their relationship and concluded that their relationship had some wrinkles in it that they said "needed fixin' before taking on the responsibilities of parenting." Jerry worked in the maintenance department at a nearby community college, and Kristin worked as a waitress in the lounge of a large downtown hotel. They felt financially secure, "had a nice little house in the suburbs," and "Jerry's truck and Kristin's car were relatively new and running well."

Toward the end of their first session, Bill drew a sketch like the one in Figure 6.2 for them. He then invited them to accept a homework assignment, saying, "I'll photocopy this sketch for each of

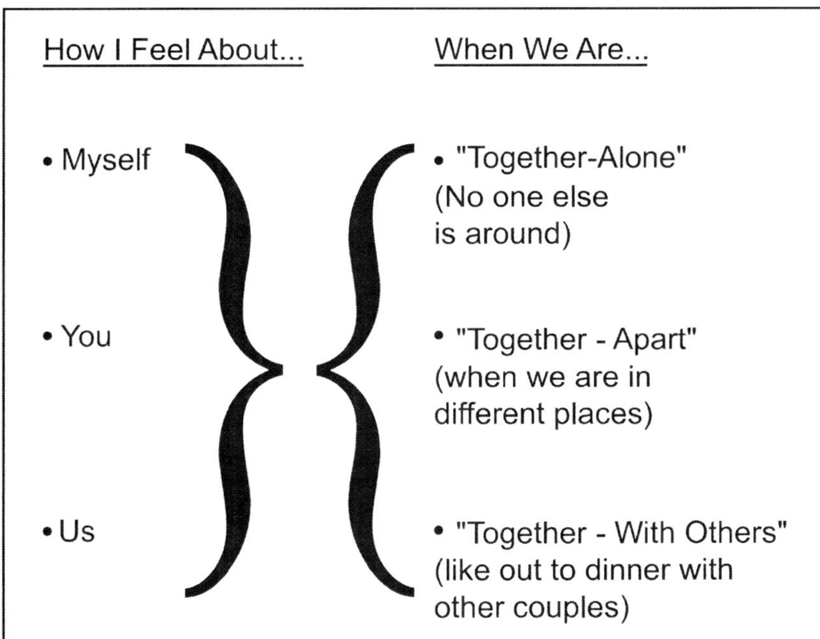

Figure 6.2. Our Feelings about "Us".

you. And between now and our next session, each of you, independently and without any discussion about it, write out your responses to nine questions. If you consider the interaction possibilities among the three *How I feel about...* and these three *When we are...* statement stems, there is a total of nine questions. For example, Jerry, you would write out your answers to your nine questions:

1. *How do I feel about myself when Kristin and I are alone-together?*
2. *How do I feel about Kristin when we are together-apart?*
3. *How do I feel about us when we are together-with-others?*
4. *How do I feel about Kristin when we are together-alone?*
5. *How do I feel about Kristin when we are together-apart?*

....and so forth. Kristin, your questions and answers would be the same, only yours would be relative to Jerry." They both told Bill that they understood what he was asking them to do and eagerly agreed to bring their nine questions and answers to their next session.

When they got together two weeks later, Bill made two photocopies of each of their sets of questions and answers so that the three of them could more easily review and discuss them. In the process of hearing and then discussing each other's answers, Kristin and Jerry learned a lot about each other and also about their relationship. For example, Jerry indicated that he felt very uncomfortable about Kristin when they were "together-apart," especially when she was at work. He subsequently shared with her that when he was younger he had found out that his one aunt had worked at a restaurant at one time and would cheat on his uncle. He said to her, "Kristin, I'm sorry, but I just can't help it... the thought of you serving drinks to traveling businessmen in a hotel lounge is nerve-wracking for me." Kristin was understanding of Jerry's "unsubstantiated worries" and tried to be reassuring to him. Kristin, on the other hand, told Jerry, "When we do things with others, I feel alone. It seems to me that you pay attention to everyone else but me. That's why I sometimes don't like us to go out with anyone else." Jerry was truly sorry for her feeling the way she did. "Gosh, Kristin," he replied in a tone of surprise, "I never knew that you felt that way."

In the process of slowly and openly processing their answers to their nine questions, Kristin and Jerry were able to understand themselves, each other and their relationship much more clearly. They agreed to keep their lines of communication open and to talk about such feelings when they arose. Importantly, they also made some modifications and adjustments in their behaviors. For example, Kristin, on her own, requested a transfer out of the lounge to the main restaurant, and Jerry began being more attentive to Kristin when they would go out with others. About two months after their last session, they mailed Dr. Emener a picture of the two of them with a six-month-old baby girl. The accompanying note read, "Elizabeth Ann – our pride and joy!"

CONFRONTING THE FEAR AND PAIN

It repeatedly has been our experience that underneath the surface feelings of anger, resentment and passive-aggressiveness are the deeper feelings of fear and pain. The following examples from our practices show this.

Dr. Lambos, who also works as a Florida Supreme Court Certified Family Mediator, was hired to negotiate a prenuptial agreement for two physicians, Grete and Carlos, who had been dating for three years but were having trouble making the commitment to get engaged. (Later in this book we will look at mediation as an alternative to family court battles in cases of divorce.) Bill's work with Grete and Carlos was simply supposed to be a non-confrontational forum for negotiating how money would be handled in the event they married and later divorced or one of them died suddenly. Each had children from a previous marriage, each owned a home and each earned roughly the same income – Dr. Lambos anticipated a single two-hour session without complications. However, it turned out to be not so simple. As they discussed the various arrangements that would meet their needs (trusts for the children, equitable distribution of joint assets into the trusts upon unexpected death, etc.), Dr. Lambos noticed the tenor of the discussion changing in a rather negative way. When he probed what was behind their questions, Grete blurted out, "He hates my children and will steal everything from them!" Carlos stood up and proffered his own accusation: "It's funny how upset you get when I pay for my son's tuition bills, Grete. Who hates whose children here?"

Bill tried to explain that by allocating the assets to trusts, the children would be protected should Grete and Carlos divorce or if one passed away. It quickly became clear, however, that money issues were not the problem at all. Both of these highly educated physicians were really expressing fear that the other person loved their children more than their partner. And as soon as that started to become apparent, their fears translated into *anger*. The mediation continued for three sessions, but no agreement was reached because of the negative feelings that arose at each session. Neither of these two intelligent professionals had the slightest ability to control his or her own emotions.

Ethical standards preclude a professional from assuming the roles of both mediator and therapist with any person or couple. This constraint exists because a certified mediator must be, above all, both impartial to the parties and neutral with respect to outcome. It is assumed for the sake of protecting the integrity of both professions that one individual cannot guarantee to be both neutral and impartial in the context of counseling. Because Dr. Lambos was acting in the role of mediator, he could not provide counseling services; thus, he referred them to another professional counselor. The last Bill heard, Grete and Carlos were still together, still living in their own homes, but marriage was off the table. Once again, unless you can learn to intelligently manage or meaningfully influence your emotions, you cannot fully succeed in a loving relationship.

Bill Emener's files contain a similar story, but one with a slightly different twist. From the moment that Wendy and Douglas entered his office, even before they sat down, they were throwing daggers of anger at each other, looking at each other with harsh resentful eyes, and reminding each other of how they were repeatedly being hurt by each other's passive-aggressiveness. After exchanging the typical cordialities and routine kinds of information exchanges, Dr. Emener looked at Wendy and said, "It is very clear to me that you are feeling a tremendous amount of anger toward Douglas." She immediately replied, with a hostile and sarcastic voice, "You're the psychologist!" After a few moments of silence, however, and after she turned back to look at Dr. Emener, in a soft and gentle voice he asked her, "Wendy, what are you afraid of? What is the little girl inside of you scared of?" Tears instantly began welling up in Wendy's eyes, and with a quivering chin she softly said, "My Daddy left us... I remember the day he pulled away... my first husband left me... and when Doug doesn't come right home from work, doesn't call and then wanders in at about eleven o'clock at night, it tears me up." Dr. Emener replied gently, "It sounds as if when that happens, Wendy, you feel abandoned." "I just can't take it anymore," she said to Douglas, "it just hurts too much. And I try not to let the kids see me worry and cry, but the hurt is just too much now." As she wept, Douglas reached out to her, held her hands and said softly, "Come on now, Punkin, you know I love you... I wouldn't leave you... I love you." After Wendy's crying subsided, they discussed what Douglas could do to be more responsive and attentive to her fears and her hurting, especially with regard to his not coming home when she expects him.

Dr. Emener later looked at Douglas, intuitively sensing what Douglas said to him: "I can't stand being told, 'You hurt me' by anyone... especially Wendy." Dr. Emener just looked at him with an understanding look. "For years, when I was younger," Douglas continued, "my mother would take any little thing I would do wrong and cry and tell me how much I hurt her... it was horribly painful. I remember those times very well." "So when Wendy..." Dr. Emener began to respond but was cut off. "When I know Wendy is hurting, I guess I just holler at her so that she won't have a chance to tell me how much she is hurting." They proceeded to process Douglas' mechanism of using anger to avoid feeling hurt. Their ensuing discussions were very helpful to both Wendy and Douglas – they were able to discover that underneath each other's intense anger was equally intense fear and pain.

As with Wendy and Douglas, people frequently respond to another person's intense surface feelings with similar levels of intensity. In a loving relationship, however, and as illustrated in Figure 6.3, it is very helpful if we can look beyond the surface

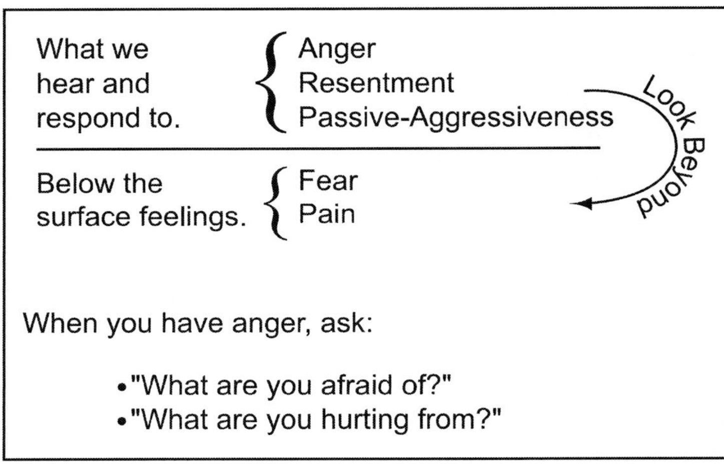

Figure 6.3. Confronting the Fear and Pain.

feelings and see and respond to the deeper feelings. We submit that when you look beneath surface feelings of anger, you frequently will find feelings of fear and pain.

What to Do with Your Feelings

From Bill Emener's experiences comes another pertinent story about managing one's feelings. "I came to see you, Doc, because I am afraid that if I don't get some help, someday I am going to lose it and hit Nancy, my wife." Andy continued. "When she is pushing my buttons, I feel the anger building up in me. But I'm good. I'm okay. I just stand there and don't do anything. But she just keeps going on, hollerin' and pickin'. Then she yells, 'How can you just stand there and not say anything?' That's when I almost lose it. And up to now, I just walk out of the house or I go for a ride. But I'm scared, Doc. What if someday..." Dr. Emener could see that Andy was genuinely scared. As they processed his feelings and reactions in situations such as the one he described, Dr. Emener suggested to Andy that when he felt his anger building up he had choices. He said, "When you feel anger building up within you, Andy, you can:

1. *Deny it...* Say to yourself, 'She's not all that angry or upset with me. She'll get over it in a minute or two.'
2. *Act on it...* Strike out and possibly hit her. Or
3. *Express it...* Say to her, 'Nancy, I am really beginning to feel angry at you.'"

As time went on, Andy discovered that because of his fear of not being able to control himself if he were to express his anger toward Nancy, he would first deny his anger. If she persisted and his feelings got too intense, he would run away from the situation. With some role-playing and other therapeutic interventions, Andy eventually began to learn how to express his feelings and trust his ability to express them. Indeed, this was very helpful for Andy as well as his relationship with Nancy.

It is important for us to try to remember that when we have feelings building up inside of us and we are aware of what we are feeling, we have choices as to what to do with them. Learning new responses and new ways of dealing with our feelings is very important, especially if our current response patterns don't work for us and at times create additional difficulties. Not learning how to effectively attend to ones feeling, such as anger, can lead to other, more serious problems, such as violence, which should be avoided at all costs.

The Importance of Feeling "Safe"

Of all the emotions produced by our brains, fear is certainly the strongest, at least in terms of immediacy. A small but very important part of the brain, called the "amygdala," is dedicated to producing the felt emotion of fear. The brain is wired in such a way that the amygdala can override almost any other impulse or choice a person might otherwise make. It is the seat of the "fight or flight" response and can cause intense changes in the mind and body nearly instantaneously. Anecdotes of superhuman strength in times of emergency (e.g., a mother lifting a car off her baby after an accident) probably reflect a massive release of adrenaline and other hormones and transmitters at the time the amygdala is activated. Interestingly, it has also been shown that the amygdala stores memories. Many are "learned" over generations throughout our evolutionary history (e.g., fear of spiders and snakes), but the amygdala can also encode new memories. Psychological trauma, including dissociative disorders such as multiple personalities, have been shown to rely on excessive and ongoing activity of this primitive, subcortical part of the brain in functional imaging studies.

But the reverse is also true. When the amygdala is quiet, we feel safe. This, too, is associated with other important emotions, and though they may be felt as less intense, they are no less important. Think of the changes our society underwent as a result of 9/11. First came fear, and Americans were willing to allow restrictions on our freedoms and even a war that were unthinkable just weeks before. But after some years, as people felt safe again, the political atmosphere reversed (along with it the popularity of our elected leaders). Fear can be a powerful motivator, but it is ultimately a negative one that normally can last for only so long. Feelings of safety, on the other hand, never seem to lose their appeal.

Many loving relationships are based on maintaining the feeling of safety. This is one of the true joys of coupledom. Problems can arise, however, when the need to feel safe pushes us to stay in an otherwise unhealthy relationship. For example, Peter and Debra came to see Dr.

Lambos because of Debra finally insisting that after years of putting up with it, "something had to be done about Peter's drinking problem." Peter, however, said, "I really don't know what the big deal is. I work all day at my lousy job, and when I get home all I ask is to have some dinner and grab a few beers while the game is on. And lately she's getting all bent out of shape about it!" Debra replied, "Peter, a few beers is two or maybe three – you're up to a twelve-pack a night, every night. Half the nights you pass out on the sofa and I can't even wake you up to come to bed. Two weeks ago, after I went to the bedroom alone, *again*, I heard noises in the house and got scared out of my wits. I thought someone had broken in and I ran out to the living room to tell you. But you were out cold and couldn't be woken up. I'm sorry, but I won't stay in this marriage if I can't feel safe in my own home."

Peter first looked as if he was about to get very angry, but then took a deep breath and sighed, "I'm so sorry, honey. I didn't realize how bad it's gotten. Maybe we should find me some help. I can't feel like a man if you don't feel safe around me because I'm in love with my beer. And truth be told, I still love you more than my beer." Bill arranged for Peter to enroll in an outpatient program for substance abuse. Peter hated it but stuck it out, and to his credit he drinks very infrequently these days – a single glass of wine with dinner on Saturdays, and no alcohol during the week. Debra feels safe now, and their romance has blossomed once again. Peter sent Dr. Lambos an email not too long ago saying he had quit his job and started over at a new company. Although he took a salary reduction, he said it was the best money he ever spent. "Ever since the new job, I don't even think about beer after work. It was the stress of that lousy job that was making me nuts."

Peter's drinking had begun to resemble an alcoholic pattern, but he was able to change the pattern in time. More importantly, his drinking was fueled not by the desire to get drunk (although that clearly was beginning to play a role), but by the need to reduce the anxiety he experienced at his former job. In counseling, we call such behavior "self-medication," and it is usually a poor solution to control stress. Like many prescription medications, it controls symptoms without addressing the underlying problem or imbalance.

ANXIETY REDUCTION

Jerry explained to Dr. Emener one of the difficulties in his and Norma's relationship for which they wanted assistance. "All of our married life, and even before we were married, at least once a week we get into a big fight, get all upset with each other, and then, as they say, 'kiss and make up'."

"It's just not fun anymore," Norma added, "We can't continue with this pattern, even though when we kiss and make up, we do have the best sex."

Jerry smiled in agreement. "But why do we do this all the time?" they wondered. As they were exploring this aspect of their relationship, Dr. Emener reminded them of a basic principle in psychology – *the reduction of anxiety can be very reinforcing*. "For example," Bill said, "ever wonder why we wait until the very last minute to go to the bathroom when we actually knew ten minutes ago that we had to go?" Jerry chuckled before saying, "Sometimes for me it's almost like a challenge, like 'How long can I hold it?' But it is true – when I finally go, for some crazy reason, it does feel good." After returning to some serious discussion of this pattern in their relationship, Jerry and Norma agreed on two things: (1) they subconsciously had been creating anxiety in their relationship because it felt so good when they would reduce it by kissing and making up, and (2) they would try to recognize the pattern as it was developing, talk about it, and try to short-circuit it. They did indeed work on this aspect of their relationship, experienced success with their new approach, and found their relationship to be much more enjoyable without their weekly fights. With a wry smile, Norma added, "And now we don't have to wait until Saturday night when we kiss and make up to have great sex."

The reduction of anxiety can be very reinforcing and feel good to us, and sometimes we may subconsciously create anxiety because of the eventual and anticipated reinforcement that comes with its reduction. However, if a pattern of anxiety enhancement followed by anxiety reduction becomes a pattern that creates serious problems and difficulties for us, it very well may be a good idea to work on changing the pattern.

JEALOUSY

For the three months prior to coming to see Bill Emener, Tonya had been feverishly busy with all of the running around involved with her upcoming wedding. Time was very precious for her. "Nonetheless," she said, "I simply have to talk with someone. I have a number of feelings about Les and our relationship that I need to sort out." The number one troublesome feeling that she identified was her insatiable jealously. "If he goes out for the evening without me, or if he gets home from work later than he said he would, I go nuts. I right away think that he has run into an old girlfriend or something." As they processed this, they discovered that she also had strong fears that Les would eventually call the wedding off "because maybe I am not worthy of his love." As Tonya and Dr. Emener therapeutically worked on her fear of abandonment as well as her overall feelings of insecurity, she found herself becoming less jealous. "Now that I'm feeling better about myself, I'm finding myself feeling better about Les and our upcoming wedding," she said in a follow-up session. About three months later, Dr. Emener received an envelope in the mail with an after-the-fact wedding announcement in it. On the bottom was written, "*Thanks, Mrs. Tonya Johnson.*"

When you are in a loving relationship and you are experiencing feelings of jealousy, it may be helpful to explore your other feelings, such as your feelings of insecurity and fear of abandonment. Quite frequently, feelings such as these are related to each other. Feelings such as jealousy also can be early warning signs of other, more serious difficulties, and in many instances seeking help from a professional counselor or therapist would be highly advisable.

EMOTIONAL SHUTDOWN

Sometimes in loving relationships, it is not uncommon for people to experience intense feelings of joy and happiness at one moment and intense feelings of sadness and aloneness a moment later. Rob said to Dr. Emener, "At times like this, it's like being on an emotional yo-yo." After feeling like this for some time, Rob became emotionally exhausted and "stopped feeling." When he first came to see Bill, Rob said, "I know I love her. In my head I know I love her. But I just don't feel anymore." As they talked, it became quite clear that Rob had been experiencing numerous difficulties with Rhonda and their relationship for a long time. Interestingly, he added, "It seems like I have been on this emotional yo-yo forever!" After a while, it appeared, Rob's defense mechanisms kicked in and he just shut down his emotional system. As he had said, "I just don't feel anymore." Moreover, Rhonda apparently was sensing Rob's emotional shut down. Understandably, yet counterproductively, she was pressuring him to be more emotional with her. "She keeps saying to me, 'For God's sake, Rob, tell me what you are feeling. You're like a robot!'"

As the therapy continued, Rob eventually was able to feel more comfortable with being in touch with his emotions. He began to be more aware of his feelings and started to trust his ability to deal with them again. He also asked Rhonda to be patient with him and to assist him in making some adjustments in their relationship. For example, he shared with her that at times he felt that she was trying to move too fast with their relationship and he was feeling smothered. From what Rob shared with Bill, she apparently was comfortable with and actually appreciative of Rob's requests and suggestions. As time progressed, they were able to more openly discuss their feelings and be more lovingly responsive to each other. For example, Rob said to

Bill in a subsequent session, "The other day when Rhonda and I were talking, it was clear that she understood what I was saying to her when she said, 'In other words, Rob, you'd like for me to slow down the movie.' I said to her in return, 'Yes Rhonda, and if you try to put your high speed film in my slow speed camera it will underexpose.' We got a good laugh out of that analogy." The important thing is that Rob and Rhonda were able to attend to their individual feelings and be respectful and responsive to them.

If we do not attend to our intense feelings, especially if they are of the yo-yo variety and left unattended over too long a period, it would make sense for us to shut down emotionally. As Rob said, "Burn your hand on the stove too many times and eventually you just start staying away from the kitchen."

A Need for Resolution and Serenity

Sometimes people will shut down emotionally when over a long period of time they feel flooded with a multitude of intense feelings regarding numerous people. At other times, people will experience great emotional upheaval and feel intense levels of anxiety. Furthermore, in such instances, it can be very difficult for them to focus and identify toward whom and for what reasons they are experiencing specific feelings. For example, when Kim first came to see Dr. Emener to talk about her feelings toward Chris, her fiancé, she "was emotionally bouncing off the walls."

During their first session, they were able to identify four people in her life, not just one, toward whom she was having some intense feelings. Bill drew a diagram for her similar to the one in Figure 6.4. Then they discussed it. For example, Bill said, "If I understand you correctly, Kim:

1. *You have strong feelings of anger and resentment toward Dean, your ex-husband, and you get nervous when your*

daughter spends the weekend with him because you do not like the way he treats her.

2. *You are angry at your daughter, Karen, because she manipulates you and Dean to get her own way, and you especially feel angry when she acts like her father.*

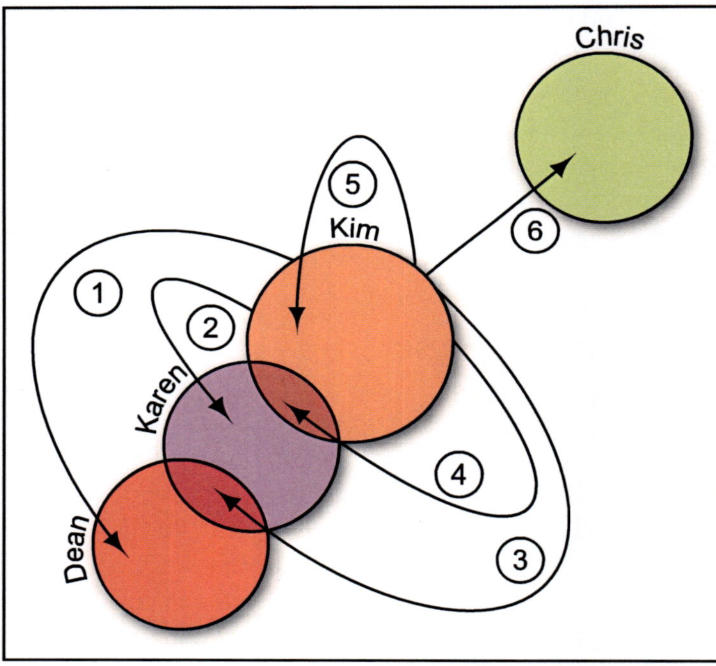

Figure 6.4. Areas in Need for Resolution and Serenity.

3. *You resent Dean and Karen's relationship, especially when she tells you what fun they have together.*
4. *You don't like some aspects of your relationship with Karen because you don't have the control over her that you think you should have because you are her mother.*
5. *You have some feelings of anger toward yourself because you allowed your bad relationship with Dean to go on for so long. And,*

6. *You have a tremendous amount of love for Chris, yet you struggle with telling him all of your feelings for fear that he may get angry at you and leave you."*

Kim nervously replied, "Yep, that's it alright. Now you know why I am an emotional basket-case!"

As Kim was able to further parcel out her feelings about herself, as well as toward whom she had all of her feelings, she was in a much better position to understand what was going on within herself. Understandably, she felt more in-control, her anxiety started to diminish, and her self-help skills began working for her again. "All I want is a sense of serenity in my life," she said to Bill. "I think I need to deal with things one at a time," she added. Dr. Emener agreed, and as time ensued, Kim was able to attend to the significant people in her life – one at a time – and move more toward resolution of her feelings toward them.

When at times we feel flooded with a variety of emotions toward and regarding other people, it can very helpful if we can: (1) parcel out and specify our feelings, and (2) target or identify them with the specific individuals toward whom we have such feelings. Getting away and sorting things out can be extremely helpful. Not only does this process assist us in moving toward resolution and serenity, but it avoids adding to our difficulties as well. For example, when our feelings and the people toward whom we feel them are confusing to us, we can inadvertently compound our problems. As Kim said to Dr. Emener, "One Saturday night Chris said to me, 'Why are you so angry at me? Karen's with Dean this weekend. And for whatever it's worth, Kim, I'm Chris – I'm not Dean!'"

* * * * * *

Among other things, a good sailing ship needs good sails and a good rudder. Think of your brain as the hand on the tiller controlling the rudder. Likewise, think of your feelings and emotions as the energy-generating sails that propel us. As illustrated in this chapter, keeping a close watch on our sails is important: an unattended small tear can quickly turn into a big rip, an unnoticed small hole can quickly send it flapping in the wind. The majority of the time, we can find a good wind. *And with a watchful eye on the sails and an occasional checking of the mast, there's nothing more beautiful than a full sail.*

Chapter Seven

PATTERNS AND TRENDS

It is not uncommon to hear from a client, "Doctor, I just want to be happy all the time," or "Doctor, our relationship is mostly good, but not all the time. What's wrong?" Although extreme swings in one's level of happiness or satisfaction can indicate deeper problems, it is more likely that such clients are being unrealistic in assuming they can be happy or that a relationship can be good, "all the time." Life, as we experience it, is not static. It has its ups and downs, and these *patterns* over time form *trends.* One's success or failure in a loving relationship has much to do with the ability to successfully adapt to change and is no exception to this common sense rule of thumb: *to deal with life means to deal with change.*

If we accept this premise that virtually all loving relationships have such patterns and/or trends, then it follows that we can learn much from studying them. Consider how frequently you have heard people say things like, "Whenever he seems to be having a lot of stress at work, a pattern emerges in our relationship in which he typically..." and "It seems that about every month or so the two of us need some time away from each other. So, about every four or five weeks I will take a fishing or golfing weekend with my buddies, or she will spend a weekend with her sister and her brother-in-law. That seems to work very well for us because..." It is important to remember that there is nothing wrong with patterns and trends in loving relationships. What is important is that people learn how to maintain a mutually satisfying relationship within the context of fluctuations in day-to-day quality and functioning.

There are four important considerations to address regarding patterns and trends: (1) *How do they affect our lives?* (2) *How do they affect our relationship?* (3) *Do I or we want to change anything about them?* and, (4) *If we do make any changes, what differences would the changes make?*

Patterns and trends can emerge in loving relationships in a variety of ways. (1) *by natural circumstances:* for example, "As part of his job, he has to go to the coast for the last Thursday and Friday of each month. And because we both enjoy the beach, I meet him there on Friday evening. Therefore, we usually spend one weekend a month away from home;" (2) *by learning:* for example, "Ever since I was a teenager, whenever I had anyone in my life who I considered to be an important person, I always expected that she would go with me to church on Sunday mornings and then join me for dinner with my family;" and (3) *by design:* for example, "Given the nature of his job and my job, we find ourselves getting on each other's nerves about every three or four weeks. So, we plan an opportunity to spend one or two nights away from home so that we can be by ourselves. When I look at my credit card bills, I can tell that there is an obvious trend there. But that works for us, and we have no intentions of ever changing it." Moreover, a pattern or trend may occur as a result of a combination of the foregoing. Nonetheless, it is important to remember that patterns and trends in loving relationships are neither good nor bad, per se. It furthermore is important for us to focus on the extent to which our patterns and trends affect our individual lives and our relationships, especially if they are harmful. On occasion, we remind a client engaged in harmful patterns of an old, flip definition of neurosis: *Neurosis is the pattern of defeating yourself by repeating yourself.*

In this chapter we will look at some of the ways in which patterns and trends can have detrimental effects on loving relationships. We'll focus on how they can emerge in relationships, their effects on relationships, and what some individuals have done to try to change their patterns or trends to result in less detrimental and more positive and meaningful effects.

LEARNED RESPONSE PATTERNS

The living experience of reality has embedded within it the properties of *time* and *change over time*. If some part of our experience becomes static or ceases to vary over time, our nervous system is strongly predisposed to learn to ignore it. Learning psychologists call this "stimulus habituation." You probably never notice the sound of your home's heating or air conditioning systems; you filter them out or ignore them. You may have known people who live near airports or train tracks and don't notice sounds that may startle you. Evolution has taught living organisms to selectively attend only to those aspects of the environment that have predictive value, and there are few aspects of our environment more important for us to predict than what will come next in a loving relationship.

To give a more concrete example, Dr. Emener was seeing Marleen, a thirty-one-year-old nurse, who was reared in a dysfunctional family. Both parents were alcoholics. Unfortunately, Marleen never learned how to appropriately and functionally deal with anger. In fact, she told Dr. Emener that when she was younger and living at home, whenever anger would emerge she would get scared and, if at all possible, leave the house. She came to see Dr. Emener because she was realizing that over the past eleven years she had had a series of eight relationships with men, none of which ever lasted more than five or six months. As they processed and discussed Marleen's previous relationships, an understandable pattern became evident.

After Dr. Emener drew a chart for Marleen similar to the one in Figure 7.1, he said to her, "Marleen, these eight relationships seem to have followed a pattern. You would begin a relationship with a gentleman then, for understandable reasons, many of which may have

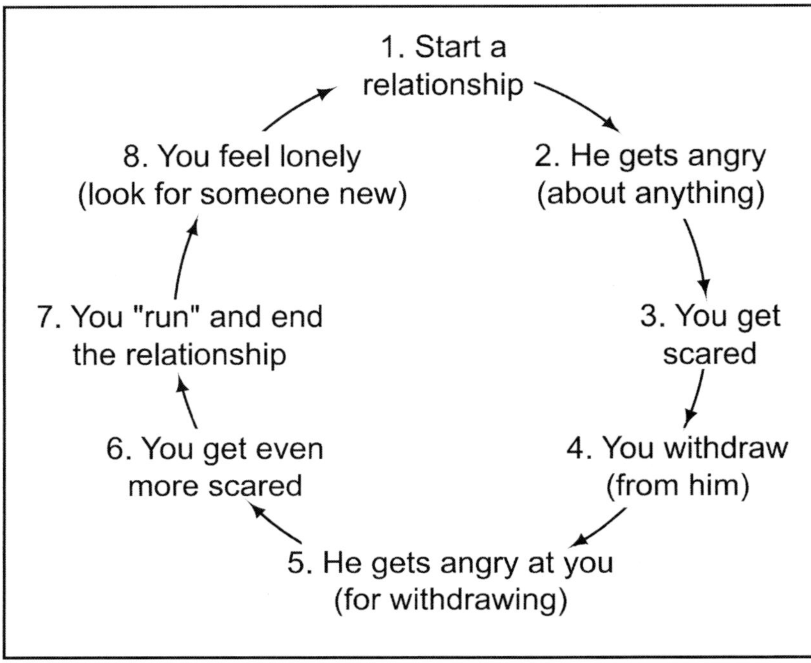

Figure 7.1. Learned Response Patterns.

had nothing to do with you, he would get angry or express anger. You would then get scared and withdraw, psychologically, and run away from him. He would then get angry with you for withdrawing from him. Then when he would express increased anger, you would get more scared. As this pattern continued, you increasingly would get more scared and he would continue to get more angry. Eventually, you would run away, leave and/or end the relationship. You would begin to feel lonely and look for someone new. Then the pattern would start all over again." With tears in her eyes, Marleen softly said, "Yes, and I have lost some beautiful relationships and have let some extremely wonderful men get away from me too."

For Marleen, this was a monumental challenge and a very difficult struggle. Learning how to deal appropriately and effectively with fear and anger is not easy. As Dr. Emener and Marleen therapeutically processed some of her earlier experiences with her mother and father and she learned that it was possible to receive and express anger without being devastatingly hurt, she began to learn how to deal with the emotion of anger in much more positive and functional ways. The last time Dr. Emener spoke with Marleen, on the phone, she said to him, "I am truly beginning to enjoy my relationship with George. He and I have been going together for about a month now. The important thing, however, is that he and I have had, and have survived, some good shouting matches and arguments. I'm learning! And that's cool. The most important thing I have learned is that I can be angry with George and he can be angry with me, and we can work through our angry feelings and still enjoy a wonderful relationship. I'm so happy!"

The ultimate turning point for Marleen was when she was able to address her feelings of anger toward herself – for not having known how to deal with anger, and then for sabotaging and losing many good relationships in her life. Once she was able to forgive herself for having been that way, she was able to get on with her life, and as she said, "enjoy wholesome relationships – not only on the sunshiny days but on the rainy days as well."

There are two important lessons we can learn from Marleen. First, poorly managed emotional responses to immediate events can prevent us from seeing the forest from the trees. In order to learn how to be comfortable over the long run, we must learn to manage momentary emotional responses that seem threatening, lead to anger or lead to overreaction. Second, the reality of both life and relationships is that the days are mixed between the good, the neutral and the not so good (and maybe even outright bad ones). It is unreasonable, or as the late Albert Ellis would say, "irrational," not to expect fluctuations in the quality of interactions. Later in this chapter, we will offer some specific guidance as to when a trend or pattern can be said to signal true dysfunction or even personal danger. For now, however, the message is straightforward: patterns and trends will always exist to some degree in relationships and for the most part play many useful roles. What is important is that you learn to manage them and *not let past patterns and trends dictate your future*.

ROLE(S) OF SABOTAGE

Like Marleen, Mick also had been reared in a dysfunctional family. For many reasons that he and Dr. Emener discussed and explored, Mick, as an adult, had a tremendous fear of rejection. As Mick said, “Whenever I think that a good friend or important person in my life might possibly tell me that he or she is angry with me or that he or she doesn’t want to see me anymore, I go crazy!”

As they discussed the patterns and trends in Mick’s relationships with women, it became clear that Mick’s fear of rejection ultimately would lead to the unconscious sabotaging of his relationships with them. When he would meet a woman who he thought was “cool and interesting,” he would work very hard to build a relationship with her. He would call her on the telephone, send her flowers, take her to nice restaurants and go for long walks on the beach together. However, once he would begin to realize that she had some positive feelings toward him, he would start to become nervous and scared. His ultimate fear was that: (1) she would fall in love with him; (2) he would fall in love with her and with their relationship; but (3) she then would reject him and he would experience what he called “gut-wrenching pain.” Thus, to avoid gut-wrenching pain from being rejected, he would stop calling her, not treat her very nicely and basically drive her away. He initially came to see Dr. Emener because his most recent girlfriend said to him, “Mick, I cannot understand you. You worked so hard to build a relationship with me and now you’re doing just the opposite. First you did everything you could to pull me in. Now you’re doing everything you can to push me away. I do not think that I have done anything wrong or different. I think you’re the one with the problem.” Mick agreed with her and subsequently came for some assistance. Among other things, Bill helped Mick work on his fear of abandonment and issues associated with toxic shame (discussed in Chapter Nine).

We are very happy for Mick. He eventually was able to understand the patterns and trends in his relationships with women, and most important, why he was subconsciously sabotaging or even ending his relationships with women – especially those for whom he had strong feelings. Once Mick realized that if a loving relationship did not last and that he would be able to survive the fear and the pain of losing it, he then would be able to risk having one.

OLD PATTERNS WITH NEW PEOPLE

A slightly different form of the same issue (one's history determining one's present and future) was problematic for Bea, a forty-year-old woman who had been engaged three times and married twice. Bea came to see Dr. Emener because she was having difficulties in her relationship with her new boyfriend, Hector. Unfortunately for Bea, all of the previous men in her life, including her father, were non-trustworthy and emotionally abusive. She once said to Dr. Emener, "The only way that I could deal with my dad and the other men in my life was not to believe them or trust them when they would say anything to me. If I would believe them or trust them, they would let me down and I would get hurt." The difficulty that Bea was having, however, was that Hector considered himself to be a very trustworthy individual. Moreover, he was growing very frustrated with Bea because she constantly acted as if she did not trust him. For example, she said to Dr. Emener, "The other night Hector said to me, 'Bea, no matter what I do, you do not seem to trust me or think of me as a trustworthy person. You never give me a chance. I always have been open and honest with you. I always have followed through on anything that I said I would do. Yet for some reason I do not feel trusted by you.'" Obviously, Bea was scared. She liked and loved Hector very much. She wanted to continue her relationship with him.

However, it became clear to her that she was having some difficulties with trust.

During their second session, Bill asked Bea, "Might it be that you are operationalizing, and continuing to use, your old patterns with new people?" She replied, "That is exactly what I said to Hector. I am so afraid of being disappointed and hurt by someone because he isn't trustworthy that I have trouble trusting anyone." Interestingly, Hector said, 'Please try to remember, Bea, I'm not anyone. I'm Hector!'"

As Bea was able to learn some new ways of dealing with people, she was able to learn to take some risks and be more trusting. It is interesting to note, however, that one time when Hector told her that he would come over by seven o'clock but did not show up until nine-thirty, she talked with him about it and realized that: (1) Hector was a human being who would occasionally forget what time he said he would arrive; and (2) it did not mean that he necessarily was an untrustworthy person – he was just human. She added, "That old cliché, 'to error is human,' is very appropriate for me in my life. For once in my life I feel that I am in a relationship with a person who is basically trustworthy, and my sense is that as long as I continue to act trustingly toward him, things should be okay. Hector is being very patient with me, and that certainly has been very helpful." We are happy to share with you that things must be going well for Bea because the last time Dr. Emener saw her was when he ran into her in a shopping mall she was proudly wearing the engagement ring she had recently received from Hector.

Treating each individual as an individual and not using old patterns from old relationships as the only way of dealing with new people, is occasionally a difficult thing to learn. For some people, it can seem like an insurmountable obstacle. However, by changing one's perspective and becoming willing to take some risks, almost anyone can free himself or herself from the trap of the past. Being aware of the basic nature of the person with whom you have a current relationship, and being sensitive to how you are responding to your new person versus how you learned to respond to people in your past, is critical.

POOR COMMUNICATIONS PATTERNS

Patterns emerge not just in the ebb and flow of the day-to-day quality of relationships, but also in the ways people become used to communicating with one another. Pioneering research by the relationship psychologist John Gottman studied such communication patterns for many years and revealed some very informative findings (which have since been replicated by other research). You may have read about his work in the popular book *Blink* or saw it on several television series in which his work was featured.

By videotaping newlyweds (with their permission, of course) for as few as four hours in his "love lab," and then carefully scoring the tapes for instances of various types of signs, he developed a system whereby he can predict, with ninety percent accuracy, whether or not a newly married couple will be divorced within four to six years. (In the behavioral sciences, that level of prediction is nothing short of astounding.) He found six types of interaction associated with arguments, each of which predicted eventual divorce. They are detailed in his books and writings for the interested reader. For our purposes in this chapter, however, we will focus on the signs Gottman calls "The Four Horsemen" – an allusion to the Biblical prophesy of doom in Revelations. The four patterns of interaction are: (1) *criticism; (2) contempt; (3) defensiveness;* and *(4) stonewalling*. Let's take a brief look at each to discern how patterns based on these types of communicating lead to downward spirals (trends) that in turn lead to divorce.

Criticism is essentially blaming one's partner for problems in the relationship, rather than taking accountability for one's own contribution to the problem and/or looking at the behaviors of both partners as the source of the problem. (Interestingly, blaming others is also one of the irrational behaviors often attacked in Rational Emotive Behavior Therapy.) We often recall our own parents telling us when we were children, "It's not what you say, it's how you say it that matters." This is the core of criticism: stating or implying that whatever is bothering you is caused by deficiencies in your partner.

Even if true (for example, if your partner has a drinking problem), criticism never helps. By turning this style around and suggesting something positive, couples can avoid falling into this destructive pattern of interaction.

Contempt is the expression of hatred. As couples counselors, we cannot remember when it ever has played a positive role in managing a relationship. Yet this pattern can develop into a two-way street, leading to a relationship style that sociologists refer to as "conflict-habituated." If you have ever watched the film *Who's Afraid of Virginia Woolf?* you will recognize this pattern immediately. Richard Burton and Elizabeth Taylor do a magnificent job in portraying such a disturbed pattern in a relationship between a university professor and his wife.

Most of us are very familiar with *defensiveness*. It is a feeling of anxiety fueled by a belief that our partner is blaming us for something. Often such anxiety is channeled into anger and unproductive "not-my-fault" declarations. Couples who fall into this type of interactive pattern are headed nowhere good.

Finally, *stonewalling* is a type of active avoidance in dealing with issues as they surface. Both of our experiences are replete with examples of how relationships have soured and ended because one of the partners refused to deal with issues brought up by the other person.

The Four Horsemen do not in and of themselves predict that a relationship will end or that a married couple will divorce. But together they can establish a style or pattern of interaction that in most cases indicates a negative trend and portends an unhappy future.

Gottman is not the only one to have studied patterns of interaction. An entirely different approach comes from the work of Eric Berne called "transactional analysis." According to Berne, interaction patterns may be looked at as a series of transactions between people. During repeated interactions, each person comes to assume one of three so-called "ego-states" – the Adult, the Parent, or the Child. In a healthy loving relationship, both partners are advised to spend the majority of their time in the Adult role, which is considered the healthiest overall pattern of interaction. But there are times when the Parent-Child pattern may be more appropriate, perhaps when one of the partners is ill and requires tender loving care. Or the couple is on vacation and just needs time to "play" and de-stress. In this latter case, the Child-Child interaction pattern may be the best. Healthy relationships are characterized both by the preponderance of Adult-Adult transactions, *and* by the flexibility to switch transactional modes when appropriate.

Another important issue in communication patterns is that of "selective attention," also sometimes called "filtering." These basically are fancy terms for "not listening" or "hearing only what you want to hear." You don't have to have a post-graduate degree in counseling or clinical psychology to figure out that this is also very frustrating for your partner and unhealthy for your relationship.

What is so interesting about selective attention from a psychological perspective is its paradoxical nature. By filtering out what they don't want to hear, people simultaneously all but eliminate their opportunity to communicate what they want the other person to hear. Communication is a two-way affair and, as anyone who has had a bad cellular phone connection can verify. Even if only one side of the line is garbled, the conversation cannot proceed. As authors, we are reminded of the central message of the recent film *Babel*: If you want to be heard – listen. To wit, in Dr. Emener's last session with Alice and Mark, a couple he had seen for four sessions, Alice looked deep into her husband's eyes and softly said, "Over the past two weeks, I have felt so loved by you, Mark. And the most powerful way you have told me that you love me has been when you listened to me."

PATTERNS ARE LIKE ADDICTIONS

Sherry, a twenty-eight-year-old single parent, originally came to see Dr. Emener because, as she said, "I am feeling incredibly depressed. I am feeling helpless. I have no feeling or sense of what is going on and now I'm almost starting to feel hopeless." Dr. Emener asked Sherry if there was anything in particular that she was feeling helpless or hopeless about. She quickly responded, "It's Rodney."

Sherry and Rodney had been dating for a year and a half. As they discussed her relationship with Rodney, a relatively clear pattern emerged: Sherry and Rodney would establish some very specific boundaries, guidelines and parameters with regard to their relationship, ones which would allow them to enjoy a meaningful relationship, yet also allow them to enjoy individual lives of their own. As time would go on, nonetheless, their relationship would seem to become "more and more involved" and eventually Rodney would end the relationship. Basically, he would tell Sherry, "I can no longer go on this way."

Rodney, by Sherry's invitation, came with her to a session. Sherry asked Rodney to share with her what specifically it was that was "driving him crazy." After thinking for a few minutes, he said, "Sherry, you and I will agree as to what we will and will not do. For example, I will plan to play golf on Saturday mornings and play softball one or two nights a week. I also will plan to spend most of Sunday evenings preparing for my upcoming week at work. You not only will agree to this, but you also will plan to play tennis one night a week and go shopping during one of the days on the weekend with one of your girlfriends. But then, over the next four-to-five weeks, it will seem to me as though I had been spending almost every night and every day with you! Either you would tell me that you needed to talk to me because you were upset about something or you were catching a cold. It's always something! You would leave messages asking me to return a call immediately, or you would have already made plans for us to go away for the weekend even though you knew I enjoyed playing golf. Somehow, Sherry, I can never seem to give you enough time. I try to tell you that, but you don't listen to me. The only way that I can get my own life back is to tell you that I do not want to see you anymore." Sherry began to cry and murmured, "I don't know why I do that." Toward the end of that session, Rodney looked at Sherry and said gently, "Sherry, I love you very much. More than anything else in the world, I want to *share* my life with you. What you seem to need, however, is for me to *give* my life to you. And I will not do that."

Over the next two months, Sherry and Dr. Emener had a number of sessions during which they took in-depth looks at her fear of abandonment, her low self-esteem and her low sense of self-worth. As she was able to identify some of her own addictive needs for love and affection from Rodney, as well as her ill-founded fear of Rodney not loving her anymore, she was able to relate to Rodney without putting high demands on him for constant attention and affection. At their last session she said to Dr. Emener, "Until I started working with you and identifying why I was the way I was, my love for Rodney was like an addiction. I never seemed to be able to get enough time with him. I am not out of the woods yet, but it sure as hell is getting better. He is such a wonderful man. And as I continue to become a stronger and healthier person, I will enjoy my relationship with him so much more. I feel so grateful!"

Paradigm Shifts: A Place to Start

Dr. Emener will never forget the first time he met Barry, a forty-five-year-old attorney who came to see him because he was having difficulties in his relationship with his girlfriend, Gladys. Part of the reason why he will never forget Barry is because he is a very engaging man who commands attention immediately – the fact that he is six-foot ten and weighs close to three-hundred pounds certainly accounts for much of this. Barry had been married for twenty years and had three children. Since his divorce, approximately three years prior to coming to see Dr. Emener, he had not dated very much – until he met Gladys, a single parent with two children. Gladys had many of the same characteristics of his first wife, "Except that Gladys is so much more loving toward me," he said. When asked if there was anything that he was afraid of, Barry said, "I am afraid that if I eventually marry Gladys, I would fall back into the same old pattern and routine that I had with my twenty-year marriage."

It is important to note that Barry indicated that on a number of occasions, Gladys would say to him, "Barry, I just wish you would pay more attention to yourself." This was very perplexing for Barry. As time went on, however, Barry and Dr. Emener were able to discover his old paradigm – that is, his old pattern of dealing with the people in his life. His old pattern was: "First comes my wife, then come my children, then come my parents, and then comes me. After I take care of everyone else, then I will take care of me." As this pattern was explored, he actually did express some resentment and distaste for that way of dealing with people. Dr. Emener suggested to Barry that it might be helpful for him to consider a new paradigm – that is, a new hierarchy of importance in terms of what and whom he would pay attention to in his life.

During their next session, Barry said, "I talked with Gladys and I told her that I am going to try a new paradigm: First, it is going to be me, then it will be my wife, if I ever remarry, then will come my children, and then will come my parents. Dr. Emener, I was shocked when she said, 'Barry, that's great! *You do not have to give up you in order to be loved by me*.'" With tears in his eyes, Barry added, "Isn't she a beautiful woman!"

Once Barry was able to overcome his codependent need to take care of everyone else in his life before attending to his own needs, he was able to form a new pattern of dealing with the people in his life. It was not easy for Barry to operationalize his new paradigm. For example, his children would become very frustrated and angry with him when he would say to them, "I'm sorry, but I have been planning to play in this golf tournament for over a month. I regret that I will not be able to go to your ball games today, but I need to do this for me. I hope you understand." The last time Dr. Emener saw Barry, however, he mentioned that his children were beginning to understand and accept his taking care of himself as well as lovingly attending to all of the other important people in his life. To her credit, Gladys was not threatened by Barry's new paradigm. The most important thing, nonetheless, was that Barry was feeling much better about himself, his life, his children, his parents, and especially his relationship with Gladys. With a typical tongue-in-cheek expression, Barry said, "I told my children that my heart is as big as my body: don't worry, there's plenty of it there for you."

RELATIONSHIP PATTERNS

Given the combination of experimental data, theoretical approaches and real-life stories we have presented so far in this chapter, you may be wondering if there is a way to summarize or condense all this information. Basically, you probably want to know, "How do I know if my own relationship pattern is productive or destructive?"

To answer this very reasonable question, we return to the four questions addressed at the beginning of the chapter with regard to patterns and trends in loving relationships.

1. *How do they affect our lives?* Knowledge is power and, for many of our readers, merely knowing that patterns and trends in life and relationships are not only natural and expected, but unavoidable and necessary, may be enough to diffuse anxiety about them. Part of our job is to educate our clients as well as to help them "fix" their problems. Therefore, when thinking about the patterns of your own life and relationships, ask yourself: "Is there really a problem here, or am I making one up because it is unfamiliar and therefore scary?" A second question is about trend: "Is there a noticeable negative trend in my life or relationship that truly concerns me, or am I merely afraid of any type of change?" Most of us can answer these questions just by giving them a little thought. If we are relatively happy overall but fear the unknown, then you probably don't need to be too concerned. If you either can't answer the question or your answer is "Yes, this pattern or

trend is a real problem," then it may be time to seek professional help.

2. *How do they affect our relationship?* This is closely tied to the previous question, except that you may want to focus more heavily on trend than on patterns. Our advice is straightforward: *If you sense a persistent negative trend or downward spiral in your relationship, you should strongly consider some type of intervention.* Whether that means seeking professional counseling, having a good heart-to-heart chat or dealing with it some other way, depends on how serious the trend is and if you think it poses a serious threat to you and/or your relationship.
3. *Do I or we want to change anything about us?* Again, our advice is to think about change over long periods of time. Are the patterns just another annoyance you can live with or do the patterns cause disturbance to the point that action is warranted? Also, look for recurring self-defeating and self-destructive patterns that form trend lines. Reviewing Dr. Emener's case examples in this chapter to see if any match your own circumstances may be a good place to start.
4. *If we do make any changes, what differences would the changes make?* This is where the rest of this book can help you, and a good piece of advice is: keep reading! But do not forget the very first piece of advice offered in the introduction to this chapter: *No person can rationally expect to be happy all the time.* If that's what you want, then you just are not looking at life as an adult.

THE RELATIONSHIP PARADOX

We end the chapter with one final case from Dr. Emener's experience. Allie, a twenty-seven-year-old high school math teacher, was increasingly frustrated with her relationships with men. "Why do they always try to control me?" she asked. As they discussed "-the men in her life, Allie shared with Bill that her father, a career military officer, was very controlling of everyone in her family. Furthermore, her high school boyfriend, her fiancé in college, her first husband and her current boyfriend, "all tended to be very controlling." Allie not only resented them for being so manipulative and controlling, but she also indicated that she resented them because "basically they were so insecure." After reading a self-help book that Dr. Emener had recommended to her, she said to him, "This is an interesting paradox, Dr. Emener. I resent the controlling men in my life not only because they're controlling, but also because they are so terribly insecure. The paradox, however, is that I am initially attracted to them because they are controlling and I am basically insecure. Maybe I just need to learn to be a controlling person?"

"Well Allie, that would be an option," Dr. Emener replied. However, maybe we ought to put that off for a while and begin by identifying some ways by which you can *take more control of your own life*."

Over the next six-months, Allie engaged in some heightened, detailed planning of her day-to-day and week-to-week activities. She identified those things she enjoyed and wanted to do in her life and made sure that she was able to do them. By doing so, she was exercising more control over her own life. Interestingly enough, her boyfriend didn't like that and eventually broke-off their relationship. Allie said with a smile, "Now that I am exercising more control over my own life, I seem to find myself less attracted to controlling men, and controlling men seem to be less attracted to me. That's wonderful!"

Bill had not seen or heard from Allie for about a year when he received a little note from her. The end of the note read, "Someday I would like you to meet my new boyfriend, Jonathan, if that would be possible. He doesn't try to control me and I do not try to control him. We each control our own lives and jointly engage in some controls so that we can enjoy our relationship together. I am so happy! Hugs, Allie."

Sometimes we exercise the most control over our own lives and those of our partners by consciously choosing not to control them. Sometimes it is necessary for all of us simply to get out of our own way and instead flow along with the patterns and trends that carry us through our lives.

* * * * * *

If we understand the patterns and trends in our own lives, and we understand the patterns and trends in each other's lives, then maybe we'll better understand the patterns and trends in our relationship, as well as the patterns in our patterns and the trends in our trends.

Chapter Eight

DIVORCE AND SEPARATION

As they sat in the parents' pew watching their son and new daughter-in-law exchanging marriage vows, they glanced into each other's eyes with a silent, understanding exchange of their shared bewilderment: *"That was us 30 years ago. What happened?"*

Divorce, the dissolution, separation and disunion of a marriage is a major life event. Commensurate with the spiraling rate of divorce in the United States over the past decade, the multifaceted aspects of divorce indeed can be appreciated in the fact that some human service professionals (e.g., lawyers and counselors) specialize in it, and books have been written with focus on specific aspects of it (e.g., the legal aspects and the psychology). Marriage, separation and divorce represent three distinctly different kinds of loving relationships. It is not uncommon to hear individuals, such as those in the parents' pew above, say things such as:

> *"The day we got our divorce, I felt convinced that we still loved each other very much. We just couldn't live together anymore."*

> *"We've been separated for almost two years, and I still love him. But I don't know if it would ever work for us."*

> *"I still love her so much, and probably always will. But, there's been so much pain and hurt between us that even if she ever asked*

me to consider trying to get back together again, I don't know if I could – or would even want to try."

"That marriage was the nightmare from hell! What in God's name ever possessed me to marry that lunatic? How could I have been so blind? All I ask for is to never have to see his face again for the rest of my life!"

Unquestionably, it is appropriate that this book on loving relationships address divorce and separation.

This chapter certainly is not designed to address all of the legal, financial, occupational, familial, economic, physical and emotional considerations of divorce and separation. We offer a set of what we believe are pearls of wisdom attained in our experiences over the past many combined years. Between us, we have counseled and/or mediated every conceivable type of relationship issue related to marriage, separation and divorce, and/or helped those undergoing divorce and separation to negotiate nearly every type of settlement agreement one could imagine. It is fair to assume that our readers are unlikely to experience or encounter any situation to which we have not already been exposed. We hope that our experiences will translate into meaningful insights for you.

We repeatedly have noticed a number of questions pertinent to divorce and separation that depict many of the recurring issues for people:

1. *What might I expect to experience? That is, what are some of the typical stages of divorce?*
2. *What do I need to consider doing to protect myself so that I can minimize my pain and sorrow?*
3. *What are some do's and don't-do's as I go through this?*
4. *In terms of what I may experience, what might be some of the effects of time?*
5. *I think I know what I will need to do as time goes on, but at what pace should I move ahead?*

6. *How can I deal with my anger after the divorce is over so that I can get on with my life?*
7. *How can we protect our children from psychological trauma?*
8. *How can we finalize this divorce without having an unfair arrangement forced on us by the family court system?*
9. *How can we retain our rights to see and care for our children after the divorce?*

These questions are not by any means all-inclusive. Moreover, you may notice they fall into somewhat different categories. For example, the first six concern personal issues related to personal adjustment and functioning throughout separation and divorce. Question 7 pertains to the psychological welfare of children in the context of a divorce. The last two questions address matters of control over economic and child visitation issues – the very important "who gets what?" questions.

Despite the wide range of issues brought out by these questions, they are all representative of the primary concerns of adults who are contemplating or experiencing separation and/or divorce. Within selected question areas, we shall discuss pertinent issues, share some relevant experiences of our clients, and offer some suggestions and recommendations that may be of assistance to you. (Those areas not addressed below are covered in other sections of this book.)

STAGES OF DIVORCE

Although we have read several theories by other specialists regarding the stages of divorce, the entire subject area is at best murky. The research is, in many cases, confounded by multiple sources of variance and/or has not been replicated. In fact, we feel it is fair to state that the stage approaches to divorce may not be appropriate as a general model. We do not know of any commonly specific stages of divorce that apply to all people. All of the individuals whom we have known in our personal lives, as well as those with whom we have worked as a psychologist or mediator, have experienced stages or identifiable processes of their divorces that were individualized. Thus, we want to remind you that there are no specific identifiable stages for all people – e*veryone's experiences are unique unto themselves*.

Our personal and professional experiences and observations have revealed five identifiable aspects of divorce that tend to be critical. Because they are typically experienced in order, you may consider them stages, though bear in mind our thoughts on the uniqueness of each experience. The following will briefly discuss each of these five critical aspects and will include some discussion pertinent to the generalized considerations within them.

I. The decision.. It is not uncommon for people to come to see us because they are having difficulties trying to decide whether or not to file for a divorce. Similarly, individuals will at times come to us and say, "My husband (or wife) has asked me for a divorce. I do not know what to do. Should I say, okay let's get a divorce or should I suggest that we try to fix our marriage?" Your decision-making process may be easier for you if you will give focused attention to two areas of concern: (1) From a cognitive perspective, *think* about and make a list of: (a) the pros and cons of trying to fix you marriage, and (b) the pros and cons of filing for divorce. Thinking it through is always highly recommended. And, (2) from an affective perspective, try to remain cognizant of how you *feel* about it. As one of our clients poignantly said, "I have thought it through and considered the pros and cons of trying to fix our marriage as well as filing for divorce. However, it just does not feel right at this point! We've been married for over ten years, so why am I in such a hurry? I think I am just going to take some time to think about it and let it settle in – when it feels right, I'll do it; if it doesn't feel right, I won't do it." We frequently have said to our friends and clients, "Slow down the movie!" – our tongue-in-cheek way of suggesting that they may be in too much of a hurry and may need to slow down. Most of the pressure to make a decision regarding a divorce tends to come from within the person. You therefore may also want to ask yourself another question:

"Why am I in such a hurry and where is the pressure coming from?" When your decision seems to be a correct decision for you (i.e., you think it's in your best interest) and when it feels right, then you are ready to act on it.

We have a colleague, a couples counselor herself, who thinks that the wedding vows should be changed to end with the phrase "to have and to hold forever, or at least until you can't stand it any longer." While we offer this anecdote in part because it is amusing, there is more than a grain of truth to it. In our experience, most people who undergo a divorce before thinking and feeling it through long enough to be sure it's the right decision, or who do so without trying to fix the relationship first, come to regret their haste. It is very easy to underestimate the emotional and economic trauma of divorce. Likewise, it is hard to overestimate the difficulty in finding a new partner that will truly be an improvement over your most recent one. In many cases, effective couples or marriage counseling is a truly worthwhile alternative to divorce. (We make this statement both from the experiences of our clients and our own previous marriages.)

We therefore recommend a person confronted with a decision regarding separation or divorce to focus on *"Why should I..."* kinds of questions. Examples of these include: *Why should I* separate from my wife (or husband)? *Why should I* file for a divorce from my husband (or wife)? *Why should I* suggest that we see a psychologist or a marriage counselor? Nonetheless, it also can be helpful to consider what we call the *contra- question.* Examples of contra-questions may include: *Why shouldn't I* separate from my wife (or husband)? *Why shouldn't I* file for a divorce from my husband (or wife)? *Why shouldn't I* suggest that we see a psychologist or a marriage counselor? During a recent marriage counseling session, John said to his wife, "Can we afford to take that two-week vacation together?" She gently, yet firmly, replied, "Can we afford not to?" It has been our experience that attending to contra-questions facilitates our having a deeper and richer understanding and appreciation of the issues and consequences of our decisions. And in the overall decision-making process, this is very important.

Finally, consider the question of reciprocity: "What does my partner or spouse think about the relationship?" "How would *I* feel if he or she were to suggest we separate or divorce?" Our society, for better or worse, reinforces self-centeredness. It is easy to forget what you have shared with your partner, how he or she may have been of great solace to you in the past. The fastest pathway from civility to anger and even hatred, is insensitivity to the feelings of your significant other.

"Why should I divorce my wife?" was a question that Ralph exclusively addressed while he proceeded to separate and move out into his own apartment and see an attorney. When he came to see Dr. Emener, "Just to see if you could be of any help to me," Bill asked him to consider a contra-question: "Why shouldn't I divorce my wife?" He called Dr. Emener three weeks later and said, "I had had a real long list of answers to my original question, 'Why should I divorce my wife?' but over the past few weeks I found myself developing an almost equally long list of answers to the contra-question, 'Why shouldn't I divorce my wife?' Last night Shirley and I were talking and we decided to explore the possibilities of reconciliation. Could you recommend a good marriage counselor for us?" Not only did Ralph help Bill appreciate the value of the contra-question, but he also reminded him that when we make important decisions such as those pertaining to separation and/or divorce, it also is a good idea to remain open to the possibility that if for some reason it doesn't seem right, you may want to revisit your original question(s) and possibly even change your mind.

A decision regarding a separation and/or a divorce is a process, not an event. While you are focusing on your thoughts and feelings regarding your decision, also try to remain aware of your decision-making process.

II. Communication of the decision. After you have made a decision, the next question is: "How do I communicate my decision?" Always keep in mind that *how* you communicate your decision is as important as the decision itself. The following series of questions tends to capture the majority of concerns that individuals have with regard to the communication of their decision. (Please note that although the following questions use male and female pronouns, they are not gender-specific and are equally applicable to both men and women). "*How* do I tell her?" "*How* can I tell her in such a way that she doesn't get hurt?" "*What* should I actually say to him?" "*How* will he react when I tell him?" "*Where* should I tell him – over the telephone or in a public place such as a restaurant in case he gets violent?" "*When* should I tell her?" We suspect that you will find most of your questions regarding how to communicate your decision will begin with: *How... What... Where...* and *When...* words. As you think through these questions, however, you also may find it helpful to ask yourself some *Why*? question. In most cases the communication of a decision regarding divorce is never easy, painless or comfortable for either party. Making the communication of your decision *easier, as painless as possible* and *as comfortable as possible*, may indeed be more realistic goals to consider.

III. Negotiation areas. Should you decide to separate from or divorce your loved one, it is understandable that you would be attending to settlement issues. Questions regarding what I will get, what he or she will get, and alimony and child support agreements are important considerations. We would suggest, nonetheless, that it also is helpful if you can negotiate some relationship issues. For example, during your separation or after your divorce, can you set some boundaries, limitations and guidelines regarding your relationship? Here are some examples to illustrate this consideration: "I appreciate your allowing me to leave all my tools in the garage, but I will never come over without calling first." "When I bring the children back on Sunday evenings, I will call you first." "While we are separated, I would be open to talk with you at anytime. However, I would appreciate it if you would not call me after ten o'clock in the evenings." "If you would like to get together so we can talk about things, that would be fine with me. However, I prefer that we meet at a public place, like a restaurant, a beach or a mall, and I will drive my own car and meet you there." "When your mail comes to the house, I will leave it in the mailbox with a rubber band around it. That way you can come by and pick it up at anytime." Again, setting some boundaries and honoring them can be very helpful.

If you find that emotional issues such as feelings of deep hurt or abandonment make boundary-setting discussions impossible, then by all means think about seeking the help of a professional counselor or hiring a family mediator.

IV. Divorce. What is a divorce? We frequently have said to our clients that there is a difference between a *legal divorce*, a *physical divorce* and a *psychological divorce*. When you think of a divorce from a legal perspective, try to remember that this is a legally sanctioned, adjudicated and finite declaration of each individual's continuing responsibilities and culpabilities regarding each other (as well as children if there are any involved). A physical divorce is when we no longer see each other, make love together, go to dinner together or live together. In essence, we are physically apart. A psychological divorce is one in which your former spouse is no longer central to your psychological and spiritual being; he or she no longer has a significant place in your heart. As one of his clients said to Dr. Emener, "I got my physical divorce in 2001 when she moved out and began living with someone else. I got my legal divorce in 2002. But it wasn't until 2004 that I felt that I had finally gotten my psychological divorce; it took me two years to get her out of my mind, my spirit and my heart. I just could not stop myself from being in love with her."

It is important to remember that everyone's experiences are not the same. For example, a client, Linda once said to Dr. Lambos, "I am convinced that I psychologically divorced Robert in 2004 but didn't get the courage to physically divorce him and move out until 2005. We've basically been gone and out of each other's lives for two years now. Can you recommend a good divorce attorney? It's about time for me to make it legal." Again, in terms of timing, *when you are physically, psychologically and/or legally separated and/or divorced from someone, is unique to, and for, you.*

V. Post-divorce processes. After a divorce is legally and physically finalized, it is not uncommon for individuals to go through two processes: (1) the grieving process; and (2) the forgiving process.

The experience of going through a grieving process (discussed in detail in Chapter Twelve) also is unique to all individuals. However, it is fair to say that it is better understood as being made up of discrete stages than is divorce. The experiences of shock, denial, desperation, anger and restitution can be very difficult at times. Nonetheless, it is important to remember that a divorce entails loss – the loss of the person, the loss of the relationship, the loss of a dream, and possibly the loss of many other things (e.g., the house that you lived in, pets, daily contact with your children, etc.). The forgiving process, which people sometimes think of as being one of the latter stages of the grieving process, is where you not only forgive the other person for what he or she has done to you, but you also forgive yourself for having allowed it to happen. As we have said many times throughout this book, recovery (not only from an addiction but from the loss of a relationship) is not contingent upon forgetting; it is continent upon forgiving.

Charting, plotting and understanding your own unique aspects of your separation and divorce can be very helpful. And try to remember, a separation and/or a divorce is not an event – it is a process.

SELF-PROTECTION

When clients come to us and say that they are separated and/or filing for divorce, one of the first questions we ask is, "What are you doing to take care of yourself?" It is very easy to be hurt as a result of ignorance and self-neglect. Protecting yourself and others in your family is important, whether legally, occupationally, financially, physically and/or emotionally. If you have been emotionally connected and/or married to another person, it is understandable that you may still have feelings of love, care, concern and possibly wanting to be helpful to that person. Once you are separated and/or divorced, however, in addition to being caring and concerned for the other person, it is also important that you pay special attention to yourself – especially to protect yourself from your own vulnerability. You may feel secure physically and financially, but that does not mean that you are secure emotionally and legally. It is understandable for a person in such a situation to be vulnerable. Thus, we highly recommend that you understand and accept the possibility that you may indeed be vulnerable and take steps to protect yourself from your vulnerability.

In your self-protection mode, it is fitting that you consider your needs and desires, and yourself in general, to be your first concern – you are Number One! As discussed above, however, you must balance this with trying to remain sensitive, yet at the same time *not* be punitive, harmful and destructive to others in the process. For example, you may indeed be able to attend to yourself without emotionally beating up, physically abusing, economically destroying and/or hurting in any way your (ex-)loved one. As Dr. Emener recently said to a friend, "I truly understand your need to consider yourself Number One at this time in your life. However, is there any room in your life for anyone to be Number 2? Can you take care of yourself *and* be a little sensitive to John, who is economically destitute and hurting like hell because he still loves you so much?" She must have heard Bill because she began to talk with John on the telephone when he called. She told John that she realized his economic situation and was sorry that he was hurting financially. Interestingly, John later shared with Dr. Emener that her responding to him with compassion was very helpful: "Okay, I know she's not in love with me anymore and that still hurts. But at least she's not emotionally beating me up anymore. For a while it felt like she was grinding me into the ground with her heels every time she got the chance."

SOME DO'S AND DON'T-DO'S

Under the rubric of self-protection, we frequently offer clients what we refer to as the *Three Don't-Do's and Six Do's.* When an individual first tells one of us that he or she is separated and/or going through a divorce, we review with them the *three and six list* to remind them of things they can be aware of and sensitive to in the process of protecting themselves.

Three Don't-Do's

1. ***Don't do anything stupid.*** We unfortunately have known many men and women to do things immediately following a separation or a divorce that in the final analysis, as they admitted, "were stupid!" For example, one gentleman said, "For the last two months, I would screw anything walking. I guess I had to prove to myself that it wasn't me." And a young woman said, "For the last three weeks I have been the easiest punch in the city. It was like I had to prove to myself that I was still attractive." Selling your house for half of what it is worth, giving away valuable belongings and quitting a good job are also examples of doing things that you may later look back on as stupid.
2. ***Don't do anything to excess.*** During a separation and/or a divorce, try to avoid doing things in excess, especially if they are harmful things such as excessive gambling, drinking or anything that in the long run is detrimental to you.
3. ***Don't avoid reality.*** As we discussed earlier in this chapter, denial is one of the first stages of the grieving process. However, if for example your husband has set up his own bank account, transferred the credit cards into his name only, has not come home from work before eleven o'clock at night for the last three weeks and has applied for a transfer to another city, there indeed may be a message there! Although it may be emotionally very difficult to accept and tolerate reality, try not to deny it.

Six Do's

1. ***See an attorney.*** Talking with a divorce lawyer in your local community who knows the laws of your state is one of the first things that we recommend. We also suggest it is a good idea not only to tell the attorney everything that is going on, but also to ask, "Is there anything that I need to know, or is there anything that I need to do, to protect myself?"
2. ***See a counselor, mediator, or both.*** Discussing your issues and concerns with a professional counselor, psychologist or mediator not only can be very helpful, but talking with a professional also can be preventative, (e.g., he or she can help you prevent further harm later on down the road). It also may be helpful for you to know that the person whom you already have met, and hopefully feel comfortable with, will be there for you should you need to talk to a professional.
3. ***Be aware of you own vulnerability.*** In the process of being separated and/or going through a divorce, you may not be able to take care of yourself as well as you would be able to under other circumstances. This does not mean that you are a weak, insecure or a less-than-strong human being! All this means is that for this brief period of time you may not understand everything that is going on, you may not be able to foresee and anticipate things that are going to occur, and you may not have the self-discipline and self-control that you typically have. Accept the possibility that you may be vulnerable.
4. ***Develop a support network.*** Surround yourself with good friends who not only understand what you are going through, but who also will be supportive and helpful (and not take advantage of you). As one of our clients said, "To some extent, I am only as strong as the people around me. Fortunately, while I am emotionally hurting very much, I'm not scared. I have good friends standing by me."

5. ***Try to get into a good routine.*** Establishing a good and nourishing diet, a restful sleeping pattern, a comfortable work schedule, and an enjoyable and relaxing recreational life are important. Many times in situations such as separation and/or divorce, people do not eat properly, they consume alcohol to excess, they do not have good sleeping patterns, and they find their lives in total chaos. Having a routine in your life not only will help you minimize, and perhaps prevent, many harmful and possibly dangerous side effects of separation and divorce, but also will contribute to your sense of security and well-being.
6. ***Stay active.*** Feelings of embarrassment, depression, sadness, guilt and shame easily can put us into a behavior pattern of withdrawal. "All I want to do is lie on the couch; I don't want to see people," is a statement we frequently hear. It is a hallmark of impending or experienced clinical depression. It is, therefore, very important to try to stay active, even if it means asking your friends to help you to stay active. During a last session with Norma, who had "successfully gone through a very difficult divorce," she said, "You're right, Dr. Emener, it was helpful for me to always remember your three don't's and six do's. I kept them on a 3x5 card on my refrigerator door as a constant reminder. Last week I took the card off of the door and it felt great! But I'm going to keep the card – in case any friends of mine ever need it."

EFFECTS OF TIME

"Time is my best ally," is a statement that is frequently made when someone says, in effect, "I will get over my divorce; it is just a matter of time." Two of the many critical aspects of time that are relevant to separation and divorce involve (1) the concern that Kim had with "When is it a good time for me to file for divorce?" and (2)

Kevin's experience with "When I finally got my psychological divorce."

When talking with Kim, a forty-three-year-old tax accountant, she shared what turned out to be a rather humorous yet poignant experience with her twenty-year old son. "A few weeks ago, my son asked me why I filed for a divorce from his father in March. 'That messed up my college spring break!' he said. I told him that I was truly sorry that that had happened to him. I had considered waiting until April, but since I am a tax accountant that would not be a very good time for me. I also thought of waiting until May, but that is when he and his sister would be getting out of school for the summer. I thought of waiting until June, but June was our wedding anniversary month. I thought of waiting until July, but since our family had always had our annual Fourth of July Bash, symbolically that would not have worked very well either. I thought of waiting until August, but that's when he and his sister would be going back to college. I thought of waiting until September, but that would have messed up my birthday. I thought of waiting until October, but that would have messed up his father's birthday. I thought of waiting until November, but that would have messed up Thanksgiving. I thought of waiting until December – oh sure, Merry Christmas! I thought of waiting until January, but here we go again – Happy New Year. I thought of waiting until February, and thought, 'Wouldn't that make a nice Valentine's Day present!' By that time, he and I were laughing, and I finally said to him, 'I'm sorry, son, but there is never a good time to file for a divorce.'"

Kevin, a thirty-six-year-old computer programmer, shared that it took him approximately three years to overcome his divorce. He brought to one of our sessions a sketch similar to the one in Figure 8.1. As he was describing it, he said, "This is what my relationship with Maria was like when we were married. We each had our own lives yet we were connected.

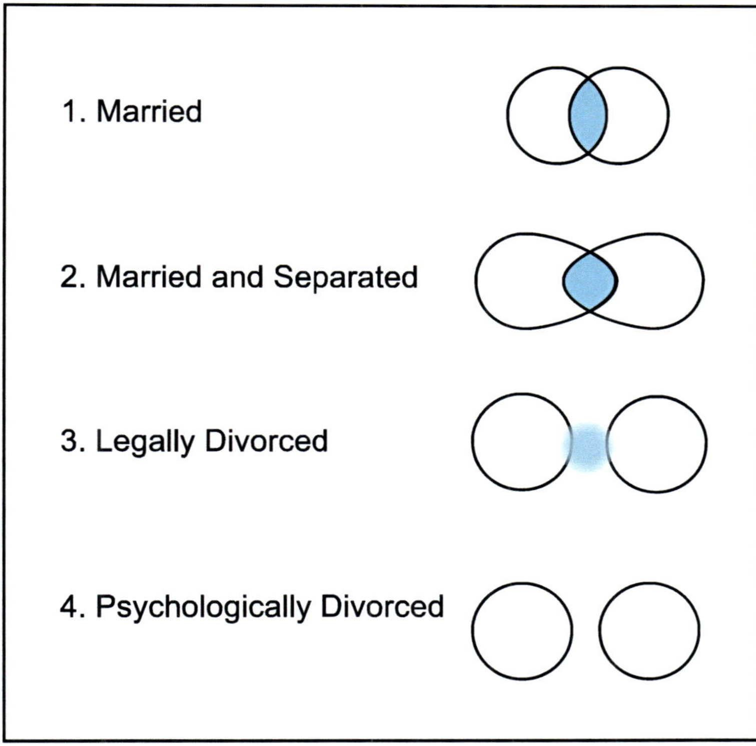

Figure 8.1. Stages of Kevin's Divorce and the Effects of Time.

In the second stage,we still each had our own lives but our life together was definitely starting to fade. Once we were legally divorced, we each had our own lives and there was nothing between us except mountains of unexpressed anger. In addition to my anger, I also was heavily grieving the loss of her and our relationship – I still loved her. To complicate matters, as we began at least to be friendly during our post-divorce times, I did not have a place for her – was she my former wife, my friend, my children's mother. I simply did not know how to deal with her because I did not have a place for her. Over time, however, I was able to forgive her and forgive myself for all of the many transgressions that had occurred in our lives. In my stage four, I feel that I am now psychologically divorced in that Maria and I have our own lives yet can still enjoy the memories of the wonderful times we had together. We now can be caring and loving toward each other and not struggle with all of the crap surrounding whether or not we will ever get back together again."

Time indeed can be our best ally, as long as we do not rush it.

ROCKING IN THE COMFORT ZONE

Jill and her husband had been married for fourteen years before their divorce. She originally came in because she was struggling with her decision as to whether or not she should file for a divorce. Approximately three months after her last visit, she scheduled an appointment with Dr. Emener and came in "Because I am feeling guilty that I have not done anything about my divorce." At that point she had seen an attorney, had all of the legal papers filled out and was separated from her husband (he had voluntary moved out). "For the last three months I have just been doing things that are comfortable. I have not formally and legally filed for my divorce yet. What's wrong?" Dr. Emener replied, "Jill, maybe you are just rocking in the comfort zone." She looked up with surprising eyes and said, "What are you talking about?"

Dr. Emener drew a diagram similar to the one in Figure 8.2. He then said to her, "For the last two years of your marriage, Jill, your quality of life had continued to go down and down.

At that point, however, you made a decision to legally separate and file for a divorce. The process of telling your husband that you wanted to separate and file for divorce, and for him to find an apartment and move out, took approximately six months. Nonetheless, even though that was a difficult time for you, your quality of life did improve somewhat. By the end of that six-months, the two of you had set some boundaries and agreed upon some rules of your separation, and your life had become relatively comfortable. However, you knew that the process of filing for divorce was going to

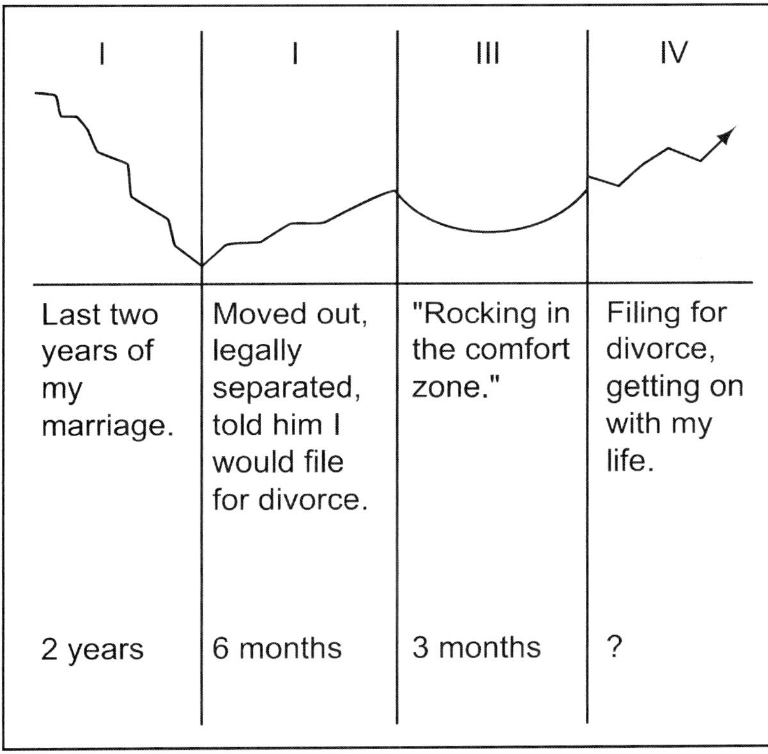

Figure 8.2. Jill's Divorce Process Over Time.

be difficult for you. Understandably, you were not in a big hurry to rush out and do it. For the first time in two and one-half years, you were feeling comfortable. Wanting to stay there in that comfort zone and, in effect, enjoy life for a little while makes total sense to me. The question is: why is it bothering you?" With a sense of relief, Jill said, "I guess it's because I have always been a believer in the philosophy that says if there's something that needs to be done, do it." Bill reminded Jill that the separation and divorce process is a process, not an event. Furthermore, Dr. Emener suggested to her that there is nothing wrong with occasionally taking some time out to catch your breath, enjoy life a little and give yourself an opportunity to recharge you batteries before moving on to the next stage. She nodded her head in understanding and said, "I see what you mean. It is sort of like calling a timeout in the middle of the fourth quarter of a football game." Bill smiled and nodded in agreement.

As a person thinks through and remains in touch with his or her feelings about an impending or in-process separation and/or divorce, having an awareness of *time* and *timing* issues is important. If we were to look at Kim's and Kevin's experiences and Jill's experiences, it would be reasonable to conclude that: (1) there is never a good time to separate and/or file for divorce; (2) the time at which we are legally divorced, physically divorced and psychologically divorced may not be the same for each partner; and (3) in the overall, long-term process of separation and divorce, there's nothing wrong with occasionally calling a timeout, especially when it may be needed.

POST-DIVORCE ANGER

Anger is a very strong emotion that a person can experience during the processes of separation and divorce. "Post-divorce anger," however, is a long-term pervasive emotion that we have observed people struggle with for years following a divorce. Walter's and Sonya's experiences may illustrate this phenomenon.

When talking about how he was feeling about being divorced, Walter said, "For the last twenty of the twenty-five years that I was married to Sonya, she deprived me of feeling loved and being loved. It was very painful for me to see her be so loving toward our children, yet so aloof and cold toward me. I resent her for that! It wasn't until after my divorce and I started dating other women that I realized that I was lovable. I am also angry because in the process of her not being loving toward me while we were married, and maybe in return I was not loving toward her, my children thought of me as a non-loving man. To this day, my daughters will not openly show affection to me or unsolicitedly tell me that they love me. Sometimes I feel incredible anger toward Sonya and my daughters, as well as toward myself. And until I am able to let go of this anger, I will not consider myself emotionally available for any other kind of loving relationship. And I am angry about that too!"

While talking to Dr. Lambos about her divorce from Henry after twenty-eight years of marriage, Becky said, "I am so enraged with Henry! By divorcing me, he deprived me of having a lifelong, loving relationship with the same person. I always had the dream of growing old together, not only with the husband of my children, but also with the grandpa of my grandchildren. And even if I were to someday find someone else with whom to fall in love, it would not be the same. Henry and I share a family root system together, and I simply do not know if I will ever be able to feel toward another man the way I have always felt toward him. Whenever I go to the beach and see an old couple hobbling along, holding hands with their gnarly little fingers, tears roll down my cheeks. Henry robbed me of my dream!"

Post-divorce anger is a strong negative emotion we can experience when we consider our marriage and our divorce from a lifelong, long-term perspective. As a friend of ours who is very depressed and angry recently said, "Whenever I see a family come into a restaurant, I think to myself, 'That used to be me. That could be me. That *should* be me. But it will never be me again.'" And in this sense, post-divorce anger puts us in a position of not only coming to terms with our divorce, but coming to terms with our life over our life span.

Sometimes, when dealing with strong, deep feelings of anger, it is helpful to engage in physical exercise, to read self-help books on anger, to talk with close friends about your anger, and to surround yourself with understanding, compassionate people. Nonetheless, strong, deep feelings of anger also are, at times, best dealt with through the assistance of a professional counselor or therapist. More often than not, a neutral and impartial third-party professional mediator can make a huge difference in settling non-emotional issues.

* * * * * *

A loving relationship is an everlasting relationship of love. Courtship, engagement and marriage are loving relationships that emanate from love. Separation and divorce are loving relationships which emanate from love. Separation relationships and divorce relationships last forever because of love – the difference is in the nature and intensity of the love.

Chapter Nine

Guilt and Shame

"In some crazy way I sort of feel guilty about the way she and I treated each other. We were forever putting each other down. In some respects, that was the only way I could keep her off my back. But you know, I would go to our national headquarters and present a proposal for a multimillion dollar deal and be wined and dined by the brass for doing such an excellent job, but during the ride from the airport to the house I would feel it coming on. By the time I got home, I would feel small, inferior, incompetent and worthless. And usually her opening remarks would be reminders of what I hadn't done around the house before leaving for the business trip and what a hardship it caused for her and the kids. 'What kind of man are you?' she would always ask me, and then add, 'What's wrong with you anyway?' I just couldn't take it anymore!"

What's being expressed here? Guilt? If so, what kind of guilt? Shame? If so, what kind of shame? Is this man feeling ashamed and sensing "Whatever I do, it's not good enough because there's probably something fundamentally wrong with me?" Yes, he is verbalizing the experience of toxic shame in a shame-based relationship. On top of that, he is also feeling guilt because of the way he treated his wife, even though he offers it as having been his only defense against her shaming.

If this scenario rings any bells, then while you are reading this chapter you indeed may want to stay in close touch with your thoughts and feelings about yourself, your loved one and your loving relationship.

In the form of Rational Emotive Behavioral Therapy known as REBT, developed by Albert Ellis and practiced in Dr. Lambos's Tampa practice, guilt is considered one of the "four blocks to happiness" (the other three are anger, anxiety and depression). According to the REBT approach, guilt is the result of two co-occurring beliefs, at least one of which is irrational. The first belief anyone who experiences guilt must feel is *I did something wrong*. The second, that is responsible for the guilt, is *I shouldn't have done that.* Since, as Dr. Ellis was fond of pointing out, "We are all fallible human beings, we all make mistakes," it is entirely possible (but by no means assured) that a person who experiences guilt or shame did in fact do something he or she regrets. If the person actually made a mistake, this first belief may not be irrational. But the second belief – that they *should not* have done so – cannot be considered rational.

Why not? *Because they already did it!* Demanding that reality be different than it is, is not only irrational, but self-defeating and hence toxic. Harboring the impossible demand that what was done cannot, and indeed *must not*, have occurred, simply adds a second (and often worse) problem. And because they then are blaming themselves for being at fault, instead of taking responsibility for their mistake and looking at how to make it better and move forward, their guilt now has become shame and the shame toxic. They have fallen into the self-defeating pattern of putting themselves down and are in worse shape than they would otherwise be.

Guilt and Existential Guilt

Eli came to see Dr. Emener for numerous reasons, among others, "I just can't seem to overcome my constant nervousness and depression. It seems like it's been this way for over a year. I think I really need help in taking a serious look at my life!" Eli, an artist with a local graphics company, had been married to Donna for twelve years. They had three children, ages six, nine and ten. Early into their first session, Dr. Emener asked Eli to identify any particular things that were going on in his life that were especially troublesome or worrisome for him. He quickly responded, "I'm sure that it's my marriage!" After assisting Eli in calming down and feeling more comfortable, Bill asked him to tell his story. In a nutshell, this is what he shared:

> "For the first couple of years of our marriage, everything seemed to be really good for us. That's when we were living in Minnesota. However, we moved down here to Florida about seven years ago, and starting about five years ago our marriage just continued to get worse and worse. We just drifted further and further apart. Being very candid with you, I basically just do not love her anymore. Over the last two years, we have gone on numerous trips, cruises and weekend getaways. I have tried everything that I could think of to rekindle my love for her – but none of it has worked. Donna is a nice person. She is one of the most wonderful people you would ever want to know. The problem is, I do not feel in love with her anymore. I know, however, that she is incredibly in love with me. She tells me that she loves me and acts like she loves me every minute of every day. At the same time, I am very close to my three children. I love them dearly and certainly do enjoy spending time with them. As a family unit, the five of us are very, very happy. Every once in a while, I think about leaving and divorcing her. I get a real warm glow with the thought of being free. The problem then is that I feel so terribly, terribly guilty! She has never done anything to hurt me, she has always loved me, and by every standard I know of, she has been and is an excellent wife. The idea of leaving her and the children just terrifies me – the guilt is incredible. On the other hand, I also feel bad because I'm not doing what I need to do to take care of me. I am still a young man – I'm only thirty-three years old. The idea of spending the next thirty to forty years in the same situation that I'm in now is very depressing. The bottom line, Dr. Emener, is that I feel like I am between a rock and a hard place. I don't know what to do."

After listening to Eli and trying to understand what he was thinking, experiencing and feeling, Bill said to him, "Guilt, rather simplistically defined, is when we feel bad because of something we have done, something we are doing, or something we are thinking about doing. And although you feel that you have a very functional and happy *family*, you are simultaneously experiencing a dysfunctional and very unhappy *marriage*. When you think about leaving Donna and the children, you know that it would cause great emotional pain for them, and thus you feel horribly guilty. At the same time, however, you are also experiencing what I refer to as 'existential guilt' – that is, the guilt that we feel when we sense that we have hurt, are hurting, or might hurt ourselves. Essentially, guilt is when we feel that we have caused a transgression against someone else, and existential guilt is when we feel that we have caused a transgression against ourselves. In a nutshell, you're feeling guilty either way. Either you are feeling guilty because you are thinking about leaving Donna, or you are feeling guilty about staying with Donna." In his tongue-in-cheek style, Dr. Emener occasionally refers to this phenomenon as Guilt 22. By that time, Eli was crying and feeling tremendously sad.

As time went on, Eli made a decision. During a subsequent session, he said, "There's good news and bad news. The bad news is that I identified another source of guilt that was bothering me. The good news is that the same source of guilt motivated me to make a decision and take action. What I mean is that I was feeling guilty about allowing Donna to continue to be in love with me, to think that I was in love with her, and to think that our marriage would last. That simply was not true. Allowing her to continue to think what she was thinking felt dishonest and very uncomfortable for me. It just didn't seem fair. I also recognized that she is also a young person. She is only thirty-two years old. Part of my decision included the thought that the sooner I tell her the truth and get on with the divorce, the sooner she would be able to get on with a real life of her own." Eli also shared with Bill that he had made arrangements for Donna to have an opportunity to talk with a psychologist herself, just in case his telling her that he wanted a divorce would be overly-disturbing to her. Interestingly, Eli added, "She handled it much better than I ever anticipated." The last time Dr. Emener spoke with him, Eli indicated that he was doing very well and that Donna was on her road to recovery. We are happy for Eli, and feel confident that Donna will get on with her life and possibly even be happier than when she was married to Eli.

It is not uncommon for people to find themselves between a rock and a hard place – simultaneously feeling that what they *have done, are doing*, or *will do*, will result in something that is or would be (1) harmful to someone else, *and* (2) harmful to themselves. Recognizing the situation that you are in and continuing to make progress toward resolution is very important. As Eli later said, "Resolving my conflict was extremely difficult. However, I will be the first to tell you that continuing to live in the conflict was even worse!"

Healthy Shame and Toxic Shame

Human beings are not perfect. We realize that, as human beings, we are not able to do everything to perfection – one cannot be all things to all people. People have limitations and are fallible. Healthy people accept their limitations and imperfections as parts of their natural make-up. For example, when talking to a client who was a sports enthusiast, Dr. Emener reminded him about Broadway Joe Namath, one of football's greatest quarterbacks, who told millions of listeners during an interview that he was quitting broadcasting football games because he simply was not good at it. His deep sense of disappointment came clearly through in his words and expressions. This, however, was *healthy shame* – he was totally accepting and appreciative of his many accomplishments (as a football player), yet also accepting and appreciative of his limitations (as a television broadcaster). More recently, Michael Jordan, one of the best basketball players in the history of the game, decided to quit professional basketball and play professional baseball. During an interview, Jordan said that if the day ever came when he would not only feel like a failure but that there was no more reason to expect improvement, he would quit playing baseball and get on with his life. Again, this is an example of healthy shame – an awareness and acceptance of one's limitations as a human being. Healthy shame is an emotion that signals our limitations.

Toxic shame, on the other hand, is an all-pervasive sense that "I am flawed and defective as a human being." It is a basic, core identity, and fundamentally irrational and damaging to the self. With toxic shame come feelings of worthlessness, failure as a person and a detachment of self from self: "I can't identify with myself because I am flawed, I am bad, and there's something fundamentally wrong with me." Thus, the person with healthy shame might say, "I lost the game" or "I got drunk last night;" and the person with toxic shame would say, "I am a loser" or "I am a drunk."

There is a quick and foolproof test of whether any shame you may be experiencing is healthy or toxic. It was alluded to earlier in the chapter. Because toxic shame always involves *blame* of oneself or others, we recommend that whenever you feel any type of regret (which is, after all, a form of shame), immediately look to see if you are blaming yourself or another for your feelings. If you are, then your shame is toxic. If, on the other hand, you are unconcerned with who is to blame, and are focused on how to make the situation better – including acknowledging your role in it – then you know your shame is healthy. Simply stated, blame of self or others is a root cause of toxic shame. It accomplishes nothing positive for anybody. The better able you are to avoid the "blame game," the more psychologically healthy you will be.

Guilt and toxic shame can erode a loving relationship very quickly. Jerome and Lindsey came to see Dr. Lambos because they were experiencing increasing conflict in their relationship. Having just returned from New York City on vacation, they described a Friday evening they spent at the Albert Ellis Institute where they sat in on one of Dr. Ellis's Friday night seminars on REBT – complete with a demonstration involving audience members with real problems. Impressed that REBT might offer a solution to their own relationship difficulties, they came to the Rational Living Foundation in Tampa for counseling.

Jerome, an accomplished jazz-rock guitarist with lots of studio work on his résumé and a band that had regular bookings but had yet to make a breakthrough, began. "Dr. Lambos, I love Lindsey and I love my work. Unfortunately, I haven't made it yet in the music business because when I proposed to Lindsey, she said she didn't want to move away from Tampa. I promised Lindsey that this was where we would live, and so we married. The problem is, in the music business, there are very few opportunities in Tampa for anything but local gigs in bars. As you might imagine, I don't make much money from the band, even working other day jobs and giving lessons." Lindsey jumped in at that point. "We've been married three years and we've been happy, but I feel strongly that it's time to start a family. We can't do that on what Jerome makes, and even if I keep working afterwards, it will be tough. I know Jerome loves his music, but he's also great with computers and he's been offered a job with a media company in town. If he took it, it would solve everything! But he doesn't want to take it because he would have to start on evening shifts and that would mean giving up the band. I am getting less and less patient, yet every time I bring it up, he says all it does is make him feel inadequate. Then he tells me I'm being selfish, then *I* start to feel guilty. We agreed when we married that we both wanted children, and now is the time. It seems like all we do now is accuse each other of who is at fault for our recurring arguments, and I can't live like this much longer."

Dr. Lambos replied, "As a former failed musician myself, I feel for you both. Let me start by advising you that you have two separate problems, and I can only help you with one of them." Both looked up quizzically. Dr. Lambos continued, "You have a marriage that is itself healthy, but you have developed conflicting goals, or at least goals that can't both be met at the same time. I am happy to help you work through the possibilities and come to some type of compromise or agreement, but as your therapist I am more concerned about your *other* problem: the blame, shame and guilt you both experience. I can tell you that until you fix this second problem, the first will never be successfully addressed. No matter what you decide, one of you will feel like they gave up something dear and blame the other for it. My bet is the other party will feel guilty about it. This blaming and guilt very well may destroy your marriage. On the other hand, if we can fix these emotional issues, the solution to the first problem may be much easier to figure out."

Over the next six sessions, Jerome and Lindsey learned about irrational beliefs, about the danger and uselessness of blaming, and about how much of the problem they thought they had actually was based on their irrational beliefs. By *re-framing* their perspectives, giving up blame, and focusing on a solution that met both their needs, they were able to work out their issues. Jerome gave up the band and took the computer job. Lindsey was soon pregnant and delighted. With some of the extra income from Jerome's job, he was able to purchase a digital music studio and continue to compose and play. Dr. Lambos ran across Jerome at an Apple Store a few months ago. He has several "indie" singles available on the Internet, is gaining recognition as a guitarist and songwriter, and even likes his computer job. Finally, he beamed with pride when he introduced Bill to his new son, Sean. "Life is good when you let it be" was Jerome's parting comment.

Guilt-Based and Shame-Based Relationships

Sometimes people in loving relationships have difficulties in figuring out why they do not do what they want to do. For example, when Dr. Emener was talking with Eduardo about his relationship with his wife, he said that she "continually got away with doing whatever she wanted to do and that he simply would never argue with her or deny her anything she wanted." She, however, was picking up on his low-level anger and resentment toward her and her "always getting her own way." The combination of his and her interpersonal dynamics was starting to seriously interfere with their relationship and their family. Eduardo was asked if he ever discussed any of this with his wife. He said, "No." Then, "Ed, do you ever tell her what you want and don't want? Do you ever tell her how you feel about her always getting her own way?" He again answered, "No." Bill suggested that it would be helpful for them to discuss some of the reasons why he was being so passive with his wife. "We have been married for eight years," Eduardo said, "and we have two beautiful children. During our second year of marriage, when she was pregnant with Pedro, our first, I went out one night with some friends. In the course of the evening, I had sex with another woman. I don't know what happened, but we all were drinking and… it happened. I felt so guilty. I told Maria. She went crazy on me. She cried for three days straight. I promised her it would never ever happen again and that I would cherish her forever. And I do! So what ever she wants, it's okay with me. But sometimes, I wonder if she uses my guilt to play me... you know – to get what she wants all the time." As they discussed this aspect of Eduardo and Maria's relationship, it became clear that they had a guilt-based relationship that was preventing honest and open communications of feelings, wishes, wants and preferences. The possibilities of manipulation and control also entered the conversation regarding their relationship. Eduardo eventually confronted Maria. He told Bill that he said to her, "Maria, I love you dearly and I truly feel sorry for what I did six years ago. But I think I have paid my penalty. I can't continue to just allow you to do whatever you want because I feel guilty about what I did six years ago. We have to get this out of the way. It's a problem in our relationship." It was not an easy task for them, but we are pleased to share with you that they worked through it, and the last time Bill saw Eduardo, he said that he and Maria were getting along much better, and that he was "feeling so much better about himself and his relationship with her." Guilt-based relationships indeed can be very trying to individuals in loving relationships. Julie and Jerry's relationship, on the other hand, was somewhat different.

Julie, a salesperson for a large, national marketing company, came to see Dr. Emener because of her difficulties with her husband, Jerry. She and Jerry had been married for approximately two years, did not have any children, had been separated for the previous three months, and she had just moved into her own apartment. Difficulties with Julie's self-perceptions were obvious right from the outset. For example, during their first session, Julie, an extremely attractive twenty-eight-year-old woman who had successfully competed in numerous beauty contests, high impact aerobic contests and photo shoot contests over the past seven years, said, "Lately I have been gaining so much weight. I'm getting so fat, and I don't know what to do with my hair anymore!" With wringing hands and a sad heart, she mentioned many times that she was "feeling so guilty about having moved out on Jerry." Basically, when she came to see Dr. Emener, she was convinced that what she needed help with was her guilt.

As time went on, however, other aspects of Julie's life began to emerge with more clarity. For example, when Bill asked her to tell him about some recollections of her childhood, she said things like, "No matter what I did, it never seemed to be good enough. I remember my mother always saying to me, 'Julie, you look like you're gaining weight again!' Whenever I would get anything less than an 'A' in school, my father would remind me of how intelligent I was and asked me what was wrong with me." Dr. Emener asked Julie whether she knew the difference between guilt and shame. She said, "I don't think so." On a blank piece of paper, he wrote out some words similar to those that are in Figure 9.1. He said to her, "Julie, guilt is basically when we feel bad because of *failure of doing*. We feel bad because of something we did.When we are feeling guilty, we tend to focus on our transgressions – things that we did that were wrong. Moreover, when we are experiencing guilt we tend to fear punishment. On the other hand, when we are experiencing shame, we feel bad because of a *failure of being* – like, 'There's something

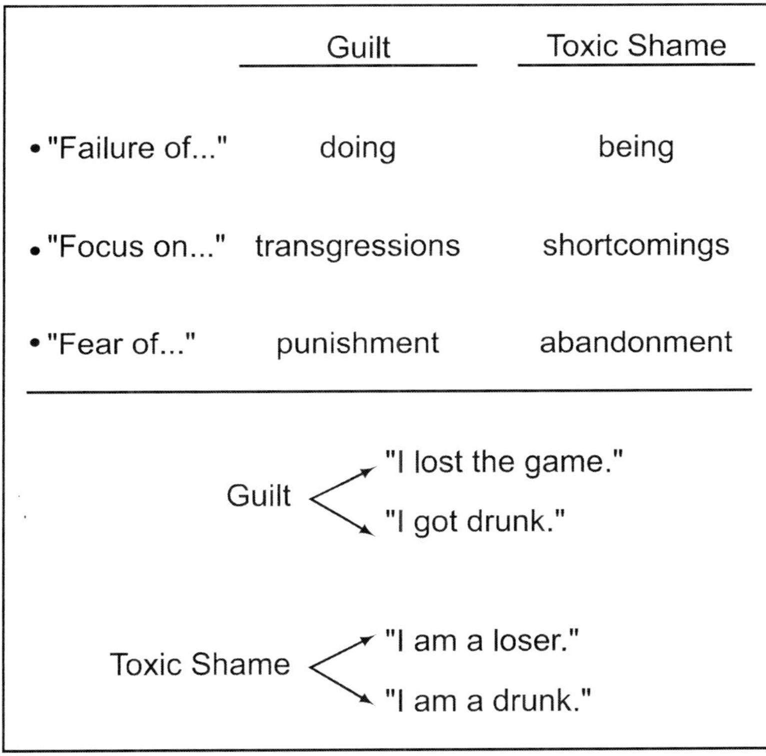

Figure 9.1. Guilt versus Toxic Shame.

wrong with me as a human being.' When we are experiencing shame, we tend to focus on our shortcomings and fear of abandonment. Do the differences between these two make sense to you in your life?" Almost with a sense of enlightenment, Julie quickly responded, "All of my life I have felt that there was something wrong with me. As a matter of fact, I have often wondered why Jerry married me in the first place! All the time that we have been married and living together, I was constantly worrying about my shortcomings for fear that Jerry would eventually leave me if he ever found out what a bad person I really am." Dr. Emener asked her if possibly she were experiencing a self-fulfilling prophecy with regard to her moving out and contemplating a divorce from Jerry. After thinking about that notion for a few minutes, Julie turned and said, "That's a good question! What you're suggesting is that possibly because I believed that there was something fundamentally wrong with me as a human being, Jerry would eventually find out and leave anyway. And with the anxiety and nervousness associated with my worrying about when that would eventually happen, I sort of moved things along for myself by moving out and telling Jerry that maybe I would file for divorce. In other words, what you're saying, Dr. Emener, is that maybe I have been shooting myself in the foot?" Dr. Emener replied, "That's something that we'll continue to talk about, Julie, because you're the best one to know the answer to that question."

In subsequent therapy sessions, Julie and Dr. Emener were able to address many of the shame-based aspects of her life. Fortunately, as she was able to work through her own shame, she noticed that her relationship with Jerry began to improve. It is interesting to note, that when she invited him to one of their sessions "so that Dr. Emener could meet him," she said, "In two weeks I am moving out of my apartment and back into the house. Things seem to have really improved for the two of us. When I used to be around Jerry, I always felt inferior and put-down. The problem was that I always felt that he was the one putting me down, when in reality he wasn't putting me down at all. I was just feeling put down. The most important thing that I realized was that I was putting myself down and blaming it on Jerry."

A few months after his last session with Julie, Bill received a brief note from her stating that she wanted to share some exciting news. In her note were the words, "Everything is going extremely well with us, and I couldn't be happier. And the doctor told me that my due date is June 5th!"

It is important for individuals in loving relationships to understand the difference between guilt and shame, and the critical role played by the destructive act of blaming oneself or one's partner.

There are two critical dimensions of guilt and shame: rational versus irrational guilt (based on blaming vs. accepting and fixing), and healthy versus toxic shame (based on mistaking our actions or behaviors for who we are at our cores). Learning to manage each of these "semantic errors," people can solve many of their worst problems by self-monitoring and catching themselves when they fall into these traps. In healthy relationships, blaming is seen as unacceptable, and both individuals tend to feel highly respected, valued and honored by themselves as well as each other.

* * * * * *

If I have any perfection about me, it is in my acceptance and appreciation of my imperfection.

If our relationship has any perfection about it, it is in our acceptance and appreciation of our imperfections

Chapter Ten

FEARS AND PHOBIAS

"I have wanted to leave Harold for a long time. I thought about divorcing him seven or eight years ago. I know what to do and probably could do it rather easily. I'd probably be good at it too. I know it would be the best thing for me. Probably would be the best thing for him too. I have even spoken to an attorney once. But I've been a married woman for the past twenty-three years, now I'm forty-four years old and the thought of being single scares the hell out of me."

"For a long time now, I have known that I want to ask Jennifer to marry me. I love her so much. I know she loves me. I'm convinced that we would make a great couple. We have a super relationship. It's simply been great these past three years! I know we would have a tremendous marriage. Children, family, the whole nine yards. Of course I know what to do. I know how to ask her to marry me, how to plan a wedding and all that stuff. I guess I'm just scared. About six years ago I had the same experience with Diane, and four years ago I had the same experience with Lynn."

It is not unusual to hear statements like these. In the course of your own life, you may have felt or expressed similar statements yourself. Many individuals experience having personal fears and phobias associated with difficulties in their loving relationships. A fear is a painful emotion, a deep sense of fright and an overall feeling of anxiousness associated with a specific event, current or anticipated. A phobia is an irrational, persistent and recurring fear associated with a particular type of event or set of events. This would suggest that the woman making the first statement is expressing a fear (a fear of being alone after a divorce), and the man making the second statement is expressing a phobia (a fear of committing himself to another person).

As we discussed in earlier chapters, fear is among the most powerful and primitive emotions. Fear is present in some form or other at nearly every level of the evolutionary ladder in the animal kingdom, from the simplest to the most complex of species. For eons, fear has served individual animals and people greatly to enhance their survival, and we could not be expected to live very long without the capacity to experience fear. On the other hand, fear is somewhat of a blunt instrument. When fears become disconnected from reality, they can dominate behavior and lead to making poor choices and decisions, even when the rational mind "knows better." Finally, when fears generalize to entire situations or sets of events – and become phobias – they are quite counterproductive. In such cases fear may greatly interfere with one's life and especially one's relationships with others.

This chapter will identify, discuss and illustrate some of the common ways in which peoples' fears and phobias can be critical aspects of their loving relationships.

Fear of the Unknown

Sharon came to see Dr. Emener because a counselor at a local crisis center recommended that she see a psychologist for some individual therapy. Sharon worked nights as a clerk in a convenience store. Her mother, who lived in her neighborhood, took care of her two children when she went to work. Sharon's husband, Nick, drove an over-the-road truck and typically was gone for two to three days and nights each week. "He's a great father to our children. And most of the time, he is good to me. He doesn't drink, gamble or run around on me. Nick brings his paycheck home every Friday and it all goes in the bank," she said. Bill then asked her what had happened that brought her to the crisis center.

"Nick has a bad temper sometimes," she replied. "I have to give him credit because most of the time he's real kind and gentle." As she took off her sunglasses, she continued, "But about once a month or so he will come home all upset about something and take it out on me. Usually I can see it coming, and I'll send the kids to Mom's. But this time it was really bad. I have these bruises all over my arms, my eyes are blackened, two of my ribs are bruised and I still have a bit of a headache. A policeman took me to the emergency room and then to the crisis center." Dr. Emener asked her if she pressed charges. "No," she said, "I didn't want to upset him and he was leaving for a three-day run anyway. I'll be alright. I'm planning to go to work tonight."

During the session, Sharon was asked if she had ever thought of leaving Nick and getting a divorce. After pondering the question for a few moments, she gazed out of the window and softly replied, "Oh yeah! I don't love Nick. I care about him, but I don't love him. The trouble is that I don't know if I could make it on my own. I married Nick after my junior year of high school. I was pregnant with Randy. Now I'm thirty years old and have no idea how I would live without Nick or someone to help me. With the house and the two kids, how could I make it on my salary? I don't think about it for long, divorce that is, because I get scared as hell thinking about being alone and being responsible for the two kids." Dr. Emener turned to her and said, "Sharon, it sounds like your greatest fear is fear of the unknown." In a wispy voice, she replied, "Yeah, I guess you're right."

Sharon was encouraged to read a book on single parenting and attend a spouse abuse group at the crisis center. "Why?" she asked. "Good question," Dr. Emener replied, adding, "I am not suggesting that you should get a divorce, Sharon. However, you have indicated to me on numerous occasions that you seriously would consider divorcing him, but you're scared. That's understandable. However, it also sounds like most of your fears are based on unknowns. You have no idea of what life really would be like for you if you divorced Nick. You should read a book on single parenting. And you could attend the group where you would hear other women share their experiences; from what I understand some of them have divorced their husbands. You then might have a better idea of what a single parent lifestyle might be like for you. And if you would do things such as these, Sharon, you would be in a better position to make an informed decision."

Bill's last contact with Sharon was via a telephone call from her. She had read the book and was attending the group at the crisis center. She said, "You know, Dr. Emener, it's amazing how often people will stay in a shitty situation based on ignorance. As you had said, 'Fear of the unknown.' And boy, am I learning!"

We do not know what happened to Sharon. She did not respond to Dr. Emener's first follow-up call, and the last time he tried to call her the operator said that the phone had been disconnected. Nonetheless, there is a good possibility that she is taking better care of herself, doing a better job of protecting herself, and possibly even filing for a divorce from Nick.

When you are experiencing feelings of fear in your loving relationship, try to identify the source (or sources) of your fear. And if your fear is fear of the unknown, try to educate yourself and inform yourself as much as you can. As Sharon wisely said, "The only thing worse than ignorance, is not rising out of it."

FEAR AND ANXIETY

Fear is closely related to anxiety, which, as mentioned in the previous chapter, we consider to be one of the four central "blocks to happiness." (As you may recall, the other three are anger, depression and guilt.) Like guilt, fear and its less salient cousin anxiety are based on two beliefs, only one of which may be rational or real. The first belief is that "I am in danger," or "Something bad is about to happen." This belief may or may not be realistic depending on your circumstances. The second belief, which is nearly always irrational, is along the line of, "I couldn't stand it if that happened." We call this second belief "catastrophizing" – elevating one's fear to the level of impending and certain doom. To catastrophize is to harbor an irrational belief because, in all likelihood, you could in fact stand it if it happened. While you might not like it very much and greatly prefer that things be different, you could sensibly plan ways to avoid or fix the situation. But unless it led to your death, it would not be the end of you.

When we catastrophize, we act as if the consequences of seeing our fears realized are unthinkable, that it would be disastrous if this or that outcome occurred. In this case, the fear of the anticipated event becomes worse than the actuality of the event itself, and in most instances our lives become unmanageable. It is therefore not surprising that we become unable to manage personal and especially loving relationships when fear rears its ugly head.

Fear of Losing Me

Dr. Emener probably will never forget the experiences of Millie, who was considering not completing her master's degree for fear that it would significantly interfere with her marriage to Paul. (Millie and Paul's relationship is discussed in further detail in Chapter Eight, "Needs and Wants," in our companion book, Our Loving Relationship.) In many ways, what Millie was saying was, "I am an intelligent, well-educated and goal-oriented woman. I want to complete my master's degree and enjoy an exciting, productive and successful career. Why do I have to be anything less than that in order to marry Paul?" One of the many things Dr. Emener said to her was, "Millie, I think it is safe for us to assume that one of the reasons that Paul loves you and wants to marry you is because of who you are and what you are. If you were not to continue to be who you are and what you are, not only would that hurt you, but it also might disappoint Paul." We suggest that there is a message in this for all of us: When someone is in love with us and wants to share their life with us, it is reasonable to assume that they are doing so because of who we are and what we are. Continuing to be who we are and what we are is not only important for us to do for ourselves, but it is also important for us to continue to be who we are and what we are for the benefit of our loved one as well as for our relationship.

Dr. Emener also was discussing this phenomenon with a client whom we shall refer to as Mary. While talking about how it personally related to herself, Mary drew a figure similar to the one in Figure 10.1 and said, "Ronald and I are currently friends and lovers. I consider us to have an 'I-thou' relationship. Part of my concern,

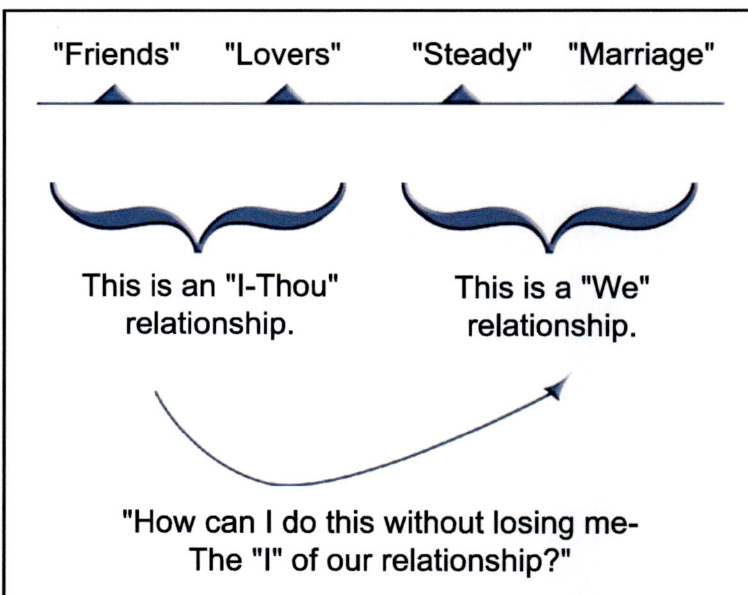

Figure 10.1. Fear of Losing Me.

however, is that if we start to have a committed relationship or eventually get married, it would be more of a 'we' relationship. And my concern, Dr. Emener, is that while I feel that I can be me in our 'I-thou' relationship, I am fearful that I would not be able to continue to be me if we had a 'we' relationship." Mary quickly realized that (1) this was a very important issue with regard to herself, and (2) if she wanted to seriously explore further potentials for her relationship with Ronald, it would be equally important for her to discuss it with him as well.

FEAR OF CHANGE

Among many other things, change in and of itself can be scary. Many times in our clinical experience, we have observed that when people fear change they subconsciously sabotage progress on behalf of themselves or their loved ones simply to avoid imminent or anticipated change. For example, Dr. Emener recalls working with Louis and Althea for the original purpose of helping Louis, who was in early recovery from alcoholism. As time went on, it became evident that on a subconscious level, Althea was actually trying to sabotage Louis' recovery "because she knew how to deal with Louis when he was drinking, but was afraid of what might happen if he ever continued to be sober."

Likewise, Dr. Lambos worked with Christina, a lady who had embarked on a regimen of regular exercise to reduce her high blood pressure. One of the consequences of her exercise program was that she lost weight and toned up to the point where she began to look at herself differently. Nonetheless, she expressed concern that her boyfriend, Donald, started buying high-calorie desserts on a regular basis, for which Christina had a considerable weakness. "It's like Donald wants me not to get better. How could he be so inconsiderate?" Bill suggested that Donald possibly was fearful that if she became more attractive, she would lose her interest in him. As it turned out, Donald had been in a comfort zone with respect to their relationship and had grave, groundless fears that Christina's feelings for him would change along with the change in her body. After several sessions, seeing both of them together, Donald was able to overcome his anxiety, and their relationship once again became stable.

Dr. Emener remembers working with Jenny who was trying to lose weight on a structured diet program. One day she shared with him, however, "It certainly appears that my husband, Philip, seems to be working against me. He does many little things to sabotage my diet program. It is almost as if he wants me to continue to weigh two-hundred and twenty-five pounds!" When they discussed this phenomenon with Philip, they discovered that because of his many insecurities, especially those related to his thoughts regarding Jenny's perception of him, Philip was fearful that if she lost a lot of weight and began "looking better," other men would find her attractive and he would lose her.

Many of our clients have said to us, in effect, "I do not necessarily like my loved one the way he or she is, but at least I can trust and predict what will happen." Fear of change indeed can be a controlling, manipulative and destructive aspect of a loving relationship.

FEAR OF GROWING UP (AND OUT)

Danny and Pat came to see Dr. Emener because they were having many difficulties with their fifteen-year-old daughter, Kristin. For approximately two years, Kristin had been continuously acting-out in school, getting into trouble and, as Danny and Pat said, "Driving us crazy all the time." Bill suggested that the three of them come in for a family counseling session.

During their first session, two very important sets of fears emerged. First, Kristin was struggling with many of the typical types of fears that teenagers struggle with as they are maturing into young adulthood. Nonetheless, she was also fearful that when she would eventually leave home "mom and dad wouldn't make it." Very succinctly and eloquently, Kristin articulated several marital problems that Danny and Pat had been having for a number of years. Secondly,

Danny and Pat were fearful of Kristin's emancipation from the family because, as Pat said, "We are not sure that we would make it when it is just the two of us." Thus, while Kristin genuinely feared that growing up would translate into marital problems for her mother and father, Danny and Pat were also having similar types of fears. Kristin was afraid of growing up (and out), and her parents were equally fearful of it.

As time went on, it became more and more clear that although Danny and Pat came for help because their daughter was having problems, it was primarily Danny and Pat who were having the problems in the family. Few nonprofessionals realize how common this situation is in family counseling. Often, the family member initially identified as the one with the problem is actually the person least in need of assistance. Fittingly, it is not surprising that as Dr. Emener continued to work with Danny and Pat on their marital relationship, Kristin was acting-out less, getting into trouble less and enjoying her life so much more. Needless to say, it was extremely difficult for Kristin to be going through life feeling as if she were responsible for "holding mom and dad together."

Dr. Emener continues to work with Danny and Pat and remains optimistic with regard to their successfully attending to their relationship difficulties. The most important thing, however, is that they were able to expeditiously identify where the problem was in the family. Fear of growing up can be extremely difficult for teenagers and families. Likewise, for parents who are having difficulties, fear of their children's growing up can be equally difficult.

FEAR OF ABANDONMENT

Fear of abandonment by one's significant other can make the establishment of a meaningful and intimate relationship extremely difficult. For example, Angie was a thirty-two-year-old hostess at a local restaurant. During their first session, Angie said to Dr. Emener, "For some reason I have always had difficulties really feeling close to, and getting close to, the men in my life. In the last five years, I have had over a dozen boyfriends and was engaged twice." As time went on, some of Angie's fears of abandonment became more evident to her. For example, she said, "I really felt close to my father when I was a freshman in college. Then he divorced my mother and within six months remarried. He moved to California and my contact with him became less and less. During that same period of time, my boyfriend, who I was hoping to marry, graduated and joined the military. I never saw him again. And, as I have already told you, three years ago my mother died." In a nutshell, Angie's experiences in life taught her that "every time I have a close and intimate relationship with someone, they leave me. I am left behind. Alone." Dr. Emener gently said, "Given your experiences, Angie, what you are telling me makes sense. And you fear the risk of having another intimate relationship with someone because you know how painful it can be if it doesn't last." As they continued to work on her fear of abandonment, Angie found herself becoming more comfortable with other people – especially those with whom she wanted to enjoy an intimate relationship. Toward the end of one of their sessions, Bill said to Angie, "Isn't it interesting how many times in life those things that we want the most are simultaneously those things that we fear the most." She replied, "That certainly has been true for me. Once you get the thing in life that you want the most, you have to constantly live with the fear of losing it."

An individual's fear of abandonment can appear to be very real and gut-wrenching at times. Unfortunately, fear of abandonment can limit or even preclude an individual from having and enjoying loving relationships. Everyone has some level of fear of abandonment – it makes sense to assume that there is always a possibility that our loved one could leave us or die. Nonetheless, when our fear of abandonment becomes a dysfunctional aspect of our life – that is, it prevents us from establishing and maintaining loving relationships – that is when our fear of abandonment can become significantly problematic.

FEAR OF INTIMACY

With tears streaming down her face, Helen said, "Yes, Dr. Emener, it is true that I have many friends, and many of my friends are men. However, I never can seem to have more than a friendship with a man. I guess maybe it's just my weight?" At that time, Helen was five-foot-four and weighed two hundred and thirty pounds. As Helen's story unfolded, it was clear that a number of significant events in her lifetime had had continuing effects on her. For example, she had been sexually abused as a child and had been abandoned by a number of men in her life. And, she said to Dr. Emener, "For a multitude of reasons that I know you understand, I am incredibly afraid of sex and intimacy with a man." Dr. Emener told her that her fears were understandable. What Helen discovered, however, was that her weight problem was significantly related to her fear of intimacy. "In many ways, I think I just use my weight as a shield. It's my protection," she concluded. "And I guess as long as I'm this much overweight, I don't have to worry about a man wanting to have sex with me or to have an intimate relationship with me. I guess in some ways this is very comforting. But I don't want to continue to be this way. I have tried numerous diet programs over the last couple of years, but none of them seem to work. I guess that before I try another diet program, it would be a good idea to spend some time focusing on my fear of intimacy."

Over the following seven months, Helen and Dr. Emener met for a total of six therapy sessions. The last time he saw her, she was down to one hundred and eighty pounds and was extremely happy with herself – not because she had lost the weight, but because she was feeling much better about herself as a person, feeling less fearful of intimacy and enjoying more meaningful relationships. In addition to continuing to read some literature and slowly explore and risk some new relationship experiences with men, Bill expects that Helen will be seeing him on an occasional basis for the next six months to a year. Fear of intimacy is not easy to overcome; it can be a very dysfunctional component of one's life and indeed devastatingly restrictive and destructive to a loving relationship.

As counselors, we understand the roles that fear of abandonment and intimacy play in sabotaging relationships. Quite often, such fears are largely imaginary and most individuals are able to quickly benefit from therapy addressing them. Because we all have more control over ourselves than we do over others, it is easier to address those problems that we ourselves create. This is an important piece of wisdom we encourage our readers to keep in mind: When you are your own worst problem, the solution is usually easier than when the problem is out of your control and in the hands of another person.

SHAME-BASED FEAR

In our discussion of toxic shame in Chapter Nine, we suggested that it is an "all-pervasive sense that I am flawed and defective as a human being," and reflects a fundamental error in confusing one's past choices and behavior with one's continuing sense of self – confusing what you did with who you are. People who go through life with toxic shame not only live with many internal struggles, daily discomforts and other assorted problems, but they also tend to experience many difficulties in establishing and maintaining loving relationships. The subconscious scenario goes something like this: (1) I truly believe that there is basically something wrong with me, my character and my makeup as a human being; (2) if anyone ever were to know that "there is something wrong with me," they would leave me and not want to be close to me; thus, (3) I better be careful and not allow anyone too close because if they find out that I am basically flawed they would back away and leave me. When Dr. Emener was discussing this in one of his lectures at the university, one of his students said, "Yes, I understand that. I have a friend like that. She seems to be very open and outgoing. But as soon as you get too close to her, she changes the subject, backs off, or puts up a wall. She's like a boxer who never gets into clinches, stays away from you with good footwork or keeps you away from her with short jabs." Simply harboring the irrational belief that we are a rotten or worthless person – the very definition of toxic shame – often will lead us to subconsciously assume others believe the same about us. In anticipating further rejection based on this fixed false belief, we then go on to sabotage any relationship that comes to bring us pleasure without conscious awareness of our actions.

Dr. Emener's client Rick is a very typical example of this. Rick expressed his primary reason for coming in when he said, "While I have had many girlfriends in my life, I finally met the girl of my dreams – Tina. I even have asked her to marry me, more than once I might add. But she keeps saying to me, 'I'm sorry, but Rick, I don't know you.' Can you believe that? We've being going steady for almost two years now and I know we love each other. We have great times together, we're very compatible, we have similar interests, we've taken long vacations together and our sex life is simply wonderful. What does she mean, 'I don't know you?'"

Rick was reared in a dysfunctional family. His mother "had her share of mental health problems – she was on medication for years," and his father "was an alcoholic who was very abusive to his mother and the kids." Rick also suggested, "Maybe that's why my older sister has been seeing a psychiatrist for the past ten years."

As Rick's life story continued to unfold, it became clear that he was reared in a home in which there was no love, no open sharing of feelings, and no true sense of acceptance. Everyone constantly walked around on eggshells being careful not to upset or anger anyone. And while he felt convinced that "there was something seriously wrong with mom and dad," he also felt convinced that "there must be something seriously wrong with me." Rick had learned to act as if – as if there were nothing wrong. But deep down inside, he was fearful that there was something wrong – with himself. He said one time, "I feel like an imposter. I basically live a lie. If anyone really knew how I feel about myself, especially Tina, well you know..." Dr. Emener gently replied, "Of course… you're afraid that she would reject you and abandon you." Rick cried.

With some suggested reading and continued therapy sessions, Rick soon began to feel genuinely better about himself, less fearful that he was a flawed human being, and more willing to let people get to know the real Rick. The last time Dr. Emener saw Rick, he added, "Tina and I are doing much better too!" Bill trusts that Rick was right because about six months after his last visit he received a wedding invitation in the mail with a personal, signed note affixed: "I hope you can make it! Rick."

Shame-based fear – fear of who we really are and what we really are – indeed can prevent the establishment and maintenance of a loving relationship. This can be especially true if the other person is healthy and sensitive to the outcome effects of our toxic shame-based fears. If you find yourself feeling a need to hide something from your loved one, especially if that something is yourself, you may be struggling with toxic shame. And if this is the case, it may be imperative that you attend to it and possibly even get some professional assistance.

FEAR OF ENDING A RELATIONSHIP

It is not uncommon for individuals in a loving relationship to find themselves wanting to end the relationship, knowing how to end the relationship, but having tremendous fear of ending it. In Chapter Nine, as you may recall, Eli was struggling with many fears regarding ending of his marriage. When he contemplated divorce, he would struggle with his fear of guilt – feeling that he was betraying his wife and children. However, it was not until Eli was able to feel comfortable with his wife and children's abilities to survive a divorce that he was able to overcome his own fear. This reminds Dr. Emener of a client named Nellie, who struggled for over two years before she was able to end her relationship with Mitch. For Nellie, it was a "fear of what my life would be like, alone in the world and without Mitch!" Thus, while Eli was struggling with ending his relationship with his wife for fear of what might happen to her and his children, Nellie was struggling with ending her relationship with Mitch for fear of what might happen to herself.

When we are in a loving relationship and fear that the ending of the relationship will bring about suffering on behalf of our loved ones or ourselves, that fear can grippingly prevent us from not only doing what we think is best but also from doing what we want to do. We have learned from clients like Eli, Nellie and many others that when we feel a need to end a loving relationship, it is helpful to identify the fears that we have associated with such an act. Then, it is important for us to explore, discuss and try to understand more deeply our fears of ending the relationship so that we can get on with our lives and do what we need to do and want to do.

Commitment Phobia

Michelle's story, in a nutshell, went like this: "I am forty-eight years old, I am a successful attorney, I own my own home, and I am head over heels in love with Ben, a fifty-four-yea-old, single attorney who lives near me. We have been going together for over a year now. I love him very much, but for some reason we have reached a plateau, a stalemate. Every time we talk about getting married, getting engaged or living together, I tell him, 'Ben, let's talk about that next week.' I don't know what's wrong with me, Dr. Emener; he surely does seem to be the perfect man for me in every way. Recently, however, he suggested that there might be something wrong within me and that it may not necessarily be him. In summation, if you will pardon my attorney talk, that's why I am here to see you. I need to find out what's wrong with me!" At the very outset, Bill told Michelle that he would prefer not to begin working with her under the assumption that there was something wrong with her. What he told her, however, was that he would be more than willing to help her find out why she is the way she is. And as her life story began to unfold, she increasingly became more aware of herself and why she was responding to Ben the way she was.

When Michelle was a sophomore in high school, her parents divorced. Her father quickly remarried and "got totally involved with his new family." Michelle then lived in a three-bedroom apartment with her mother. She said, "My mother was a wonderful mother to me. Almost too good. I felt that she was smothering me all the time. Yes, we were very close, but I'm glad I eventually went away to go to college because I think I needed to get away from her." When Michelle was twenty-eight, she fell madly in love with José, a very successful, thirty-five-year-old businessman from Spain. José was in the United States for one year to help with the establishment of an American-based satellite company. After knowing each other for approximately six months, Michelle moved in with him. "It was wonderful!" However, when José's year was up, he returned to Spain not only to continue his work in the corporate office of the company, but also "to see if he could renew his relationship with his ex-girlfriend." With tears in her eyes, Michelle said, "I was devastated. Fortunately, my firm gave me a three-week paid vacation so I could try to get my life together. I was a basket case!" Over the next decade, Michelle never dated or had any more than a friendship relationship with any other man.

During their second session, Michelle said, "After reading the book that you suggested, I think I understand myself much more clearly – I have commitment phobia. When I was in high school, I loved my father very, very much. He left me. I loved my mother very, very much. She smothered me. Thus, I guess I subconsciously concluded that if you commit yourself to someone they will either leave you or smother you. Then about ten years later, I took a risk and made a lifelong commitment to José. What happened? I was abandoned again! I guess maybe that's why I'm having difficulties making any kind of commitment to Ben." She then went to her portfolio and pulled out a figure similar to the one in Figure 10.2 that diagrammed these experiences. As Dr. Emener looked at Michelle's diagram, she said, "I guess my fear of abandonment and my

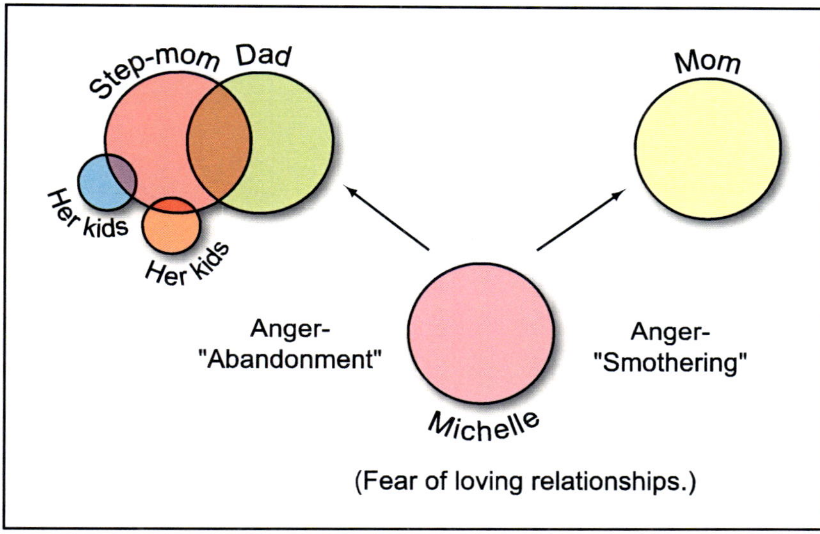

Figure 10.2. Michelle's Commitment Phobia.

commitment phobia became really locked-in. But I love Ben so much! Maybe if I just continue to be patient and share all of this with Ben, it might be easier."

Not only was it very helpful for Michelle to share her commitment phobia with Ben, it was also very helpful that they decided to establish a "living together relationship" on a gradual, approximation basis. Michelle moved some of her clothes and other belongings into Ben's house and spent three nights a week there. Then, after approximately one month, she spent four nights a week at his house. After six-months, she was living almost exclusively with Ben and going by her house once a week to water her plants. Eventually, she became more trusting of Ben and more trusting of herself. She put her house up for sale. With a somewhat "let's celebrate" attitude, she came into Dr. Emener's office and said, "If you want a good deal on a house, I've got one for you!" Basically, that was her way of telling Bill that she had overcome her commitment phobia and had made a commitment to Ben.

Commitment phobia can be a very dysfunctional and destructive aspect of life. As Michelle observed, "It can rob us of the most exciting joy and sense of meaningfulness that life can behold." When you find yourself truly fearful of making a commitment to another individual, in addition to asking yourself what is wrong with him, what is wrong with her or what is wrong with our relationship, ask yourself if possibly you are experiencing a phobic response to commitment.

The core ideas of this chapter can be summarized rather succinctly. First, fear is a powerful and necessary emotion, but it too easily can become divorced from the realities of our lives. When this happens, and fear becomes generalized or otherwise without basis, it affects us adversely. We have seen many examples in which the fear of a perceived reality (e.g., "There is something wrong with me…") that is not shared with others can make it difficult or impossible to manage – especially if you are in a loving relationship. And remember, such fears typically do not go away by themselves. Attending to them, and if necessary with the assistance of a professional therapist, can be incredibly liberating and ultimately contribute to a healthier, more meaningful and happier life.

* * * * * *

When you have fears regarding another person or when you have fears regarding a relationship with another person, chances are that you also may have fears regarding something within yourself.

Chapter Eleven

DEPRESSION

> *"Ever since his girlfriend broke up with him and moved out about a month ago, he has been utterly dejected. He sounds helpless and hopeless when he talks about anything. He seems to have lost interest in everything, especially people, and he talks about himself as if he is totally worthless."*
>
> *"Ever since he divorced me, everything I do requires effort. People tell me that I will answer their questions but will not initiate anything. I just feel blue, down and lonely all the time. It bothers me that people won't talk with me, but then again, I don't want to talk to anyone anyway. And even if I did, it wouldn't make any difference. I have nothing to say or add. Why would anyone want to be around me? I'm a loser. I wish people would just leave me alone."*

These two scenarios are not uncommon. When a person has painful emotional experiences within or as a result of a loving relationship, it is understandable to feel depressed. The first scenario is an illustration of a person's description of a friend who is feeling depressed because his girlfriend ended their relationship. The second is an illustration of what a person who is feeling depressed as a result of a divorce may say. We suspect that there is a high probability that you may have heard statements like these in your life and possibly may have expressed statements like them yourself.

Feeling depressed, feeling and behaving like the individuals in these two illustrations, can result from biochemical and/or psychopathological etiologies (e.g., a person may have an illness called "depression" for many years) or from situational conditions (e.g., when a person is divorced and feels abandoned by an individual with whom they were, and still are, very much in love). The first of these two conditions is known as "endogenous depression" (coming from within), while the latter is referred to as "reactive depression" (due to causes outside the body). Sometimes a person can suffer from both types of depression at the same time. For example, a middle-aged woman recently said, "I have had bouts with depression ever since I was a teenager. However, with some occasional visits to my psychologist and by sometimes taking medicine prescribed by my doctor, I have been able to live a good life. But this recent breakup with Jerry just brought me down. I emotionally hit bottom."

There also are several different components to depression. Feelings of sadness are part of what we call the *affective* component, whereas difficulty initiating behavior (i.e., just wanting to lie around all day) reflects the *motor* component. Finally, there is a *cognitive* component of depression, in which a person experiences difficulty solving problems, remembering, or being able to think clearly about things. Neuroscientists now know from brain imaging and mapping studies that these components reflect dysfunctions in different parts of the brain. Affective depression, for example, is closely associated with the left frontal lobe (in a right-handed person), while motor depression stems from brain disregulation in deep sub-cortical areas, particularly the brainstem. We include this information to make sure our readers understand that depression is an illness, not some type of character flaw.

Although endogenous and persistent depression is among the most serious and widely diagnosed mental illnesses in our society, in this chapter we focus on the reactive depression that many times results from relationship issues. We will look at some of the ways by which feelings associated with depression may be related to loving relationships and what some people have done to help themselves. We also will look at depression as one of the "four blocks to happiness" we frequently address in counseling, where our focus is not on underlying biochemical factors, but on one's beliefs about themselves, significant others and the world around them.

Ultimately, we want our readers to understand that the experience of depression that results from relationship issues is shared by nearly everyone at some point or other. Reactive depression is quite normal and even expected at times, and it is a mistake to believe that you are somehow inferior or to blame if you suffer from it after a loving relationship ends. The fact that our culture tends to characterize such reactions as evidence of weakness or shortcomings of character is in fact more of a shortcoming of our culture. The often unspoken but widely assumed philosophy of rugged individualism that permeates our society is often the cause of great harm because it equates seeking help with weakness. If ever there were a better example of blaming the victim, we are unaware of it. Depression in all its forms is a treatable illness. If you wouldn't feel right about labeling someone with a broken leg a loser because he or she can't walk without crutches, then we urge you never to make the mistake of blaming yourself or another person who is suffering from depression.

I Don't Know How to Act

Wayne, a thirty-eight-year-old construction worker, not only told Dr. Emener that he was feeling blue and depressed for a long period of time, but his behaviors and mannerisms tended to indicate it as well. When Dr. Emener asked Wayne to tell him what his life was like, Wayne said, "Ever since my divorce about a year ago, I go to work, sleep and every other weekend I see my two children. Sometimes it seems like the walls in my one-bedroom apartment are closing in on me. I basically live a very boring and sterile life. Part of the problem is that I just don't know how to act. I don't know what to do. And let me assure you, that bar scene, that single life scene, and that running around trying to meet someone, basically sucks!" In almost a humorous fashion, Wayne added, "It's almost funny – on the weekends I really find myself not wanting to talk to anyone. I screen my telephone calls with my answering machine. Quite frequently when someone calls, I listen to them talk to me and ask me to call them back, but then I just sit there and stare at the walls. I guess I just don't feel like talking to anyone. By Sunday evening I start feeling sorry for myself because I haven't talked with anyone all weekend. Sometimes I just don't know what to say, I don't know what to do and I don't know how to act!" One of the first things that Dr. Emener did to help Wayne was to identify some ways that he could continue to keep himself active. Prior to his divorce, he was a very active man; he played on a softball team, he and his wife went out together at least one evening a week and he was very actively involved in the lives of his two children. Wayne agreed that it would be important for him to try to continue to be active. He felt that he could do this successfully by surrounding himself with active friends, buying tickets ahead for plays and ballgames, and joining a softball team. "Basically," he said, "I need to take control of my life and plan things so that my depression doesn't get the best of me."

There is an important message here. Although depression often leads to a loss of motivation, committing oneself to staying active is one of the more effective ways to combat its symptoms. As paradoxical as this may seem, as counselors we have experienced this time and again. In the case of Wayne, for example, the last time Dr. Emener saw him he reported that he was doing much better. When asked specifically what was going on in his life, Wayne said, "First of all, I took your advice and I have been making sure that before I go to bed on Wednesday nights, I have at least one planned activity for the upcoming weekend. You were right, waiting until Saturday morning or Saturday afternoon to call people to see if they want to go out was simply too late – everyone already has plans by then. In fact, last night I called some friends of mine and we are going to meet at the beach this coming Saturday night to have some dinner and listen to some reggae music. I'm looking forward to that! I've been playing softball one or two nights a week and have tickets for four – for a buddy of mine, his girlfriend, her roommate and me – to go to a concert the last Saturday night of this month. By being careful, going slowly and planning things, I'm gradually learning how to act. Having been a married man with children for the last fourteen years, it's hard to learn again how to be a single person. But I'm getting there!"

As is illustrated by Wayne's experiences, it is easy to understand that when a significant change occurs in one's life, especially if it has to do with changes in loving relationships, it is not uncommon for people to simply not know how to act. The alternative of doing nothing may seem like a sensible choice, but it usually only makes one's condition worse. On the other hand, by planning activities and committing oneself to them, by surrounding ourselves with good role models, by spending time with friends who understand and are helpful to us, and by not putting pressure on ourselves to live up to everyone else's expectations in addition to our own, it indeed is possible to stop the perpetuation of what can feel like a meaningless and sterile life and overcome depression. As time goes on, as Wayne experienced, a person can know and learn or relearn how to be involved.

ALONE – LONESOME – LONELY

In the introduction to this chapter we looked at how tacit or unspoken assumptions of our culture can lead to making poor choices and to inaccurate ways of understanding our issues. Another one of these tacit cultural values is gregariousness – the belief that it is always better to be with others than to spend time alone. As counselors in private practice, we have been surprised at how often this is expressed by our clients. Learning how to enjoy one's own company for varying periods of time is both healthy and undervalued. Teenagers seem to understand this naturally, as anyone who has had to spend time while their sixteen-year-old child spends hour after hour in his or her bedroom with the door closed can readily attest. Time spent alone allows one to *process*, or think through, many aspects of their recent past and to better understand their world and the role they play in it. As we grow older, however, we somehow seem to lose this affinity for soulful reflection and assume that if we are not in the company of at least one other person, something is wrong with us. There is no doubt that we are highly social beings, and that most of us cannot survive or prosper if we go for long periods of time without quality company and interactions with significant others. But in the short run, time spent alone is much underrated, as the following example makes clear.

When talking with Paula, a twenty-eight-year-old stenographer, it became clear to Dr. Emener that she was confusing the phenomena, or conditions, of being alone, being lonesome and being lonely. *Being alone*, in simplistic terms, is just that – being by oneself, spending time without others around and not being in a significant or meaningful relationship. *Being lonesome* is an experience that we typically think of as pining over or painfully missing a special, significant, identifiable individual. *Being lonely*, on the other hand, is the missing, pining and feeling down because there simply is no one else in one's life at that time. "So in other words," Paula said, "when I stay in my apartment by myself or go to a movie by myself, I am simply being alone. When I am feeling down and depressed because I miss Harold, I'm being lonesome. And when I am feeling down, depressed and sad because I do not have a significant other in my life to share things with, I am feeling lonely." Dr. Emener nodded and replied, "Yes, that's right. In many ways these three conditions are mutually exclusive and independent. Being alone, feeling lonesome and feeling lonely can be three entirely separate kinds of experiences. It might be helpful, however, if we could identify some things that you could do to try to reduce your feelings of depression resulting from each of these three conditions."

The next time Dr. Emener saw Paula, she shared with him that she had gone back to the spa where she had been a member for years and began working out and attending aerobic classes again. Moreover, she renewed some of the friendships that she used to enjoy with the other women whom she knew from the spa. Furthermore, she began doing some of the things that Wayne had found to be helpful, such as planning for future activities with people she knew, felt comfortable around and could trust. Interestingly, Paula said to Dr. Emener, "I think there is a reason why I have been feeling less depressed. By not being alone all the time, as I used to be, I'm now finding that I'm not feeling as lonesome or as lonely as I used to feel either!"

When we are experiencing feelings of depression as a result of significant changes in, or the loss of, a loving relationship, it is understandable that we may feel lonesome and/or lonely. If, however, we simultaneously allow ourselves to spend all of our time alone, we can: (a) magnify the intensity of our lonesome and lonely feelings; and (b) find it difficult to work our way out of the depression and find a way to enjoy life again. There is nothing wrong with being alone; as we have said, sometimes it is very important for people to spend time with and enjoy themselves. However, when spending too much time alone contributes to feeling lonely, lonesome and depressed, it is frequently helpful to do some things, as Wayne and Paula did, to reduce the amount of time that we are alone.

Loneliness: It Could Be Worse

Bill Lambos was counseling Mike, a thirty-one-year-old restaurant manager who had recently given up drinking after a DUI arrest. "Dr. Lambos, the restaurant business is like this: First you spend an hour or more prepping tables and the kitchen before the crowd arrives. Then, you spend five or six hours running around like mad serving customers and making sure they are happy with their food and the service. Finally, you spend the last hour cleaning up and decompressing from the stress of the evening. That's when all the staff starts drinking – I mean, the bar is right there, and everybody feels like they need one or two just to calm down. *Then,* since they feel so much better, they all go out and party half the night until they are plastered, crash – in bed if they're lucky, or into a pole like I did – and the next day they do it all over again." After taking a sip of water, Mike continued, "The problem is, now that I've decided to clean up my act, I can't spend time with any of my former friends. If I do, I'll just end up drinking again, and I'm not going to let that happen." Mike's new problem, however, was loneliness. "I end up spending night after night in front of the TV by myself, and it only makes me depressed. I'm starting to wonder if this is any better than drinking myself to death."

Dr. Lambos and Mike spent the next few sessions doing what he likes to call "advocational counseling." They created a list of things Mike enjoyed doing besides watching television, which included racquetball and hiking. Mike also expressed an interest in learning to practice yoga. A brief time on the Internet revealed a local fitness club that offered opportunities for doing all three, and Mike reluctantly joined. (One of Mike's issues was that he was shy; meeting new people socially was hard for him.) With a little prodding, however, he forced himself to start by getting a free day pass to the club, where he took a lesson from the racquetball pro and was introduced to several other players at his level. He also joined a yoga class. After more than a year of not hearing from him, Mike recently dropped by Bill's office early one evening to say hello. "Life is good, no complaints at all," he said. "I switched to the lunch shift, which is just as busy, but now I get off at four PM. Three nights a week I head to the club for regular games and classes, and on weekends there is a group that goes hiking. I thought things couldn't be better until my regular racquetball partner pointed out that a certain young lady was paying a lot of attention to me, and I was clueless." He laughed. "We've been going out for seven months now, and I'm starting to think she's the one. I just came by to say thank you."

From Dr. Emener's files comes a similar story. A significant contributor to Glen's depression was his horrible feelings of loneliness. After sixteen years of marriage, he filed for and received a divorce from Betty. At one point during their first session, Bill said to Glen, "It sounds to me like you have been experiencing some strong feelings of loneliness." Glen replied, "Yes, that is true. I'm not spending as much time alone as I used to, nor am I necessarily feeling lonesome. But I am experiencing tremendous feelings of loneliness – sometimes I just feel deeply depressed because I miss Betty so much!" Following a few minutes of silence, Bill asked Glen, "Are you missing Betty as she actually was, as she had been at one time, or as you wished she were? Which Betty are you missing?" Glen pondered that for quite some time. He then turned and said, "That is an excellent question to think about. To tell you the truth, I think I am feeling lonely because I miss the Betty who I first married – the Betty who loved me so much, the Betty who I felt such incredible love from." Dr. Emener continued to explain to Glen that sometimes it is helpful for us to identify to what extent we are grieving over the loss of the person who we married, the person who we divorced, or the person who we think of as "the person who could have been."

About one month later, Dr. Emener received a letter from Glen in which he told Bill that he was doing much better and that he felt no need to continue to see him. He said that his continued deliberations regarding "Which Betty he was grieving over?" and "Why he filed for a divorce from her?" were good, thought-provoking considerations that were very helpful for him to think about. Interestingly, he added, "There is only one thing worse than feeling alone alone, and that is to feel *alone in a relationship*." We know what Glen meant by that; for the last three years of his marriage, he emotionally and psychologically felt very alone. Glen also said that he was able to differentiate among his feelings regarding *the Betty he married, the Betty he divorced* and *the Betty in his dreams*. Having witnessed his progress with his emotional recovery from his divorce, we trust that he is doing well and enjoying life.

Helplessness and Hopelessness

We have mentioned that depression is one of the "four blocks to happiness" that is routinely addressed in Dr. Lambos's practice, along with anger, anxiety and guilt. Like these others, we believe that depression is often sustained by the irrational beliefs we come to harbor. As with the other blocks, in the case of depression, there are two sets of beliefs people hold – one realistic and the other usually not. The realistic belief goes something like "I am sad and I want to feel better." This is entirely expected from someone who is depressed, regardless of the reason. The irrational belief that accompanies it, however, is "My situation is hopeless and I am helpless to change it." Once again, this is irrational. It is almost never true, it is illogical in that it doesn't follow from any premises, and it is dysfunctional – it won't help you get better. From our years of professional practice, we have learned that the faster we can help clients realize the irrational nature of this belief, the sooner they will begin to recover. This is not to say one can snap one's fingers and overcome such beliefs and the feelings that accompany them. It takes effort, a commitment to change, and a sincere desire to climb out of the hole. Hopelessness is a self-fulfilling prophecy – a prediction that comes true because of the behavior it evokes in those who believe it.

Each of your authors has many times said to clients and friends, "The only thing worse than a feeling of helplessness is a feeling of hopelessness." This postulate became eminently clear when Dr. Emener was talking with Lonnie, a thirty-year-old schoolteacher who had been living with her boyfriend for two years prior to coming to see Dr. Emener. After Lonnie and her boyfriend agreed to end their relationship, she moved into her own apartment and soon began feeling very depressed. As he was talking with Lonnie, Dr. Emener shared three statements that she had made to him during their conversation: (a) "I don't like what happened between Reggie and me;" (b) "I am feeling very down and depressed about it;" and, (c) "There's nothing that I can do about it." As she looked at the three statements that he had written on a piece of paper for her, Dr. Emener said, "Lonnie, it looks to me like you went from feelings of disappointment, to feelings of depression, to feelings of despair. First you were disappointed because of what happened, then you began feeling very down and sad about what had happened, and then you began feeling that no matter what you did it would not make any difference." As she nodded in agreement, she began sobbing. By the time Lonnie composed herself, their session was just about over. Nonetheless, Lonnie was asked if she would agree to a homework assignment. She nodded. She was asked to pretend that her therapist, Dr. Emener, had just ended a three-year relationship with a girlfriend with whom he had been living. She was also asked to pretend that Bill had been feeling incredible disappointment, sadness, depression and despair. He also asked her to assume that she and he were good friends. Dr. Emener then asked, "Lonnie, what would you suggest that I do? I would like you to write a letter to me and put it in the mail by the end of this week. Give me a list of suggestions and recommendations, things that I could do, to help myself." As she left his office, she said, "You will have my letter by next Monday."

When Lonnie came in two weeks later, Dr. Emener handed her the letter she had written. The only difference was that he had crossed off his name, "Bill," and wrote the name "Lonnie" wherever his name had appeared. He then said, "Lonnie, I would like you to assume that you have just received this letter from a good friend. Please read it out loud." She read the letter aloud and by the time she got to the end she had a big smile on her face. Looking up, she wryly said, "You know, Dr. Emener, for whatever it is worth, these ten suggestions that are listed here are really very good recommendations!" Dr. Emener replied, "Yes they are, Lonnie, whoever wrote that letter really knows what she's talking about!" She laughed. He then looked at her and said, "There is only one question remaining, Lonnie. If these are such good recommendations, and if they come from such an intelligent person, then why can't *you* listen to them and try to do what is being suggested?" Lonnie answered by saying, "The last time I was here in your office, I was so emotionally caught up in my feelings that I totally shut off my brain. Not only did I think that nothing would work, but I didn't even think that I was capable of coming up with any halfway decent ideas or recommendations of what to do about my situation." In fact, she was correct.

At their next session, Lonnie spoke about all of the exciting and helpful things she had been doing to help herself. Many of these were similar to the kinds of things that Wayne, Paula and Mike had been doing – things we considered earlier in this chapter. The fact that Lonnie was not only doing helpful things, but doing things that were her own ideas, also contributed to her self-efficacy and sense of self-worth. That was the last that Lonnie ever came in. A few months later, when the weather had turned colder, Dr. Emener received a postcard from the island of Nassau. On the back was an inscription that said, "I am helplessly and hopelessly in love with this place! Having a wonderful time! Your good friend, Lonnie."

Mixed Depression and Secondary Depression

Throughout this chapter, we have been looking at situational depression as it relates to loving relationships. The essential experiences illustrate what is termed *primary reactive depression* – the depression that one experiences as a result of a specific situation and/or other related considerations. In our clinical work, as well as in our personal lives, we also have experienced and observed *secondary depression* – the experience of feeling depressed because I recognize and realize that I am, and have been, depressed. Closely related to secondary depression are anxiety-related depression and its cousin, depression-related anxiety, both forms of *mixed depression*. These arise when one experiences depression or anxiety *as a consequence* of feeling the other. One of our favorite acronyms from the *Diagnostic and Statistical Manual of Mental Disorders* (the diagnostic bible of our profession) is MAD, which stands for "Mixed Anxiety and Depression." Rarely will you hear of anything better described by its own acronym!

For example, Dr. Lambos spoke with Carol, a twenty-four-year-old young lady who was concerned about her situation. Carol had finished a two-year college degree but dropped out of her four-year degree program because she found dormitory life "idiotic." To save money, she moved back in with her parents. But as soon as she did, she found herself embarrassed by her friends, who told her that she was a "loser" because she still lived at home at the age of twenty-one. Her anxiety over being so labeled was strong enough for her to want to stop attending classes altogether, and so she took off some time to work, intending to resume classes later. After a while, however, she found coworkers classifying her in the same way as her fellow students had, only then because she still lived at home at age of twenty-three. She again felt so anxious about being labeled a "homebody" that she quit work as well as school. Finally, too anxiety-ridden to return to school or work, or to dating, she became quite depressed. Dr. Lambos recalls telling her "Carol, first you built a castle in the air, and now you have moved into it."

Over the next several sessions, Carol was asked to create a list of all the things she thought were "wrong" with her. When she brought the list in, every item was either a statement about her situation ("I am twenty-five and still live with my parents") or her reaction to her situation ("I am a zero because I'm not working or going to school"). Dr. Lambos looked her in the eye and asked, "Is there anything on this list, Carol, which could not be fixed by taking a few steps toward changing your life right now?" She agreed there was not. The two made a pact. Since, by her own description, there was "nothing inherently wrong with her," Dr. Lambos would continue to see her only if between each visit she would make at least one change in her situation. She started going back to school at nights. She found she fit in much better with the older population and was able to continue and even to make a few friends. Next, she began working part time and using the money to attend acting lessons – her real passion. Finally, she started saving up enough money to move out of her parents' house and rent a small apartment. By the time she got to this stage, she no longer felt it was necessary to keep coming to see Dr. Lambos.

"My depression was all a reaction to my own anxiety," she said when she called to stop her appointments. "Things are fine now, I just had to claw my way out of that hole. Thank you." To which we say, "Well done, Carol!"

Dr. Emener remembers working with Greg, a thirty-one-year-old school teacher and basketball coach, who had been very depressed following the break-up of a three-year relationship with his girlfriend, Cindy. He said, "I know that for the past year or so I have been somewhat depressed, on and off. Over the last six months, however, it has continued to get progressively worse. In the last few weeks, I've been feeling very down, sad, blue and sorrowful, primarily *because I realize what a depressed person I have become.* I feel that I have become depressed because I'm depressed." With a look of understanding, Dr. Emener replied, "Yes Greg, that is what I refer to as *secondary depression*." Greg looked at Bill and added, "This crazy thing that I'm experiencing, and that you refer to as secondary depression, is like trying to go back to sleep at night. Occasionally I will find myself waking up in the middle of the night and not being able to go back to sleep because I am thinking about things that I need to do the following day. After a while, however, I find myself not being able to go back to sleep because I'm thinking about the fact that I'm not able to go back to sleep." Greg's realization and awareness of what he was experiencing was an excellent first step for him. The two were able to build on Greg's self-understanding and begin to identify some specific things that he could do (similar to what Wayne, Paula, Mike, Carol and Lonnie had done) that, as he said, "Started to help me get out of the funk!"

Secondary depression can also affect couples. For example, Mark and Ginger had been trying very hard to reconcile their engagement and improve their relationship. They lived in their own apartments; but since their apartments were in the same complex, they were able to spend large amounts of time together. During their second counseling session, Ginger said, "Yes, Dr. Emener, our relationship does seem to be improving. We talk more than ever. But sometimes I think we talk too much. It seems that the only thing we do nowadays is sit around each other's apartment and talk about our relationship." Bill looked at both of them and suggested, "You may be experiencing what I think of as *the paralysis of analysis*. Collectively analyzing your relationship and working on it is very important. However, sometimes it also is important for people to enjoy doing things together. For example, when is the last time the two of you went away for a day and did nothing but have fun together?" They looked at each other with saddened expressions. Mark said, "I can't remember. I think Ginger is right, all we do now is sit around and talk about our relationship!"

The weekend following that session, the two of them went away to the beach for the day. They left their watches and cell phones locked in the trunk of the car. They also went with the agreement that they would not talk about their relationship or each other; they would just try to enjoy having fun. When Dr. Emener saw them the following Tuesday, it was clear that they had been to the beach – their sunburns were quite revealing. The two of them had had a wonderful day together and, to a large extent, they felt that they had reduced their "paralysis of analysis." With a chuckle in his voice, Mark said, "You can only sit in front of a scrumptious meal for so long without finally shutting up and eating! Sometimes the only way to enjoy good food is to eat it, not talk about it. And I truly believe that the best way for Ginger and me to enjoy our relationship is to live it!"

Living the life of a couch potato is easy: you just keep doing the same thing. Living the life of a runner is easy: you just keep doing the same thing. However, the transition from couch potato to runner can be very difficult. Simply said, it's really tough sometimes to get running again, getting the muscles accustomed to being used and getting into a routine of running. The transition from couch potato to runner can be made a little easier, however, if a person has a plan of attack, a schedule of incremental increases in running, and a genuine sense of patience with this incremental progress. With regard to Dr. Emener's couch potato-runner analogy, Ginger said, "We are not ready for a 5K or a 10K race yet. However, we are up to one mile per day, three times per week, and that feels good!" Mark added, "And within that analogy, Bill, we've also quit bitching about what bad shape we're in!"

At one time or another, depression will become a challenge for almost everyone. To the degree that a person is able to accept periods of reactive or situational depression as part of life, he or she normally will be able to cope with it, sometimes alone, other times with the help of friends, family or a professional counselor. When the fear of depression prevents an individual from engaging in the things once enjoyed, however, it typically becomes very dysfunctional and self-defeating. This is especially true of moving on to the next loving relationship. Similarly, when a person becomes depressed over a situation that he or she has the control to change, depression becomes a self-fulfilling prophecy. Finally, when an individual reacts to depression with more depression and/or with other negative emotions, a downward spiral has begun. We trust that after reading this chapter, you, our reader, will keep these things in mind when depression rears its ugly head in your own life, and respond accordingly. If you do that, chances are that it will last no longer than necessary.

* * * * * *

Situations and conditions within and/or surrounding a loving relationship can result in depression, which among other things, includes feeling sad, down, blue, helpless and hopeless.

Without our intervention and our actively doing something about it, however, these feelings associated with depression easily can become our reasons or excusesfor not doing anything about it.

Chapter Twelve

GRIEVING

"I can't believe it. I came home from work today and found a note on the kitchen table next to her engagement ring. All of her clothes and her portable TV were gone. I just can't believe it!"

"I know our divorce was finalized a few months ago, and now he's living with her. But he still loves me. He'll be back. As soon as he gets this thing out of his system, he'll be back. He loves me. He'll eventually want me back."

"She deprived me of my dream of growing old together with the mother of my children. I still love her, but what she did to me is unforgivable. And now she's playing the children against me. What a manipulator she is – and always has been. Well, wait until she needs something. She better not come crying on my doorstep!"

"I took all of his fishing equipment and roller blades to his mother's house today. There's no need to punish him. It's time to bring closure to our relationship so I can get on with my life."

"We went together for four years and lived together for the past year or so. In many ways it was wonderful. But in many ways it wasn't so wonderful either. I'm sad that it's over, but that's behind me now. I'm making new friends, going out some and beginning to again enjoy life."

These are examples of statements people may make during the process of *grieving* – the process of dealing with loss. As we will see in this chapter, there are different kinds of loss that can be experienced within, and as a result of, a loving relationship. How people experience loss, the effects of loss on people and their lives, and what people may do as a result of their feelings of loss, are different and unique for all people. *Grieving is not an event, it is a process* – a process that typically evolves in stages. The individuals expressing the five statements above are illustrating shock, denial, anger, restitution and adjustment, which respectively, are common stages of grieving. It is helpful for people to understand their grieving process, to be aware of the loss for which they are grieving, and to appreciate that there may be some things that they can do to help themselves with their grieving.

There are different ways in which the grieving process can impact your loving relationships. Most books such as this one typically focus on the grief that follows the loss of one's significant other in a break-up initiated by the other party. But the subject of grief and its impact on relationships also must consider another type of grief, known to counselors (and funeral directors) as *bereavement* – the grief that follows the loss of life of a loved one. Bereavement stemming from the loss of a family member other than one's spouse or significant other also can have a significant impact on current and/or future loving relationships. Finally, the loss of a child is probably the most difficult thing a couple can experience and occasionally is responsible for ending many otherwise well-functioning relationships.

In this chapter we will focus on the grief associated with breaking up. However, we also will examine these other sources of loss and the impact they may have on you, your significant other and your relationship. In so doing, we hope to help you more efficiently and effectively deal with each of these sources of loss and to better understand the process of making the transition through them. We also trust that you will benefit from some of our helpful advice, designed to help you (a) manage your own sense of grief that results from these various sources of loss, (b) be of more assistance to your significant other, and (c) caringly aid those outside your dyadic relationship (e.g., children and family).

Grieving: A Process

It is not uncommon for people to experience the evolution of their grieving process through identifiable stages, such as: (a) shock; (b) denial; (c) anger; (d) restitution; and, (e) adjustment. These stages were first described systematically by Elizabeth Kübler-Ross, a Swiss-born psychiatrist, and the author of the groundbreaking 1969 book, *On Death and Dying*, in which she first discussed what is now known as "the Kübler-Ross model." Her work originally focused on how one prepares for one's own death, rather than on bereavement or loss due to the end of a loving relationship._Psychologists and counselors soon came to realize, nonetheless, that her work, with minor adjustments, generalized to these latter areas as well. Her contributions to our understanding of the process of coping with and overcoming loss are enormous, and she will long be honored for her work.

From our perspective, however, it is important to remember that every individual's grieving process is different and unique. A person can experience various aspects of grieving at almost any time during a day, an evening, a week, a month or a year. Furthermore, an individual may experience the process of grieving as a sense of loss while in a relationship as well as after a relationship may have ended. The most important thing to remember, however, is that *grieving is not an event – it is a process*. And if an individual is experiencing a sense of loss and going through various stages of the grieving process, it also is critical for that person to remember that these stages tend to be fluid. For example, while an individual may experience denial on Monday, he or she may experience intense anger on Tuesday and Wednesday, and by the end of the week be back to experiencing various aspects of denial. Being patient with yourself and allowing yourself to experience these facets of your grieving process are paramount.

Among many things that you can do to help yourself when you are grieving over a sense of "loss" within, or upon the ending of, a relationship, it is helpful to: (a) recognize and accept the process that you are experiencing; (b) allow yourself to experience whatever you are experiencing (e.g., if you feel like crying, cry; if you feel very angry, go out and chop some wood or punch a pillow); and, (c) allow yourself to obtain and accept some assistance (e.g., having a close network of friends who are helpful to you, seeing a psychotherapist and/or reading self-help books can be extremely helpful). To reiterate: grieving is not an event – it is a process, a very understandable, natural, human process.

We begin our case reviews by looking at the loss associated with one's loving relationship that is caused by break-up or divorce. Then we will look at bereavement due to the death of a partner or spouse, and finally we will look at how the loss of a child or partner's loved one may be expected to impact an intact relationship.

What Are You Grieving?

Dr. Emener will never forget the first time he met Wilma, a thirty-one-year-old legal secretary who had recently gone through an emotionally embattled, draining divorce. "I came to see you because I feel so depressed all the time, and I don't know what to do about it," she said. As they talked about her five-year marriage to John and some of the details of her divorce, they quickly realized that Wilma was experiencing many aspects of grieving. For example, at one point she softly said, "I have a very intense feeling of loss."

Later in their first session, Dr. Emener said, "It might be helpful, Wilma, if you could somehow identify your feelings of loss as well as the *objects* of your grieving. That is, what are your feelings of loss associated with? Are you grieving over the loss of John, the person? Are you grieving over the loss of the relationship that you had with

John? Are you grieving over the loss of a relationship, in general? And/or are you grieving over the loss of your dream of having a future with John?" As tears welled up in her eyes and she stared out the window, she slowly and softly managed, "All of the above. There are many things about John that I loved so much. And I guess I still miss them incredibly. At the same time I miss our relationship; we had many good times together. I also miss having a person to have a relationship with – hugging my pillow as I fall asleep at night is no fun. Likewise, I think that my dream of having a little 'John Jr.,' who would have the same cute little ears that John has, is gone." For Wilma, this was a very good beginning of her journey toward overcoming her grieving over (a) the loss of John, (b) the loss of her relationship with John, (c) the loss of being in a relationship, and (d) the loss of her dream of the growing-old-with, and raising-a-family-with, John. As time went on, it also was helpful for Wilma to understand how her sadness, denial and anger were associated with each of these various objects of her grieving.

As was discussed in Chapter Eleven, it is important to know the difference between being *alone*, being *lonesome* and being *lonely*. For Wilma, knowing specifically what aspects of John and her relationship with John that she was grieving over, was very helpful. The last time Bill spoke with Wilma, she said to him, "I think that there will always be a place for John in my heart. And I hope I never will forget the wonderful memories of the times we enjoyed together. But now that I am able to have a place for John and my relationship with John as a part of my past, I can get on with my life. What you said during our last session is true: it is very difficult to start to write a new chapter in your book of life until you have started to bring closure to the previous chapter."

GRIEVING CAN SNEAK BACK ON OCCASIONS

Chuck, a twenty-eight-year-old videographer, was trying very hard to improve his current relationship with Irene. Chuck and Irene had been "going together" for about six months and had even begun discussing the possibility of a long-term relationship, including engagement and marriage. "Even though I truly believe that I have overcome the ending of my relationship with Linda, to whom I was almost engaged two years ago, I sometimes have the feeling that all of my issues with Linda are not totally gone," he said. Dr. Emener suggested to Chuck that there was a definite possibility that he was still emotionally involved in some aspects of his process of grieving over the loss of Linda and their relationship. "That could very well be true," Chuck replied, "because just the other day when I was driving home from work, a song came on the radio that reminded me of the time that Linda and I took a two-week vacation together. Visions of Linda and visions of the two of us playing together on the beach flashed through my head as I was listening to the song. Tears began rolling down my face. A couple of months ago, I was going through some boxes in my storage bin and ran across a Christmas ornament that Linda had given me. A lump in my throat, a knot in my stomach, and a strong feeling of sadness quickly engulfed me. I just stood there holding the ornament in my hand, speechless."

Dr. Emener sketched a little diagram for Chuck similar to the one in Figure 12.1. He then suggested to Chuck that although he was currently very much in love with Irene and enjoying his relationship with her, he was still experiencing some of his grieving process – grieving over the loss of Linda and his former relationship with her. Chuck took the diagram with him and shared it with Irene. When he first said that he shared it with Irene, Dr. Emener got a little nervous. Sharing with a current loved one that you may still be grieving the loss of a previous loved one and/or a previous loving relationship indeed could be explosive and/or destructive to a current relationship! He felt relieved, however, when Chuck said, "That was a very helpful thing for me to do. First of all, I recognized that my grieving had nothing to do with Irene, my love for Irene, and my love of my relationship with Irene. Luckily for me, Irene responded in a very

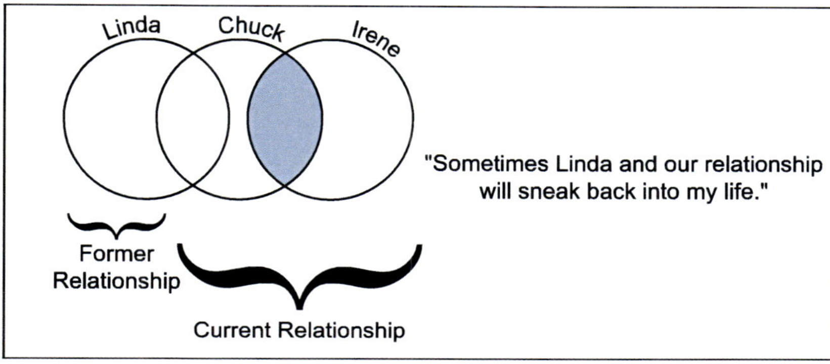

Figure 12.1. Grieving Can Sneak Back on You on Occasions.

Linda. In fact, she very lovingly told me that she would be patient and allow me to experience whatever I had to experience in order for all of that part of my past to finally stop interfering with my relationship with her. And since we had that conversation, I find myself not grieving half as much as I used to."

It was clear to Chuck that his grieving over the loss of Linda and his former relationship with her was a process – a process that was taking time and could not be rushed. He also recognized that while he was writing a new chapter in his book of life – the chapter with Irene – he simultaneously was writing the ending of the former chapter of his life – the chapter of his life with Linda. It is also interesting to note that while it was helpful for Chuck to talk with Irene about his occasional grieving, it also allowed Irene to talk with him about some of her occasional remembrances of her former relationship with Tom, a gentleman to whom she had almost become engaged about three years prior to meeting Chuck. By allowing each other the freedom to experience their residual grieving over previous relationships and to share their grieving experiences with each other, Chuck and Irene further enriched and strengthened their relationship with each other. During his last session with Dr. Emener, Chuck said, "The more I am able to find a place for Linda in my past and the more Irene feels free to find a place for Tom in her past, the better we seem to feel about our present relationship and our future."

The Stalls in Your Barn

Dr. Emener will never forget his first counseling session with Lynn, a thirty-three-year-old elementary school teacher. Her divorce from Rob had been finalized six months previously and she had primary custody of her five-year-old son, Jason. However, she was having trouble sleeping, staying focused and basically getting on with her life. Her primary care physician gave her a thirty-day prescription for antidepressants, but told her to see a therapist to work on her post-divorce issues.

During their first session, Lynn not only appeared depressed but fidgety and somewhat anxious as well. About halfway through that session, Lynn pointedly said, "Sometimes I feel like my head has a hundred ping pong balls bouncing all around in it. No matter what I am trying to do, I just seem to be thinking about a hundred other things and a thousand other people all the time. I'm managing, but I can't get on with my life! For example, my neighbors invited me to join their Friday night co-ed bowling team. It's a lot of fun – it's me, my two neighbors, Jerry and Sally, and Sally's father, Roy. And not only do they have to remind me when it's my turn a lot, but… Well, last Friday night Sally told me that this real nice guy on another team, Scott, was asking about me. I could tell he was looking at me a lot. Sally said she thought he might ask me out. But every time I would look at Scott, I would think about Rob. I left and went home as soon as I finished my last frame. Jeez, I can't get Rob out of my head! I know I have to see him two or three times a week – we have shared custody of Jason. But… I just wish I did not have to 'see him' when he's around."

After talking more about Lynn's experiences, Dr. Emener asked, "Didn't you tell me that you grew up on a farm in Wisconsin?" Lynn smiled and replied, "Yes." While starting to draw a diagram similar to the one in Figure 12.2, Bill said, "Lynn, I want you to think about what it would be like to be a farmer up there in Wisconsin, in the wintertime, with a barn full of animals with no stalls or pens in the barn. What would that be like?"

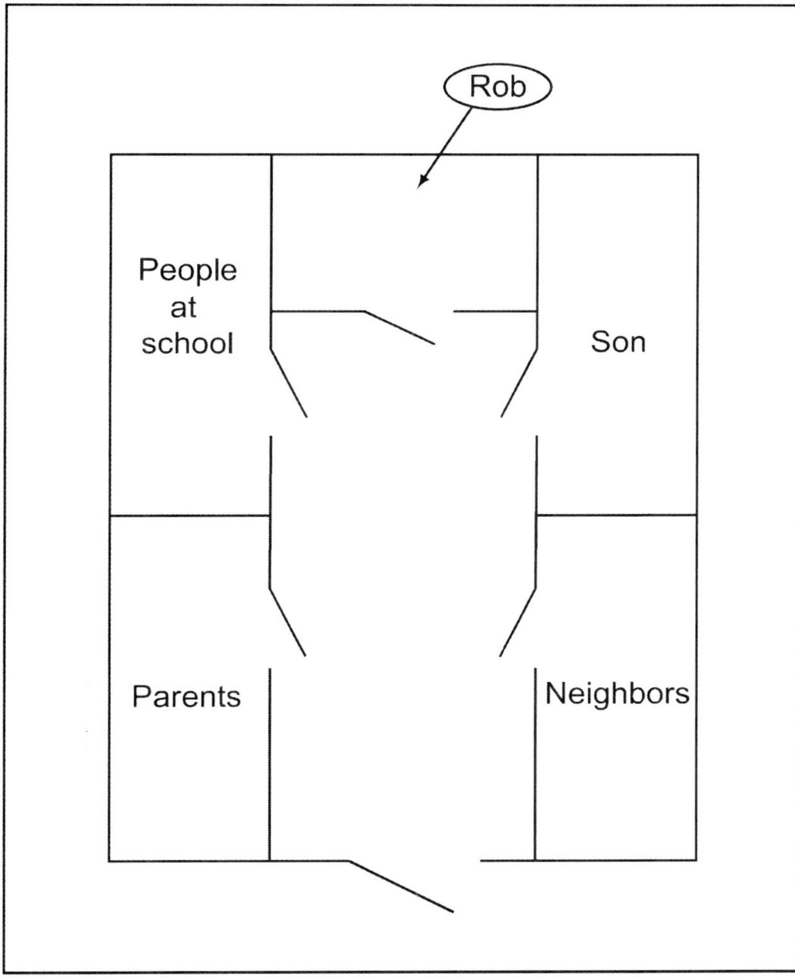

Figure 12.2. The Stalls in Your Barn.

"Crazy… on a good day," Lynn said through a chuckle. "With all of the animals free to go wherever they wanted to go in the barn, it would be 24/7 chaos." Dr. Emener continued to draw the diagram and said, "So you would have all of the animals in their respective stalls or pens, and when you wanted to milk the cow you would bring it out of its stall into the middle of the barn and milk it and then put it back in its stall, and then when you wanted to groom the horse you would bring it out of its stall into the middle of the barn and brush it and then put it back, and so forth." Lynn knowingly smiled and said, "Of course. Can you imagine…?"

"Well," Dr. Emener began, showing Lynn the Figure, "the good news is that if we were to think of this as your current barn, you have stalls or pens for your parents, the people at your school, your son and your neighbors. And based on what you have told me, you may have to reinforce and mend some of the walls on those stalls and pens. *However, you don't have a stall for Rob.* And if this is true, no matter what you do in the barn, he just wanders in and around you and whatever you're doing whenever he feels like it."

A thin smile slowly splayed across Lynn's face. "Jeez, that makes so much sense," she softly said. "So what you're saying is that I need to make all the existing stalls in my head more secure and build a stall for Rob so that he only comes out when I want him to – like on Wednesday nights and every other weekend?" Bill smiled and replied, "Well, that's up to you, Lynn – it's your barn."

Two weeks later when Lynn came for her next appointment – her last appointment – she introduced herself as "Farmer Lynn." In addition to saying that she had been feeling less depressed and less anxious, she told Dr. Emener that the self-help book he had recommended had been very helpful to her. "I also have rebuilt some of the stalls and made one for Rob," she proudly stated, and then through a wry smile added, "That one has a lock on it, and I have the key."

At the end of the session, Lynn happily said that she was much better and would call to make an appointment if she needed to come back. "Oh and by the way," she added with a grin, "I may need to build another stall – this Saturday night Scott's taking me out to dinner and a movie."

Sometimes it simply is important to make sure that you have control over those parts of your life – especially the people in your life – that you can have control over. As Lynn aptly said, "If you don't, your life will be crazy… on a good day."

Have Something to Take Care Of

A large part of struggling with loss is the consumption with and hyper-vigilance on one's self. When we are hurting and in pain, paying attention to ourselves is understandable. Nonetheless, even though being self-absorbed and self-focused, all or a majority of the time, may be unconscious, it still mitigates against healing and getting on with one's life. Thus, from a logical perspective, it makes sense to identify ways of making yourself focus on and pay attention to some things outside of yourself. One of Dr. Lambos's case files provides an excellent example of this suggestion.

Alex came to see Dr. Lambos because, as he had said, "I'm still so caught up in Sherry, I can't relax or enjoy myself anymore. Okay, our divorce was finalized three months ago and we have agreed not to have any contact with each other. But I think about her all the time… I miss her so much!"

Toward the end of their first session, Bill suggested a self-help book for Alex and said, "Alex, a while ago you said that you like dogs… you said something about Sherry having taken your collie with her. Well, I would like to suggest that you think about getting a puppy." Alex thought about it for a moment and with a small smile said, "My sister's terrier just had a litter a few weeks ago. I'll see."

Two weeks later when Alex came in for his next appointment, he had a terrier puppy with him. After an exchange of greetings and comments about Alex's new friend, Blackie, he said to Bill, "When I told my sister that I felt like a family man without a family, she handed me this little guy and said, 'Here, he needs a good home.' And ever since I got him, I've slowly been feeling better. I take him with me wherever I go." Then as he petted Blackie and set him down on the rug, Alex said, "You're my buddy, aren't you."

In addition to Blackie giving him something to attend to outside of himself, Alex also was enjoying the unconditional love people tend to receive from a puppy. Alex was feeling special again. That was Dr. Lambos's last session with Alex, and Bill believes that Alex is progressing, feeling better every day and getting on with his life.

When appropriate and if you enjoy animals, getting a pet indeed can facilitate your working through the grieving process. (It is not recommended, however, that you take your pet with you to your doctor's appointments – especially if it's not housebroken yet!)

When a Loved One Dies

The death of a significant other, especially when unexpected, can be a devastating experience. Most people are not well prepared for it, and such losses can be especially difficult for people in long-term or life-long relationships. The probability of a person dying within two years following the death of a spouse is statistically quite high after twenty-five years or more of marriage. This is true even if the individual was healthy at the time of the loved one's passing.

One reason for this was proffered by the well-known Viennese psychiatrist, Victor Frankl. A survivor of nearly four years in Nazi concentration camps where the odds of making it out were estimated at only one in twenty-five, he witnessed his parents, brother and pregnant wife perish. Based on his experiences, Frankl went on to develop both a theory of human motivation and a form of psychotherapy based on the human need to ascribe *meaning* to one's existence. In his famous book, *Man's Search for Meaning*, first published in 1959, Frankl stated that his survival depended on his focusing on the one thing his tormentors could not take away from him: *his choice of how to view his situation*.

In one of the more poignant recollections from his book, Frankl describes an elderly man, a retired medical doctor, who came to see him because he was suffering greatly over the loss of his wife of forty years. Frankl asked the man a simple question: What would life have been like for her if you had died first? Upon reflection, the man realized that his suffering had spared his beloved partner of having to experience the same terrible fate. This gave such a profound sense of meaning to the man's situation that he shook Dr. Frankl's hand, thanked him and left the office.

As counselors, your authors tend to be eclectic in their choice of theoretical perspectives, looking for explanations and treatment approaches from many theories of personality, motivation and change. For example, one of us (Dr. Lambos) is quite heavily involved with the neuroscientific origins of psychological phenomena and also has an extensive background in Rational Emotive Behavioral Therapy. The other (Dr. Emener) originally was trained within the Rogerian model, but since then also has made use of many other approaches, including behavioral, cognitive and solution-focused models. Nevertheless, neither of us is prone to underestimate the importance of one's perspective in matters of mental life – a perception-based orientation sometimes called *phenomenology*. No matter what else life throws one's way, as long as one is conscious, one retains the choice to adopt one or another perspective for their situation. This is among the more important messages we convey in this book.

The Loss of a Child or Another Loved One

Many a marriage or relationship is put at risk when parents lose a child. This is especially troubling, because an ensuing breakup often becomes a second source of grief, and can make an already difficult situation seem unbearable. There are several signs to look for in one's relationship when a family member or other loved one dies.

The first is *isolation*. Although a person may need to spend time alone for a period following the death of a loved one to process the change it involves in their life, extended isolation is associated with depression and mental instability. It can be difficult to judge the balance between needing to process a loss privately and the need to remain in social contact with others. Should your partner react to such a loss by separating from you and others for an extended period, one must combine patience while monitoring for depression along with the need to remain functional at some level.

Another warning sign to look for is extended *denial*, which counselors sometimes refer to as "stuffing it." The grieving process must be allowed to unfold, and this cannot happen when one cannot or will not face the reality of a loss. Again, there is a fine line to be walked here, like Somerset Maugham's rhetorical "razor's edge." If you are helping your partner cope with the loss of a loved one, try to engage them in conversation about their feelings and encourage them to recount the joys they experienced by having previously had the deceased in their life. If they refuse to deal with it for a prolonged period, gently suggest they seek the help of a licensed counselor or other professional.

Sometimes a person will find it necessary to *blame* you, the partner, for the loss. As irrational as this may seem, it is very common and you must remind yourself that it is a part of the grieving process and should not be personalized. Although you should not blame your partner for experiencing or expressing such feelings, if it does not resolve itself over the course of a few weeks, we once again recommend encouraging your partner to seek professional help.

Another warning sign is *self-destructive behavior*. Abusing alcohol or other substances – a means of self-medicating – is never a healthy response to loss. In addition to substance abuse, look for behaviors such as excessive risk-taking, self-cutting, or other compulsive, self-destructive behaviors. If discussing them with your loved one does not resolve such behavior patterns, immediately seek professional help.

Among the most important things you can do to assist a loved one who is grieving, is simply to be there for them and to accept them and their situation – within the limits discussed above. Pressuring them to "get over it" will do little other than to generate resentment and put your relationship at risk.

Loss and the grief that accompanies it are ultimately a part of life. To move beyond it, one must allow oneself to undergo the grieving process, to search for and find meaning in the loss, and ultimately move on. This is, like so many of the issues we address in this book, more often easier said than done. Nevertheless, one of the wonderful benefits of loving relationships is that they can lead us to grow and become more than we were before. In the ideal world, everyone can find some solace in the "meaning" their former partner brought to and added to their life.

* * * * * *

Grieving is a process of attending to loss:
of a loved one in your life,
of a loving relationship,
of a loving lifestyle,
of a dream.
Loss is painful.
Grieving is painful.
Recovery from loss and grieving is a process
that is highly contingent upon forgiving,
not forgetting.
And although a time may come
when you may think you are fully recovered
from the loss of a love,
you may not truly appreciate
the depth and breadth of the wounds,
the thickness of the scars
and the healing still remaining,
until you fall in love again.

A wound is not a wound until a memory makes it bleed.

Chapter Thirteen

TIME AND TIMING

"I still miss Richard so much. It's been over two years now since his death. But I still miss him so. I would give up the insurance money, his car, the house, everything – if I could just spend one more day with him."

"I know what life has been like being married to Alice for these past ten years and I have an appreciation for what it is like now. What it will be like to be with her in the future, however, is a big unknown for me."

"By the time we get home from work and attend to the children and the usual house things, we never seem to have any time left for each other – not to mention ourselves."

"As I think about our relationship over the past five years, the things that bring the biggest smiles to my face are not the rings, the expensive presents or the new house we had built. It's the wonderful times we spent together and the precious moments we shared."

All of these four statements have something in common. They illustrate the importance of *time* in loving relationships. In this chapter we will focus on the construct of time, its characteristics and attributes, and take a look at how time, if unattended to, can have detrimental effects and influences on us, our loved ones and our loving relationships. We also will address and take a look at how some people were able to attend to their time issues for the purposes of improving their own quality of life, their loved ones quality of life and their loving relationships.

TIME: A PRECIOUS COMMODITY

There is an old cliché that suggests that the way an individual spends his or her time and money is the best indication of his or her values and what he or she considers important in life. We would argue that of these two, time and money, that *time* is the more precious commodity. On numerous occasions we have suggested that time is the most precious commodity in a human being's life; we do not know how much of it we have left, we are constantly running out of it, we have no way of knowing when we will run out of it, and there is no way to get more of it. Fittingly, one of the first questions we frequently ask individuals who come to see us with a relationship problem or concern is: *How do you spend your time?*

It also would appear reasonable to assume that if you love another person and you want to give to them and share with them the one thing that is most precious to you in your life, it would be your time. As we shall see in this chapter, it is not only the *amount of time* that you give and share, but it is the *quality of that time* as well. We always have believed that one of the most helpful things two individuals in a loving relationship can do is to remain cognizant of (a) how each of them individually spends his or her time and (b) how they spend their time together.

Pursuant to the issue of *quality of time*, many individuals are unable to experience the passing of time without feeling either anxious or bored, and in fact spend the majority of their time toggling back and forth between these two states. Others feel that time is wasted unless they are sufficiently stimulated or experiencing some thrill (e.g.., the "adrenaline junkie"). Many such people eventually give up trying to feel any sense of quality of life, and give in to the mindless distraction of television or, in some cases, work. Others succumb to the lure of self-medication and often develop serious problems with alcohol and/or drugs. Yet it is quite difficult, if not impossible, to develop a healthy and sustainable loving relationship if one is unable to enjoy periods marked by the mere passage of time. Counselors often refer to this as learning to feel "comfortable in one's own skin."

It stands to reason, therefore, that learning not only to manage one's time well but also to learn how to make the most of it across a wide range of circumstances, is a core skill needed for loving relationships. Our case reports look at many of these issues in hopes of illuminating our readers about this important subject. Toward the end of the chapter, we also suggest some ways of learning how to live well in the moment of the present, or "in the now," and how this can also enhance the quality of your relationship with your significant other.

You Can't Create It – Just Allocate It

John and Mary, both of whom were single parents in their early forties with four small children between them, "had been going steady for the past six months" before coming to see Dr. Emener. Both of them expressed and demonstrated a tremendous amount of frustration: John was frustrated with Mary because she did not spend enough time with him, and Mary was frustrated with John because he did not understand why she was not able to spend more time with him. John, who lived in his house with his two children, owned his own lawn service and worked nine or ten hours a day, six days a week. Mary, who lived in her house with her two children, was a co-owner of an answering service, and not only put in long days during the week but also had to be on call every other weekend. "But why can't you just spend more time with me?" John repeatedly asked Mary.

Not to help Mary defend herself but to assist her in explaining herself and communicating her frustration to John, Dr. Emener drew a diagram similar to the one in Figure 13.1. He then said to Mary, "It appears that this circle on the left represents your life as it is now in

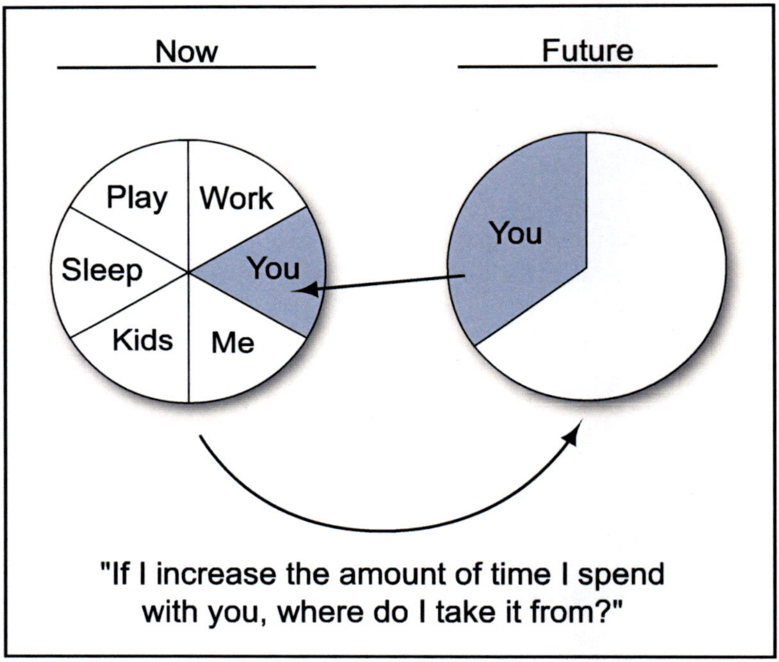

Figure 13.1. You Can't Create Time – Just Allocate It.

terms of the relative amounts of time that you spend at work, at play, sleeping, with your two children, with John, and for yourself. And what I hear you saying, Mary, is that although you would like to increase the amount of time that you spend with John, the "You" in the diagram..." Mary interrupted Dr. Emener and looked at John and said, "That is exactly it, John. I do want to spend more time with you, but where do I take it from?"

The important thing that John was able to understand was that Mary, like all human beings, could not create time, only try to reallocate it. Much pleasure was gained by the two of them when, over the next few weeks, they were able to reconfigure some of their work schedules, as well as their social activities, so that both of them were able to comfortably allocate more time to be with each other. There was no doubt that they were in love with each other. However, their intense emotions, specifically their frustrations, were preventing them from identifying ways to arrange their lives so that they could comfortably spend more time together. And as John poignantly said at their last session, "I used to say to Mary, 'If you loved me you would spend more time with me,' but I eventually realized that given all of the things going on in her life, it was not that easy, and the amount of time that she could allocate to me and to us was not necessarily an indication of how much she loved me. Once we were able to get over that hurdle, Dr. Emener, we were able to work things out and improve things rather quickly."

A Sense of Time and Space

Gary, a thirty-eight-year-old air conditioning repairman, came to see Dr. Emener because he was contemplating filing for a divorce. He said to Bill, "Gail and I went together for four years and then married. We have been married for five years now. For many reasons, I am thinking about divorce. However, I want to make sure that this is the right thing for me, and it would be helpful to me if I could try to figure out why I am so scared."

During the two subsequent therapy sessions, they addressed many aspects of his life, his relationship with Gail and many considerations pertinent to his filing (or not filing) for a divorce. One of the things that was helpful for Gary was his enhanced understanding and appreciation of his sense of time and space. Bill drew a chart for him, similar to the one in Figure 13.2, and said, "Gary, from what you have been telling me it appears that the time you have spent with Gail in the past has been somewhere between *okay* and *good*. The time that

"My Time"	In The ... Past	Present	Future
With Her:	Ok/Good	Ok	Optimistic
Without Her:	Ok/Good	Terrible	?

"Not knowing what my time would be like in the future without her, is scary."

Figure 13.2. A Sense of Time and Space.

you spend with her in the present is *okay*. And although you are contemplating the possibility of divorce because of the numerous understandable reasons that you have expressed, you still have a sense of *optimism* when you talk about a possible future with her. As you think of your time without her, however, your recollections suggest that in your past you tended to feel *between* okay and good without her – for example, when she was away on a two-week vacation or you were on a one-week hunting trip with your buddies. Since you moved out last month and now are living in an apartment by yourself, however, you are feeling *terrible* without her and you have no idea what your life might be like without her. In fact, that seems to be a very scary thought for you." At that point, Gary's six-foot six, two hundred and seventy-five pound body melted into the couch while tears streamed down his face.

When he left Dr. Emener's office, Gary asked if he could take the figure with him because it was helpful in understanding and appreciating his life over the course of time – *with Gail and without*

Gail. And although he was emotionally upset at the time he was leaving, he said to Bill, "This has been extremely helpful, Doc. I think I understand things much better. I will get back in touch with you."

Dr. Emener never heard from Gary again. Two weeks later Bill called Gary's home phone number and left a message on his answering machine asking him to call if there were anything he could do, then or in the future, to be of assistance. Although Bill has not heard from Gary, we trust that whatever has happened in his life he is doing well. What Gary helped Bill to appreciate, however, was that when an individual is emotionally caught up in the day-to-day, moment-to-moment difficulties with a loving relationship, it is helpful to also give consideration to the relationship and its difficulties from the perspectives of *time* and *space.*

PRIORITIES CHANGE OVER TIME

Katie, a twenty-nine-year-old nurse, made an appointment to see Dr. Lambos because, "For the last year or so I have been feeling empty and aimless. My marriage is okay by all the usual criteria, but my husband, Phil, an insurance salesman, is happy just to come home, have supper and watch TV or play on the computer. Then the day ends, and it starts all over again. I mentioned I wanted to go back to school to work on my master's degree in nursing, and he couldn't believe it. He couldn't understand why what we already had wasn't enough. He even accused me of having an affair with the doctor I work for and asked if my employer wasn't behind it all!"

Bill asked Katie more details about their situation. She was unable to have children because of a medical condition, and her husband accepted this when they married. Neither of them wanted to adopt a child, so they fell into a comfortable set of routines. But after a few years, Katie developed a need for becoming someone better and more accomplished – something psychologists refer to as the need to *self-actualize* – whereas Phil was fine with things as they were. Since Katie's situation, rather than their core relationship was the main issue, Dr. Lambos suggested they come to sessions together. Bill explained to Phil that as some people move from one life stage to another, their priorities can change. Moreover, Dr. Lambos suggested that Phil could choose to see Katie's need for growth and self-actualization as a positive and admirable quality, rather than to feel threatened by it. Phil looked down and said, barely loud enough to hear, "What happens if I'm not good enough for her after she gets her degree? I'm happy as a salesman and don't want to change."

Over the course of several sessions, Phil came to realize that it is unrealistic to expect a loved one to remain the exact same person as the years pass by. Although Phil remained nervous that Katie would not remain in love with him, when Dr. Lambos last saw them Phil had accepted that Katie's need for self-growth was not about him at all – it was about her changing priorities. To our knowledge, they remain together.

In a similar vein, Donna, a forty-eight-year-old computer programmer, came to see Dr. Emener because she was experiencing "mild levels of anxiety and worrisome levels of depression." She tended to focus her conversation not only on her job but on her twenty-four year marriage to Daryl, a fifty-year-old life insurance salesman, and their "three almost grown children." She also said, "I keep telling Daryl that I feel like I'm going through some kind of transition, but I don't know what it is. For reasons that I do not understand, I just feel off balance, off-center and not really focused on what's going on around me." As Donna and Dr. Emener continued to talk, the "transition" to which she had referred became evident.

Dr. Emener drew a chart for Donna, similar to the one in Figure 13.3. He then said to her, "Donna, from what you have been telling me, it appears that you went through your *first lifestyle transition* in your late twenties to early thirties, and now you are going through your *second lifestyle transition.* When you and Daryl were first married and did not have any children, your priorities were relatively clear: first came you, then came your relationship with Daryl, and then came your work. By the time you were in your mid-thirties, your

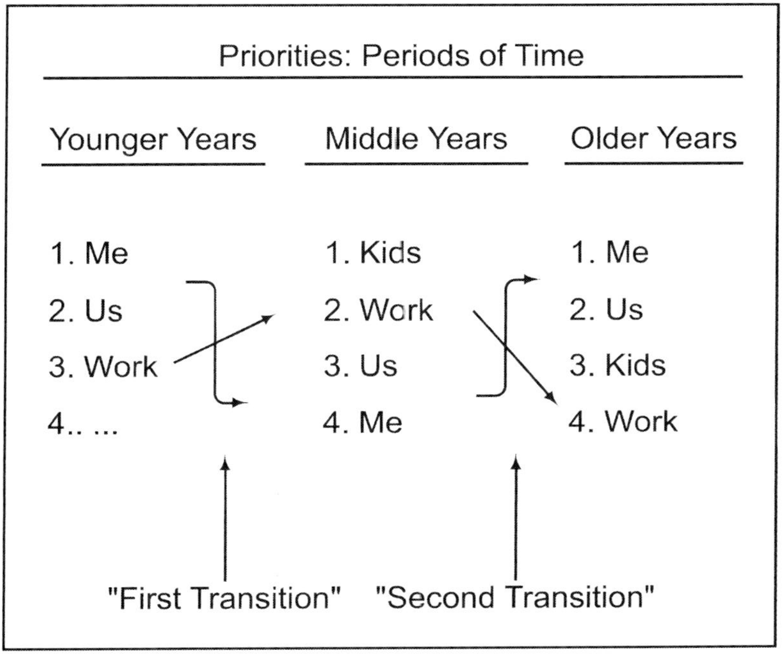

Figure 13.3. Priorities Change Over Time.

priorities had shifted: first came your children, then came your work, then came you and Daryl, and then yourself. Now that you are getting older and your children are moving out on their own, you are transitioning into a new set of priorities: first it is you, then it is you and Daryl, then it is your children, and then it is your work. Does this make sense to you?"

After pondering the diagram, Donna replied, "Yes, it surely does. That's me!" She then added, "This second transition, however, seems to be a hell of a lot more difficult than the first one! If I continue to attend to and dote on the kids, they get frustrated with me and say, 'Leave me alone!' Then when I leave them alone, I feel guilty because I still have a sense of responsibility for them and don't know how to continue to be their mother." Dr. Emener could not help but smile as he looked at her and said, "Yes, Donna, that's very true they... they keep changing the rules on us. Just when we learn how to be parents of child-children, they become adult-children and we have to start all over again." She laughed and nodded in agreement.

Donna took the chart home with her and shared it with Daryl. "It's amazing," she said in their next session. "When I went over the chart with Daryl, he immediately told me that he had been experiencing the same thing, but was afraid to share it with me for fear that it would bring me down." Donna then went on to explain the many ways in which both she and Daryl had been struggling with how to allocate their time during their transition phase.

Toward the end of their last session, they were interrupted by a knock on the door – it was Daryl. Earlier, Donna had told Dr. Emener that Daryl was going to try to stop by to join them for a few minutes when he got out of work. That provided them with a very enjoyable opportunity to collectively review how the two of them were doing with the transitioning of the time priorities in their lives, and how they were doing in assisting each other in allocating their time. "Now that we have been helping each other with this," Donna said, "it has been so much easier." About three months later, Bill received a postcard from the Smokey Mountains that included the following inscription, "For many reasons, we are having a wonderful week's vacation – two of which are: we do not have the children with us (for the first time in many years), and we don't feel guilty about it! Thanks again, Donna and Daryl."

This May Not Be the Right Time

Jack, a thirty-four-year-old plumber, came to see Dr. Emener because he was feeling extremely frustrated with his relationship with Sharon, a woman he had been dating for about two and a half months. "A little over a year ago, I finalized my divorce. We had been married for nine years and had no children. A few months ago, I began occasionally going out on dates. Then I met Sharon. She is really neat! Sharon is twenty-eight, divorced, is the head receptionist in a law firm in town and has the most adorable little three-year-old daughter that you would ever want to meet." It was clear, however, that Jack also was feeling some depression and anxiety regarding his life, as well as a growing level of frustration with his relationship with Sharon. Dr. Emener asked him whether there were one or two specific issues that he and she tended to have the most difficulty with. With a big sigh, Jack said, "There's only one. And, I don't know what to do about it."

As their discussion continued, the primary nature of Jack's difficulty with Sharon became relatively clear. Sharon had been divorced for approximately two and a half years, and as Jack said, "has her life together: she is comfortable with her divorce, she has worked out a comfortable and cordial relationship with her ex-husband, and basically she is ready to settle down. The problem for me," he continued, "is that I am still reeling a little bit from my divorce. I don't really feel like my feet are firmly on the ground yet. I have tried to tell Sharon that, but somehow she just has difficulties hearing me. Just the other night, I said to her, 'Our timing is terrible!' Whenever I tell her that I'm not ready to see her as often as she would like or that I am not ready to consider living together, she right away thinks that either there is something about her that I do not like or that she has done something to upset me. I don't know why, but for some reason I cannot get through to her."

At Jack's invitation, Sharon came to their next session. After each of them had the opportunity to express some individual feelings and thoughts, Dr. Emener asked them to identify some boundaries for their relationship that would be comfortable for the two of them. When they left, they were planning to go to dinner together and to discuss what boundaries each of them needed in order to feel comfortable with and enjoy their relationship. Jack said, "Thanks a lot, Doc. I don't feel any need to schedule another appointment at this time, but I will get back to you. I really feel that the two of us are heading in the right direction." As Sharon threw her arm around Jack's waist, she looked at Dr. Emener with a smile of understanding and agreement. Dr. Emener had not heard from Jack and Sharon for about six months when he received an envelope at his office in which there was a photocopy of a newspaper clipping announcing their engagement. Across the bottom was written, "I finally felt ready – it feels good. Just wanted to share this with you. Thanks again, Jack."

Needless to say, timing is a very important consideration in any loving relationship. Moreover, most of the time it is futile for us to try to hurry another individual's timing if he or she is not ready. As Sharon had said, "I guess for the time being, *patience* is going to have to be my middle name." And given what eventually happened, it apparently had been – and it worked.

A Long-Term Trade Off

Betty, a forty-eight-year-old instructor at a junior college, had been married to Henry for twenty-five years. Their two children were no longer at home – one was married and living in another city and the other was in graduate school. "It's just the two of us now," Betty said. Following a relatively lengthy discussion about her life, she finally said, "The truth of the matter, Dr. Emener, is that while I love Henry very much and truly believe that he loves me very much, I simply do not feel *in love* with him. In fact, I haven't for a long time. I have come very close to having an affair or two, but up til now nothing like that has ever happened. It is not that I have a bad relationship with Henry; in fact, it's comfortable. But for me, the spark is gone, I no longer feel romantically involved with him. He is more like a friend than a lover or husband, and I guess from a romantic point of view our relationship is somewhat dull, meaningless and empty." Dr. Emener suggested a couple of self-help books for Betty to read and invited her to return for another session at which time they might take a serious look at some of her options. She agreed and scheduled another session.

Within two minutes of entering Dr. Emener's office, Betty said, "I read the two books you had recommended and have made a decision, at least for now, and I feel okay about it! I made a list of the pros and cons of either staying with Henry or leaving him. On one side of the ledger, I have a good friend. He is a good man and is very good to me. I live a very comfortable life. Considering that he is fifty years old, he is still in pretty good shape and we enjoy a relatively active life together. From a romantic point of view, however, our relationship is about as exciting as a dial tone. I guess that is a sadness I will have to live with because I have decided to stay with him." While wiping back some tears, Betty continued, "At this time in my life, I guess I simply just don't want to go through all of the hassles involved in separation and divorce. Furthermore, I don't want to screw up my relationship with my children or create any difficulties for my future grandchildren. If I was twenty-eight and felt this way, there is a chance that I might be more inclined to end my relationship with Henry. But at forty-eight, I am simply at a different place in time." Betty's body language and facial expressions, while communicating the sense of sadness that she was verbalizing, also communicated a sense of peace and tranquility with her decision. As she was leaving, she turned and said, "If I ever change my mind and/or need any further assistance from you, I will call you."

Time is relative and it impacts every human being's life differently. *What* we ultimately decide to do when we are at a relationship crossroads, many times is influenced by *where* we are along our journey of life. To say the least, this indeed was an important and critical consideration for Betty.

TIME MARCHES ON

After "bouncing around from job to job over the last fifteen years," Terry, a thirty-five-year-old, married man with two children, decided to take some time to see if he could find out what he really wanted to do to earn a living. "This cashier's job that I currently have," he said, "is just a tide-me-over job. I'm only going to stay there until I figure out what I really want to do." Following some conversations regarding his occupational and career interests, Dr. Emener directed him to some literature regarding paramedical occupations and careers that he was able to find in a local library. When he returned for his next session, Terry said, "Given that I will have to continue to work while going to school, it would take me five years to complete the local paramedic training program. By the time I graduate, I would be forty. For some reason, that doesn't make sense to me."

With a wry smile Dr. Emener looked at him and said, "Terry, let me ask you something: How old will you be in five years if you don't go through the paramedic training program?" With a look of amazement on his face, Terry said, "No shit, forty! That surely is an interesting thought!"

A week later, after discussing the details of the training program with his wife, Terry enrolled in the local paramedic training program. When he telephoned to relate his decision, he said, "I am really excited about this. So is my wife. And you never can tell, Dr. Emener, someday we may meet again!" They both laughed. Continuing with their joyful and playful communication mode, Dr. Emener said, "Hey, I ride a Harley, Terry – study hard!"

The next time that you have a decision to make regarding doing or not doing something and you calculate that you will be a certain age by the time you finish doing it, ask yourself how old you will be at the end of the same period of time if you don't do it. And if you come up with a different answer, please – see someone!

STAYING IN "THE NOW"

Many times clients complain of generalized feelings of *ennui* – low-level anxiety, or a pervasive sense of restlessness that leads to risk-taking, thrill-seeking, or substance abuse. Invariably, such individuals also tend to experience difficulties in their loving relationships and may even blame such feelings on their significant other. Furthermore, we believe such experiences to be pervasive in our culture, which emphasizes continuous and ongoing need for stimulation and immediate gratification. As psychologists, we can advise our readers that this frequently is a common but serious trap of unrealistic expectations. Any given moment or period of time will either be positive, neutral or negative, and the degree to which a given period of time is judged as one or the other is as much determined by one's expectations as the quality of the moment or time period itself. We simply cannot be "up" all the time, if for no other reason than our "ups," "downs" and "neutrals" are experienced relative to our perceptions and commensurate expectations.

Many people dream day after day of winning the lottery as if it would make them happy forever. Research reveals, however, that most lottery winners turn out to be unhappy people – some even commit suicide. In order to have a fulfilling, loving relationship, we must first learn to achieve a level of contentment with the ebb and flow of time over the course of each day. Those who have difficulty with this many times look for help through meditation, yoga, spiritual fulfillment, or other methods of learning to be at peace – living in the current moment. Increasingly, a therapy offered in Dr. Lambos's practice called EEG-biofeedback (or neurofeedback) has helped many of his clients achieve the same result by helping clients change their brainwave patterns. Regardless of how you get there, however, remember that you cannot be happy with another person for very long if you have never learned how to appreciate life and your situation as it is right now.

* * * * * *

While walking on the beach early one morning, Dr. Emener met an elderly couple. Both of them were in their eighties and had been married to each other for over sixty years. As they rambled along on their tired legs, clutching each other's hands with their gnarly fingers, they epitomized what he refers to as "gnarly love." Their deep sense of bonding, love and oneness was evident in their every thought, feeling and action. As Bill rambled along with them and they chatted, the gentleman said,

In our earlier years we did a lot of things together, not just with our children and our friends, but with each other. The most important thing we have ever given to each other has been our time. But now that we can't move along as well as we used to, the only thing we really have left to give each other is our time. Now that we can't play tennis, fit in a round of golf or spend a day Scuba diving together, I guess you could say that our relationship has lost some of its shine.

With the winningest smile on her face, the man's wife pulled his body flush with hers, looked up at him and said,

No my dear, I tend to think of that differently. I prefer to say that the shine of our relationship hasn't been lost – it's been replaced by a deep luster.

Chapter Fourteen

HAPPINESS AND JOY

"All I want is to be happy!" is probably the most frequent response we get when in therapy we ask, "What do you want?" or "What are you hoping for?" Happiness and joy are in many ways synonymous. *Happiness* implies the enjoyment of pleasure without pain, felicity, blessedness, satisfaction and/or bliss. *Joy* implies a very glad feeling, happiness, great pleasure and delight. To have and experience happiness and joy in a loving relationship, to have and experience them in one's life in general, are expectations and desires common to most people in the world. Assuming this is true, it certainly would be important to consider what is meant by "happiness."

When we think of happiness, we look at it from a number of perspectives in order to expand and enrich our understanding of it. This is because the construct itself – "happiness" – has many facets and refers to different things to different people. Indeed, happiness, or at least how to achieve and sustain it, may be seen as something quite different across cultures. For example, whereas Americans typically equate happiness with "feeling good at this moment," Eastern cultures tend to look at happiness as more of a "state of being" that results from achieving a balance of work and play, reward and sacrifice, and of duty and honor over long periods of living. It could be said that Americans want to be happy now – and all the time.

Our individual professional backgrounds also influence the ways in which your authors define happiness. For example, as a counseling psychologist with strong underpinnings in humanistic psychology and phenomenology, Bill Emener tends to look at happiness as "*a by-product of effective living... a manner of traveling, not a station you arrive at.*" To wit, he embraces thoughts such as: "If you pursue it, you'll never find it." Thus, for example, if he had been working with Mr. Franklin, Mr. Jefferson and Mr. Washington when they were writing the Declaration of Independence, he would have objected to "life, liberty, and the pursuit of happiness." He would have recommended, "life, liberty, and *the opportunity to live an effective life that would increase a person's chances for happiness.*" Although Ben, Tom and George may not have disagreed with Bill, his language probably would not have sounded as good to them. Bill Enemer's contention is that happiness is not a single, isolated experience or incident that a person may have or may get from someone else. *Happiness is the outcome experience of a process – a process of living an effective life.* While talking with a client recently, Bill suggested that, "Pursuing happiness is like chasing a butterfly. The more you chase it, the more it just eludes you. But if you sit down quietly, turn your thoughts to other things and become intellectually and emotionally involved in what you are doing, the butterfly may come and sit upon your shoulder." When he shared the butterfly analogy with one of his clients, he replied with a tongue-in-cheek quip, "Yeah, and knowing me, even if I did chase it and were fortunate enough to catch it, my grip would probably kill it."

Bill Lambos, a neuropsychologist, cannot help but to think about happiness as an emotional state of the brain that naturally arises when one's basic needs are met, perhaps when one is successfully engaged in the longer term pursuit of higher aspirations, and when other incompatible emotions such as grief, anxiety, and depression are not preventing its expression. In essence, when the brain can maintain homeostasis and effectively regulate itself, the natural result is happiness.

It is important to note that our perspectives are not incompatible. Both of us focus on happiness as a result of living well. We also recognize that since happiness can be experienced only in comparison to other feelings, one simply cannot expect to be happy "all of the time." Finally, both perspectives recognize the viable role of significant others in achieving happiness.

In this chapter we will look at issues pertinent to happiness as it relates to your individual life and loving relationship, ways by which you may influence your potentials for happiness and joy, and critical aspects of how people tend to experience happiness and joy via their loving relationships.

YOUR "HAPPINESS POTENTIAL"

As part of Bill Emener's pro bono work with people in recovery in his local area, he occasionally meets people at a nearby restaurant and talks with them over coffee. Late one recent balmy afternoon, Bill was talking with Hank about some of Hank's many frustrations with his wife. For example, Hank, a fifty-two-year-old high school math teacher, said, "I know Sandy and I have only been married for three years and are still adjusting to being married again. And considering that both of us are recovering alcoholics, there indeed are numerous challenges for us. But sometimes she drives me crazy! All the drama. Every time I turn around there's another problem, issue or pebble-in-the-shoe that demands concentration on her, the issue or whatever the hell the problem du jour is. And when I try to explain to her that all of the crisis-focused drama is really getting to me, she simply reiterates why it's so important. Sometimes it just seems like she can't stand prosperity! Whenever things seem to be going well in her life, in my life and in our marriage, I start to prepare because I know it's merely the calm before the next storm." Then with a chuckle Hank added, "Jeez, there are only three hours a week when I know I can enjoy myself without having to worry about what she's doing or when the new crisis will come to a boil – the three times a week when she's in her AA meetings."

"It sounds like you feel like you're constantly walking on eggshells," Dr. Emener said before asking, "Have you explained to her that it would be helpful to you if she could change some of the things she's doing?" Hank's brow furrowed as he said, "Eh! Last week I went with her to one of her sessions with her counselor and practically said those same exact words to her – including specific examples of what she's been doing and how it's affecting me. All she said was, 'Hank honey, every one of those things were out of my control, and they were critical things. And anyway, that's the way I am! Why can't you just deal with me the way I am? Why are you always trying to change me?"

Later, after further discussing Hank's frustrations with his wife and before ending their talk, Dr. Emener said, "Hank, I'd like to suggest something for you to think about." Hank smiled with an accompanying "please do" nod. "From what you have told me, between your divorce from your first wife fifteen years ago and your marriage to Sandy three years ago, you lived by yourself with your dog, enjoyed your teaching, had fun with your hobbies, and basically were happy." Hank again smiled and gave a "yes-that's-right" nod.

"Think of a 10-point happiness scale," Dr. Emener said. "A '1' would be akin to 'miserable' – a horribly unhappy life, and a '10' would be akin to 'ecstasy' – a simply wonderful life." Sensing that Hank understood what he was saying, he continued, "So, Hank, let me ask you this: if you were to assume that you could control those things which you reasonably could control, *as an individual* – that is, not thinking about Sandy at all – on a scale of one-to-ten, how happy do you think you could possibly be? What's the best you could hope for?" Hank looked away, deep in thought, and then turned back and said, "An 8. Considering that I'm in recovery, I have to keep an eye on my diabetes issues and I have some financial issues, I suppose that it would be reasonable to expect myself to be able to be happy at 8." Dr. Emener smiled, and after allowing that consideration to settle for a moment, he then said, "Okay Hank, now revisit my question with an additional consideration: if you were to assume that you could control those things which you reasonably could control *and being married to Sandy* and *assuming that she would continue to be the way she is*, on a scale of one-to-ten, how happy do you think you could possibly be? What's the best you could hope for?" Hank's eyes narrowed as he again turned away.

A minute later, Hank returned from his deep-level thinking, looked at Dr. Emener, and with a sense of sadness said, "A 4 or a 5." Tears began welling up in Hank's eyes. "As much as I love that woman, that's probably the best I could hope for."

Before agreeing to get together the following Thursday afternoon, Dr. Emener looked deep into Hank's eyes and said, "Hank, I strongly encourage you to ask Sandy if she would be willing to see a professional marriage counselor with you. And if she says yes, do it as soon as possible."

The following Wednesday, Hank called Dr. Emener and said that he and Sandy had made an appointment with a licensed marriage and family therapist and that he would call Bill to schedule a talk as soon as he and Sandy had seen the marriage counselor. That was a month ago; Bill is still waiting to hear from Hank.

As we have said numerous times, among the many reasons why people get into and stay in loving relationships is because "compared to what my life would be without him or her in it, my life is better with him or her in it." In essence, this is saying that your significant other is positively contributing to you life – including your happiness. To wit, evaluating "your happiness potential *without* him or her in your life" versus "your happiness potential *with* him or her in your life" indeed can provide you with important and helpful information.

HAPPINESS IN A RELATIONSHIP

Dr. Emener first began working with Tom approximately four years ago because he "was experiencing some deep levels of depression." One of the many things that he and Tom focused on was his "commitment phobia with women." For example, Tom said, "All I want to do, Dr. Emener, is to be happy. I am thirty-two years old, fairly good-looking, I have a good build from working out all the time, I don't have much trouble going out on lots of dates, and I usually enjoy myself when I do go out on dates. In the main, however, I am simply not happy!" After Dr. Emener's initial work with Tom, which totaled four sessions, Tom would schedule an appointment about every six months, as he said, "Just to stay in touch with you; I still haven't been able to find the happiness that I'm looking for." Recently, however, when he came in for what he called his "regular six-month checkup," he seemed to be very excited in a way that Dr. Emener had never seen him. After their usual, brief, get-reacquainted conversation, Tom said, "I think I finally found the woman I've been looking for!" Surprised and somewhat taken aback, Dr. Emener said, "Your excitement seems to be coming out of every pore in your skin – for gosh sakes, Tom, tell me all about it!"

With a penchant for detail somewhere between that of a fine jeweler and a neurosurgeon, Tom proceeded to describe every aspect of Judy. And each detail within his description, from the softness of her skin and the smell of her hair to the shine of her smile and the depth of her character, Tom continued to demonstrate emotional excitement at a geometrically increasing rate. When he finally completed his exhausted, detailed description of this incredible woman, Bill said to him, "Tom, I need a rest. Your excitement and enthusiasm have captured me, my heart rate is up to about one-hundred and forty and I would appreciate it if you would give me a moment to catch my breath!" As they jointly chuckled and relished this new excitement in Tom's life, his entire body sank down into the couch. Then with a soft and deep look in his eyes, Tom said, "Isn't it wonderful?!" Dr. Emener felt almost too tired to respond. After a sip of water and a few deep breaths, he then said, "Tom, my friend, I am so happy for you. Nonetheless, I have a feeling that you are here for more than just to share this great news and information with me." With that "yep, you got me" look in his eyes, Tom softly replied, "Even though everything with Judy seems to be wonderful, perfect, and simply beyond my wildest dreams, I still do not know whether or not I am happy with her."

Following some revisiting of their previous conversations regarding *happiness* and how it interfaces with a loving relationship, Dr. Emener said, "I would like to invite you to try a little experiment. Would you be willing to try something?" With a look of respect and trust in his eyes, he nodded. Bill continued, "Every time you are with Judy over the next few weeks, ask yourself three questions: (1) *Would I rather be anywhere else?* (2) *Would I rather be with anyone else?* And (3) *Would I rather be doing anything else?*" As Tom looked at his watch, noting that their time was almost up and he had to return to work, he said, "That's a deal, Dr. Emener! And just for the record, I think that what you are saying is that if I am able to answer yes to each of those three questions, then chances are that I am happy in my relationship with Judy?" Dr. Emener responded, "Yes, that's what I am suggesting." Tom scheduled another appointment to see Dr. Emener three weeks hence. However, two weeks later Tom canceled and Bill did not hear from him for quite some time. Approximately four months after seeing Tom at their last session, Bill received a postcard in the mail from Key West. The entire inscription read, "Bill, yes, yes, yes! We got engaged last night! Your good friend, Tom."

Bill carried Tom's card around in his attaché case for quite some time. It reminded him of the excitement that Tom must have been experiencing, possibly for the first time in his life! Furthermore, it added some credibility to the hypothesis that when we are happy in a loving relationship – *when we are with the other person: (1) we would rather not be anywhere else; (2) we would rather not be with anyone else; and (3) we would rather not be doing anything else.* And knowing Tom, we feel sure that he invited Judy to ask herself those three questions as well.

We are tempted to say, "We are so happy for Tom. From the way he described Judy, he certainly is a lucky man." But the more we think about it, we have a greater tendency to believe that they both are lucky.

CONTROL YOUR HAPPINESS AND JOY

Dr. Emener vividly recalls Greta, a thirty-eight-year-old sales manager at a large department store. Her striking and exquisite skin tone, her long, soft brown hair, her perfect, pearl-white teeth, her bright blue eyes, her tall and slender body with perfect posture, and her warm smile that would stop the best running back in the National Football League provided an incredible contrast to all of the beneath-the-surface emotional scars that were immediately evident the moment she began to speak. In spite of all of her successes and accomplishments, her horrid memories of having been sexually abused as a child, of having been reared by two alcoholic parents, and of having been in an abusive marriage for three years, collectively produced an emotionally ravaged but galvanized young woman. "After my divorce about six years ago, I was in therapy for about eight months. I ended it because I was actually doing very well. My life over the past five years, however, has been about as exciting as a dial tone with an occasional busy signal." At that point, Greta could no longer hold back the tears. She began to cry profusely.

By the time Dr. Emener got back from getting Greta a glass of cold water, she had dried her eyes and collected herself. "I am so afraid of getting hurt again that I simply don't ever go out. I know that I would be so much happier – actually I would be *happy* – if only I could be involved in a *good* loving relationship with someone," she softly said. The next three sessions, in addition to some selected self-help books that Greta read, were very helpful to her in working through some of her abusive experiences and overcoming some of her fears regarding relationships.

Toward the end of their most recent session, Greta learned that part of her "do nothing at all" lifestyle was associated with her subconscious focusing on her ultimate dream – to have a long-term loving relationship with a significant other. Dr. Emener sketched a diagram for Greta similar to the one in Figure 14.1, and while discussing it with her said, "For the past few years, Greta, it appears that you have been engaged in a variety of safe, yet self-defeating behaviors, here on the diagram at Level III. These 'go nowhere behaviors' include either bitching all the time, avoiding men, or

I. "Dream"	• "A sign. Other"	"What you are hoping for!"
II. "Maintenance People"	• date • go out with • occasionally go out with	"Better than nothing."
III. "Self-Defeating"	• occasionally talk to • avoid • "bitch" all the time	"Self-defeating," "Go No Where Behavior."

Figure 14.1. Control Your Happiness and Joy.

occasionally talking with men. This is understandable because these types of behaviors are the least fearful and the least threatening types of behaviors. Rather than focusing on the Level I category, 'the dream category' in which you would have a loving relationship with a significant other, I suggest that we try to focus on what it might take for you to move into a Level II category in which you would involve yourself with 'maintenance people.' For example, you could occasionally go out with someone, or you could go out with someone on a fairly regular basis, or you even could date someone on a fairly regular basis. I would consider this to be a 'better than nothing' category. Let's talk about this, Greta, because I have the sense that you are looking at your current situation and your future situation with a dichotomous eye: you either do not involve yourself with a man at all, *or* you involve yourself in your ideal or dream relationship with a significant other." (As you may recall, dichotomous thinking and emotions were discussed in detail in Chapter Five.) Greta's ensuing verbal expressions and body language clearly indicated that she understood what Bill was saying. "It almost appears to me, Dr. Emener, that this is somewhat of a sequential, developmental hierarchy of relationships. I think I see what you mean. It's like the person who lies on the couch all the time and dreams of running a marathon." Dr. Emener quickly responded, "Yes, Greta, that's exactly what I'm trying to say." From that point on, they spent much time discussing Greta's fears, as well as her specific thoughts about what she could do to start inching her way from doing nothing toward her ultimate dream.

The last time Dr. Emener saw Greta, she not only was excited and happy with herself because she was beginning to go out on dates, but she was beginning to date one particular gentleman on a regular and frequent basis. As she was leaving his office, she turned and said, "I think that one of the things I have been doing that is so helpful, Bill, is that I am no longer looking for happiness; I'm just looking for opportunities to enjoy myself with another person. I figure that if I can just continue to do that, happiness will find me. As long as I am enjoying myself, enjoying the person who I am with and enjoying my relationship with him, I don't care whether happiness finds me or not. Lately, I also have thought that I will know I am happy when the day comes that I no longer have to ask myself if I am happy. The most important thing is that I am in control of my life. And you have no idea how good that feels!"

As Bill smiled and warmly waved goodbye, he thought, *and therefore, Greta, you are in control of your happiness.*

HAPPINESS AND ENJOYMENT WITH A SIGNIFICANT-OTHER

For approximately twenty years of their marriage, Andre and Roberta had tremendous happiness and joy: "At least until Andre had a heart attack and was no longer able to play golf or tennis," they said. Throughout the four sessions that Dr. Emener had with them, they specifically focused on many aspects of *their relationship* and *their individual lives*, as well as *their expectations of each other*. Nonetheless, when they focused their attention on some of the activities that "used to bring them happiness and enjoyment in their relationship," they discovered the possibility that their relationship "had not been as good as they had thought." For example, Dr. Emener said to Andre, "You said to me that before your heart attack, you and Roberta had a perfect marriage. You had a perfect relationship. Well Andre, let me ask you a question: for all of those years that you and Roberta played golf and tennis together, was your happiness and enjoyment coming from the fact that you were playing golf and tennis, *or* was it from the fact that you were doing something, no matter what it was, with Roberta?"

As he pondered Bill's question, Andre said, "Like when I thought I used to be so loving toward my son when I took him to the football games every Sunday, there was the possibility that I may have just been taking him to the football games so that I could go myself and not feel guilty about it. Is that what you are implying?" Bill looked at him and said, "I don't know, Andre, that's a question that you have to answer. Possibly your son could shed some light on that question as well." Andre gazed out the window for about thirty seconds, which seemed like two hours to Bill and Roberta. They could tell, however, that Andre was engaged in some very deep soul searching.

As time went on and as Bill continued to work with Andre and Roberta, a painful recognition surfaced: "The truth of the matter, Dr. Emener, is that we should have been trying to improve our relationship for the past fifteen years," Roberta said. "I agree, Roberta," Andre commented, "but I guess we were able to hide in our activities so well that we simply were getting joy, excitement and happiness out of the activities that we were doing and not necessarily the fact that we were simply *with each other*."

Dr. Emener recommended some selected readings to Andre and Roberta and suggested some homework assignments between sessions that were very helpful in renewing their love and their expressions of their love toward and with each other. In a tongue-in-cheek fashion, Andre once quipped, "I am pretty damn angry about this heart attack. I just can't do many of the things that I used to be able to do. But on the other hand, it may have been a blessing in disguise in that it showed me how negligent I have been in attending to my wife, my marriage and my relationship with Roberta, not to mention our son."

Needless to say, we are very happy for Andre and Roberta because they were able to overcome many potentially devastating effects of Andre's heart attack on their marriage. What they helped us learn was significant: *When two individuals in a loving relationship are experiencing happiness and joy "almost exclusively" through the regular, routine, mutual involvement in activities, it is helpful if they can remain cognizant of the fact that the activities can become the primary source of their joy and happiness and not each other.* As Andre said the last time Bill spoke with him, "What I am able to do or what I am not able to do with Roberta is not important – the fact that it is Roberta is what is important!"

THE A-B-CS OF HAPPINESS

One of the first ideas Dr. Lambos tries to impart to his clients regarding happiness is that every person is largely responsible for his or her own sense of happiness, misery or whatever else might fall in between. This is not the same as blaming the victim of a tragedy or situation out of their control. Rather, it is a philosophy and a theory of personality or counseling that focuses on the central roles played by one's *beliefs* about oneself, others, and the world. This model, diagrammed in Figure 14.2, is based on the approach of Albert Ellis and his model of Rational Emotive Behavior Therapy.

A	B	C
Activating events Past, present (or possible future) adversities or aggravations	**Beliefs** Thoughts, attitudes, and assumptions	**Consequences** Emotions Actions/behaviors

Figure 14.2. The "A-B-C's" of Happiness.

Most people automatically assume that when some action or event happens to us (the "A" in the diagram), it causes us to respond to it – that is, it generates a "consequence," either feelings, behavior, or both (the "C" in the Figure). Ellis' insight was that the connection between "A" and "C" is mediated by, or is a function of, our beliefs. When these beliefs are irrational in nature – when they are unrealistic or illogical – we may experience unwarranted feelings or engage in inappropriate behaviors because of them. It is much healthier to recognize that:

1. The activating event – what happens to us (the "A") – does not automatically cause "C," but rather "A" activates a belief in us about how the world (or we, or other people) should be, and
2. It is the combination of the event and the belief that causes the resulting feelings and behaviors. Furthermore, since each of us has the power to alter our beliefs, we are ultimately in control of how we react to the things that affect us.

Road rage is one of the best examples of this paradigm. When some inconsiderate driver cuts us off, we often immediately become furious. But if we realize that the world is full of inconsiderate motorists and that to believe otherwise is unwarranted, we will not experience the rage. We are more likely to sigh and say to ourselves, "so what else is new?"

The point of this discussion is that individuals – all of us – have much more control of our day-to-day happiness than we typically realize. To the extent that we make irrational and selfish demands about the way our partners *should* or *must* treat us, we allow ourselves to experience anger or deep disappointment when they fail to live up to these expectations. On the other hand, when we focus on our role in responding to them and to the beliefs we harbor about them, positive strategies for managing our loving relationships naturally present themselves. This is a very powerful and effective philosophy of being, and we advise you to think about this the next time you are about to blame your significant other for something he or she did or did not do, and then inappropriately act out to the detriment of the relationship.

YOUR SENSE OF MEANING AND PURPOSE

In Chapter Twelve we described the work of Victor Frankl and the theory of counseling he created (Logotherapy) from his concentration camp experiences. To briefly review, Frankl's work is based upon the postulate that human beings must be able to find meaning and purpose to their situation in order to experience satisfaction and happiness in both life and in relationships. This sense of meaning and purpose is different for every individual. For some, it may be tied to spiritual beliefs such as God's will. For others, meaning and purpose are derived from an appreciation of the existence of karma, harmony or balance in the universe. Yet for others, the true purpose of existence is to help one's fellow human beings to the best of their ability. Many people in the helping professions hold this percept and thus endured long educations and internships for far less monetary reward than typically would be available in the business world. Regardless of where one finds *meaning and purpose*, it is fair to say that a healthy person rarely would expect to be happy without it. Perhaps the ultimate enemy of happiness, in relationships and elsewhere, is the existential philosophy of *nihilism*: to believe that existence is meaningless and that life has no purpose is to accept a life of despair and emptiness.

It follows that "being happy" in and of itself cannot be the basis for such meaning or purpose. If happiness *requires* an overarching sense of meaning, then happiness per se cannot also be the purpose of existence. Our culture, unfortunately, seems to forget this simple reality. If you feel you can never achieve happiness no matter what you do, or if your only goal in life is to be happy, you may well have fallen into the trap of existential despair. Look beyond yourself and your situation, find your inner sense of purpose, and you will then be ready to share your vision with another soul in a loving relationship. And along the way, you are sure to experience a good deal of happiness.

* * * * * *

When two people in a loving relationship
intentionally pursue happiness,
their experience will be akin to
chasing butterflies,
and the butterflies
will always just elude them.
But if they lovingly attend to themselves,
each other and their relationship,
and if they individually live effective lives
and collectively enjoy a meaningful relationship,
Then the butterflies will gently sit upon their shoulders
and grace the beauty of their love
and their happiness.

Chapter Fifteen

THE INTERNET

On Saturday, September 15, 2007, the following headline and first four paragraphs were on the front page of *The New York Times*:

Tell-All PCs and Phones Transforming Divorce
(by Brad Stone)

> The age-old business of breaking up has taken a decidedly Orwellian turn, with digital evidence like e-mail messages, traces of Web site visits and mobile telephone records now permeating many contentious divorce cases.
>
> Spurned lovers steal each other's BlackBerrys. Suspicious spouses hack into each other's e-mail accounts. They load surveillance software onto the family PC, sometimes discovering shocking infidelities.
>
> Divorce lawyers routinely set out to find every bit of private data about their clients' adversaries, often hiring investigators with sophisticated digital forensic tools to snoop into household computers.
>
> "In just about every case now, to some extent, there is some electronic evidence," said Gaetano Ferro, president of the American Academy of Matrimonial Lawyers, who also runs seminars on gathering electronic evidence. "It has completely changed our field."

There can be little question that the management of loving relationships has been affected in important ways by our society's transformation in the digital, information-based age. As is made glaringly clear in the above article, privacy has become far more difficult to maintain. Virtually all of our electronic transactions and communications leave a record of what we wrote and did. An entire industry has been created to collect and analyze such data – the electronic trail of our daily behavior and the consequences for loving relationships are sweeping beyond imagination. For example, anyone who cheats on a spouse or significant other using a cell phone, PDA or computer had better realize that the evidence of their tryst is permanent and mounts with each communication.

On the other hand, many people – millions, in fact – have met and been able to enter into loving relationships because of the Internet and the advent of so-called "digital dating." The Internet and related electronic communications have facilitated relationships that otherwise never could have happened. Many of these relationships are seen as a blessing for those involved in them and welcomed alternatives to their otherwise lonely and isolated daily existence. Moreover, the nature of digital dating allows people to get to know one another in a relatively safe context, in which if they decide they no longer wish to remain in contact with someone they can end the relationship instantly and in most cases without fear of reprisal or embarrassment. The multibillion dollar industry of Internet dating services such as eHarmony and Match.com has grown seemingly out of nowhere to meet the needs of people who wish to meet others with whom they can have a meaningful relationship. In 2002, *Wired* magazine predicted that:

> Twenty years from now, the idea that someone looking for love without looking for it on-line will be silly, akin to skipping the card catalog to instead wander the stacks because 'the right books are found only by accident.' Serendipity is the hallmark of inefficient markets, and the marketplace of love, like it or not, is becoming more efficient.

These two aspects of the Internet – *new opportunities* for meeting people and *digital espionage* – may be considered examples of "the

Good" and "the Bad" of how the Internet has changed loving relationships in very profound ways. But there is also "the Ugly" – ways in which the Internet has acted as a fertile growth medium for some of the worst examples of human behavior. Child pornography, the electronic advancement of prostitution and the sex-slave industry, and violent sex offenders gaining access to unsuspecting victims are examples of this terrifying aspect of our modern age.

A Brief History of the Internet, Electronic Communications and Social Networking

As you might imagine, millions of people worldwide use various on-line "love sites" daily, and as such there are some Internet dating statistics that reveal an interesting picture. Here's a few for starters:

- Up to 30% of American singles have used matchmaking sites.
- U.S. residents spent $469.5 million on on-line dating and personals in 2004, and over $500 million in 2005, the second largest segment of "paid content" on the web.
- Women, on average, receive over 5 emails daily.
- Men, on average, receive 1 or 2 emails daily.
- Around 40% of men say they don't feel confident meeting women the first time.
- The overall cost of personal sites has dropped over the last 2 years.
- On the first date many women think men aren't truthful.
- Generally, men prefer women younger than themselves.
- 60% of women prefer men older than themselves.
- Most people would prefer to be in a relationship than not.
- Over a third of women don't like men being clingy.
- Most women say personality is much more important than looks.

Statistics such as these may reveal only individual facets of very complex "gestalt" phenomena, but they do help us think about the subject matter at hand. When thinking about a subject with as many different aspects as the Internet and loving relationships, facts such as these remind us that it is wise to look for a broader, unifying perspective. One way to accomplish this is to step back a bit and look at the development of electronic communications and communities over the last twenty or so years; among other things, this would give us a handle on where these new media came from and why they have been adopted so readily and by so many people.

It is not our purpose to describe in detail the history of the Internet, email, blogging, social networking sites, or other forms of digital interaction. This is, after all, a book about loving relationships. But we feel it adds useful perspective to take a brief look at how the new media arose, if only because it greatly helps to understand the purpose it serves.

Firstly, let's look at the traditional telephone – a highly centralized system built around a "hub and spoke" architecture. The line connecting you and all of your neighbors' landline telephones to the rest of the world travels more or less directly to a telephone company network switching station, called a "network operations center" or NOC. From there, calls are routed to other NOCs, each of which handles either a single area code or a single prefix (the three digits after the area code) and eventually finds its way to the receiving telephone line. The process is reversed for incoming calls. In major population centers such as Washington, D.C. and other big cities, the destruction of a single NOC could wipe out telephone use for long periods of time during a crisis. The government, in particular the Defense Department, feared that a nuclear strike on a major population center would so disrupt the ability of military and government leaders to communicate that the country might be unable to respond rapidly and effectively to a surprise attack. They wanted a decentralized alternative means of communication that could withstand a nuclear assault and still allow leaders to communicate and respond as needed.

To achieve this, in the 1990s, the Defense Advanced Research Projects Agency, or DARPA, envisioned a non-centralized alternative to the telephone system that could absorb localized nuclear strikes and continue to function. The idea was to use a distributed architecture instead of a hub and spoke system. If information trying to get from computer "A" to computer "B" couldn't make it via one relay station (which later came to be called "servers"), the system allowed for the information to automatically find an alternative route via a different server. Therefore, the destruction of one or more servers wouldn't prevent communication.

"DARPANET," as the Internet was first called, was limited to include only key government offices, military installations and some universities. Commercial traffic was prohibited. But the system proved to include the seeds of its own undoing – it was very efficient and easy to add servers and the associated hardware (like routers and switches), and the increased connectivity was so useful that the "Net" started to grow exponentially. To text messaging was added graphics and a naming system to replace the numerical addresses, which evolved into the World Wide Web – the "www" at the start of most of today's web sites.

Once the genie got out of the bottle, there was no getting it back in. The distributed nature of the Internet meant that ultimately, no one person or agency could control it. Early attempts to stop commercial traffic (as well as content related to sex, gambling, and everything else, good or bad) proved useless. The truth of the matter is, even if the same government that created the Internet wanted to shut it down, it could not. Repressive regimes around the world fear the Internet, and while they try to limit its use, they can only be so successful (mainland China comes to mind as the most prominent example).

So, for better or worse, the Internet, email, social networking sites like MySpace and Facebook, dating sites such as eHarmony, and the rest of the world of digital relationships are here to stay. They have had an enormous and growing impact on loving relationships and will continue to do so. With the foregoing perspective on how all this came to be, it's now time to look at what the Internet has to offer those seeking loving relationships. We like the analogy of the "Wild West" when thinking about the Internet and relationships – a new frontier only partially explored, one like the Clint Eastwood movie of the same name, that offers some aspects of "The Good," "The Bad" and "The Ugly" to those intrepid enough to explore it.

The Good

What does the Internet have to offer those of us looking for a loving relationship that the older alternatives such as singles bars and clubs don't? Here are a few of the "good" aspects of the Internet and relationships:

- The variety is almost limitless.
- On-line dating is safe and secure, when used with a little common sense.
- People of any interests or backgrounds are almost guaranteed to find a match; you can meet people based on career, qualifications, looks or any other criteria.
- It can be fun – imagine meeting a millionaire or a movie star?
- In most cases it's affordable and low cost. Options on many sites allow you to join for just a few days, a week, a month, quarterly or even a year.
- It's very easy to do: simply create a profile, place it on the on-line dating site and start emailing other members.
- Many sites cater to people with disabilities.
- Many dating sites include instant messaging, flirting, photo exchanging, etc.
- If you don't connect with the first person you meet, there are always plenty more fish in the on-line dating sea.

Is it possible to find love on the Internet? There is no question that it is. In fact, eHarmony claims that ninety of its members get married every day! Though many other dating sites won't give out specific information about nuptials among their paid membership, we personally know of many happily-married couples who admit they met on the Internet. Indeed, it is possible to find your soul mate in cyberspace.

There are several different avenues for meeting others on-line. The most direct approach is to sign up with one of the reputable services (again, such as eHarmony or Match.com) that specialize in loving relationships. These sites offer significant assistance with profile development that is designed to filter out the thousands of others that do not fit your wants, needs and desires. They therefore offer to maximize the possibility that each person you meet on-line will be of interest to you, and vice versa.

Other avenues include social networking sites such as MySpace and Facebook. Although these are not intended primarily for meeting other people for the purpose of loving relationships, they are free and filled with millions of profiles. And, of course, you typically have the option of limiting your search to your own geographical area.

Regardless of the avenue you choose, the best strategy we know of for finding love in the on-line world includes the following core recommendations:

- *Be honest* when developing your profile or answering the on-line interview form questions. If you are a male looking for a younger female companion, say so. If you are a female looking for someone who is financially secure, state it up front. It is also a "must" to include a recent, unretouched photo of yourself. Honesty is truly the best policy in relationships, on-line or otherwise.
- *Keep an open mind* and "meet" as many potential partners as possible. All too often, love happens when we least expect it. Sometimes, the harder you look, the more elusive it may become (the metaphoric "butterfly").
- *Hone your on-line profile* continually and keep searching for the right chemistry. For each person you have met, tailor your

profile to reflect the experience gained, both for the better and for the worse.

- If you want a partner for life, *look for a friend first.* No matter how strong the initial chemistry between two people or how good the sex seems at first, relationships that last are based on mutual compatibility and not on puppy love or physical aerobics. The pleasure derived from these cannot be other than fleeting in nature.
- *Don't give up.* You may have to kiss a lot of cyber-frogs to create a real-life prince or princess.

It should be apparent by this point that the Internet represents a powerful tool – perhaps the most powerful that has ever existed – for meeting potential partners. Just remember the old adage: "There is no such thing as a free lunch." Expect to have to work at finding your significant other, and don't expect instant results. But if you follow the recommendations above, you have a good chance of being successful sooner or later.

THE BAD

What are the downsides to the world of Internet romance? Here are few mentioned by various people with experience:

- You normally can't see the person with whom you are communicating (video chatting, if both parties have a web cam, is an exception).
- The person you meet may live quite far away. You may therefore have to deal with a long-distance relationship, or one of the two of you may have to relocate in order to be together full time.
- It's easy to pretend to be someone else, as identity is not verified. Approach new acquaintances with a healthy dose of

skepticism. Because of the anonymous nature of the web, it can and does attract some undesirable characters.

- On most sites you have to pay a fee; there are some free ones but most are not too great.
- You very well might be nervous meeting someone from the Internet you have never seen before.
- It can be time-consuming.
- If you're a female, you can usually expect a deluge of emails.
- If you are a male looking for an attractive partner, expect to compete for the most attractive females.

Other than these caveats, and the material in the next section, there are not too many additional drawbacks to looking for a meaningful relationship, or even just a friend, in the on-line world.

The Ugly

The anonymity of Internet dating has afforded con artists a new playground for scams and allowed people to be anyone they think you want them to be because they are engaging you primarily through the written word. This is not meant to bring forth the message that it is impossible to find love through Internet dating, but to inform people of the dangers that are out there. For example, the Internet dating scene is one of the easiest places for someone to cheat on their spouse or significant other, or to use the Internet dating area as a source for promiscuity.

Internet dating is still a relatively new way of people connecting with people from all over the globe, and people need to understand the dangers so they can make their search a safe one. Interestingly, movies and T.V. have focused on the lighter side of Internet dating as opposed to the darker side. What's tricky here is people want to believe they are going to find what they are looking for (nothing wrong with that) and don't want to believe someone may be lying to them or playing games. People easily can think they are "too smart to fall for B.S.," and it is that attitude that leaves them wide open to be proven wrong.

Dr. Emener recalls the first time he met with Marion, an attractive, thirty-one-year-old owner of a successful lawn service company, who came to him for help with her relationship issues. During their first session, she shared with Dr. Emener her less-than-successful attempt at Internet dating.

"One evening I was fooling around on my computer," Marion said, "sending emails back and forth to some of my girlfriends. One friend kept pressuring me to try Internet dating since my dating life seemed to be going nowhere fast. She sent me a dating site and we started going through the profiles; then she helped me to make one of my own. We decided to leave it to fate and go through the ones that contacted me first. That was how I met Greg, who lived in another state, but said he put an ad in mine because his job was relocating him: 'So I may as well look for love where I am going to be living,' he said. This sounded reasonable at the time, but now, looking back on it, this was red flag Number 1. He and I exchanged emails with more and more frequency and seemed to have a lot in common. He asked for my phone number, but I asked for his instead. He said that since he was moving he had disconnected his home phone number and only used his cell in preparation for his move. Again, this sounded like no problem, but should have been red flag Number 2. We chatted on the phone, and he seemed anxious to meet me, adding that he would be in my area in a few weeks because he would be house-hunting. So, we kept talking on the phone. However, I began to notice that he didn't answer my calls during evenings and weekends. He said that since work was paying for it, he had to limit his evening and weekend calls. Once again, this guy had an excuse for everything – I should have seen this as red flag Number 3. When I went back on the dating site, I saw his profile was still active, even though we spoke every day and planned to meet the following month! This red flag, Number 4, I did pay more attention to. When another friend told me she was writing to some men on the Internet dating site from out of state, I decided just to browse… just to see what was out there.

Guess who was out there? Greg! Actually, he was in several different states, with several different handles, but the one thing he did was keep the same photo. Yikes! So, I asked my friend to help me set up a phony profile on the site to try and find out what he was up to. I wrote to him pretending to be a woman from a different state, far away from where I actually live. We wrote back and forth and I got an email from him saying how he was going to be moving to that state in a few months! I was fuming. I realized this was all a bunch of lies, this man was never moving to my town or any other, he was just using this site as a way to make false promises to women looking for something long term, and it was obvious he had no plans to deliver! Now when I go to dating sites, I only choose people that live in my area, now. I recommend people looking for a long-term relationship to start in their area!"

Needless to say, Marion was lucky; she easily could have gotten hurt. If you are planning to surf the web with high hopes and expectations, arm yourself with the knowledge of what to avoid and what to watch out for, so you have the best possible chance of a positive outcome.

RECOMMENDATIONS

The day has come when Internet dating is considered a legitimate way of meeting new people in the endless search for the "right" person. Chat rooms have replaced bar rooms, and dating sites and personal ads no longer have the stigma they once had. You may still get a raised eyebrow when telling people you are using the Internet for your search for the perfect mate, but far from the negative reaction you would have gotten only a few years ago. Internet dating has gained popularity by leaps and bounds, and unfortunately, so have the dangers and horror stories some have encountered.

There are many hidden dangers in the world of Internet dating, and it's up to you to recognize the red flags so that your experience stands the best chance of success, rather than leaving a bad taste in your mouth. We urge you to heed the following recommendations.

Get a secret email address, create a persona, use a cell phone, and if necessary a P.O. Box. Many times, before someone can verify what they've been told over the Internet, they are already emotionally invested and don't want to hear the truth or get hurt by hearing the truth. You must realize the Internet dating scene can be dangerous for those who don't approach it carefully, as well as for those too trusting in nature. Arm yourself with the knowledge you need to Internet-date safely, watch out for the signs of danger, and as Marion's experience demonstrated – *pay attention to every red flag you see!*

KEY INTERNET DATING TIPS

Here are some quick Internet dating tips. As always, take them with a pinch of salt and have a great time using the net to meet like-minded people:

- Decide on want you want from on-line dating sites: marriage, long-term partner, quick fling, friends, and/or some fun?
- Read reviews of any sites you consider. They're out there; just search for them.
- Decide if a particular site is within your budget. Don't be fooled by "Join for a buck for three days!" Believe us: you can't do much in three days.
- If you can afford it, we would recommend joining at least two Internet dating sites. That way you're more likely to meet more people and as a consequence achieve your goals quicker.
- Never give out any personal information whatsoever until you are completely satisfied the person you are in contact with is trustworthy. Before meeting someone, tell your friends and relatives of your intentions, and tell them where you are going.

* * * * * *

When using the Internet for loving relationship purposes,
avoid the Bad and the Ugly
and enjoy the Good.
And above all –
BE SMART,
BE SAFE, and
HAVE FUN

Chapter Sixteen

SEEING A PROFESSIONAL COUNSELOR, THERAPIST OR FAMILY MEDIATOR

"We read some self-help books over the past year or so while we tried to fix things in our relationship. Sometimes things would get better, but then after a while we'd be right back where we started. I guess that's why we're here. In their own way, our friends and relatives try to be helpful. They offer advice and suggestions. But that hasn't made any difference either. We need some help – professional help."

"She doesn't know I'm here. I just thought I'd come in to see you by myself first. I've been trying to get her to understand that I still need to see my first wife on occasions, like every other week when I get the kids for the weekend or when we both go to one of their school functions. She's just so jealous. She just doesn't understand. I can't take it anymore."

"You are the fourth therapist we have seen in the last three months. All the rest didn't 'get it.' We've heard you're really good, so we expect you will understand what it is we are trying to say when we say it."

"As soon as I can get back to working day shifts, everything will be fine. We really don't need to be here! She just blows things

out of proportion all the time. This is unnecessary. That's all I have to say!"

"Now that Luke has finally agreed to come to counseling, I can finally take a deep breath, a sigh of relief. I am convinced our problems are almost behind us just because we're here."

"This is embarrassing. We live in a real nice neighborhood. We both have professional jobs. Our families know we're doing just fine. Our two kids know we're okay; the four of us do a lot of things together all the time and have a lot of fun. Alright, so we have a few arguments once in a while, but to have to come here to see a psychologist... I don't know."

"He agreed to meet me here today, but this afternoon he called me from his office and said that some honcho from the regional office was flying in and that he had to pick him up at the airport and take him to his hotel. 'Otherwise I'd be there,' he told me. But I don't know. He wasn't all that excited when I scheduled this appointment for the two of us. So I thought I'd come anyway, so at least I could fill you in on what's been going on."

"Being here, seeing you... I know this is the end. I'm so scared..."

"I can't believe we're seeing a counselor! We've been living together for over two years now and everything is really going great. We used to have our problems, but we worked them out. But now, because I just have a few beers when it's hot, she thinks I have a drinking problem. I don't have a drinking problem. She's the one with the problem."

"We've made appointments to see counselors in the past, but then she would cancel them. She would say, 'Look, I bought this new book on communications,' or something like that. I know we have problems and we need help. I'm just glad that the two of us are finally here."

"Yeah, we argue sometimes. It's usually because she gets on my case. She really knows how to push my buttons. Then when I get

mad, she won't leave me alone. She just keeps pickin' and pickin'. Yeah, I may push her or slap her on rare occasions, but I don't mean anything by it. She just needs to learn to leave me alone when I'm mad. She just needs to learn how to let me cool off."

"We really wouldn't have to be here if he would just listen to me. I've been telling him for years that everything would be okay if he would just..."

"I came ready to negotiate and settle our differences. Lord only knows what you'll hear from her!"

When one or two individuals first come to see either of us for assistance with their loving relationship, it is not uncommon to hear them say things similar to the preceding statements. Seeing a professional counselor, therapist or mediator, especially for the first time, as is revealed in this baker's dozen of illustrative statements, understandably can be:

- **depressing** ("Reality has hit me. We really do have problems.");
- **saddening** ("I've tried so hard, but it hasn't helped.");
- **demanding-unrealistic** ("We're paying you good money, so 'fix us' and be done with it!");
- **threatening** ("My denial has worked so far. Who wants to look at the truth.");
- **optimistic-unrealistic** ("Now that we're in therapy, we have no more to worry about.");
- **embarrassing** ("I have my pride, you know. And what will others think about me when they know we're seeing a therapist?");
- **self-focusing** ("If he doesn't want to do anything about our situation, that's up to him. But I've had it! I'm going to do this for me if that's the way it has to be.");

- **scary** ("I know we have some very serious problems, and I'm afraid that if we ever look at ourselves as we really are, it may be over.");
- **relieving** ("We've talked about getting help in the past, but something always came up. Now maybe we'll get some help and actually improve our relationship. At least now there's some hope.");
- **denial inducing** ("I'm not the one with the problem. If only she would just...");
- **anger producing** ("I've been telling him what's wrong for years and he just won't listen to me… he never has!");
- **utterly unrealistic** ("I can agree to *anything*, as long as it is *reasonable*.")

If there is a common thread or theme to these reactions or expectations regarding professional help, it is this: *Going for, receiving and benefiting from professional assistance with a loving relationship, is frequently easier said than done.* Thus, in view of the possibility that someday you might find yourself thinking about seeing a professional counselor, therapist or mediator, we will share with you some of our experiences, reflections, thoughts and suggestions that will be helpful to you.

So far we have used the terms "counselor," "therapist" and "(family) mediator" more or less interchangeably, and you may be wondering if there are differences among such professionals. Indeed there are, although the boundaries between them are fuzzy and getting yet fuzzier with time. Nonetheless, from this point forward in the book, the terms *couples* or *marriage counselor*, *therapist* or *relationship therapist*, or *mediator* or *family mediator*, imply or mean the same:

> *A person with at least a master's degree in mental health counseling, marriage and family therapy, clinical social work, or a doctorate in psychology from a regionally accredited university who is licensed by his or her state to practice as such, or a person*

who meets these educational requirements and is certified by the Supreme Court of their state as a family mediator.

For purposes of readability and prose, in this Chapter and beyond we also use the terms *helping professional* and/or *professional assistant* to refer to those in our profession.

If you and your loved one have never talked with a helping professional before, then one of the biggest hurdles you face may be simply not knowing what to expect. One reasonable prediction, however, is that your first several sessions with a helping professional are more likely than not to be *different* from your expectations. The only experience most people have is their recollection of "therapy" scenes from television shows and movies. For reasons we have assumed to be due to dramatic necessities and ratings, screenwriters rarely if ever manage to create a realistic impression of therapy. The therapy process is either depicted as unstructured and trivial chit-chat, or as complete emotional breakdown and catharsis, but seldom anything in between. We hope that the actual stories from counseling sessions interposed throughout this book have helped you gain a more realistic understanding and appreciation of what actually transpires. We also hope that the material we discuss in this part of the book will help to alleviate any fears and apprehensions you might have regarding your decision to see a helping professional.

SEEKING PROFESSIONAL HELP

The following will address five questions that are often asked by people who are (a) struggling with problems or issues in their loving relationships and (b) thinking about seeing a professional assistant.

1. "Why would a person go to see a professional assistant?"

It has been our experience that most people go for one (or a combination) of the following reasons:

- *Anxiety and Stress.* "I spend every minute of my free time worrying about what will happen next. I can barely sleep or function anymore."
- *Danger associated with Anger.* "Lately when we have been arguing a lot, there's been some violence. I'm afraid that if this goes any further, one of us or possibly even one of our children may get hurt."
- *Pain and Hurting.* "I've been living with a lot of emotional pain for a long time. I'm just hurting too much. I can't take it any longer."
- *Guilt.* "Because of what I did, I just can't look at myself in the mirror any longer. This has to be dealt with, and now."
- *Helplessness.* "I know that some things need to be done. We need to make some changes in our relationship. But we don't know what to do."
- *Hopelessness.* "The both of us have been trying to make some changes and do some things differently, but none of it seems to have made any difference. So before calling it quits, we thought maybe you could help us."
- *Ignorance.* "We want to make things better and improve our relationship, but we just don't know what to do."
- *Required.* "The last time we got into an argument we started hitting each other. So the judge said that if we want to be able to have the kids with us we have to see a professional."
- *Improvement.* "I wouldn't say that our relationship is bad. It's okay. But that's the problem – it's just okay. We love each other and have a great, fun-loving family. However, we need to try to improve our relationship because someday the kids will be grown up and out, and then it will just be the two of us."

2. "How would I go about finding a helping professional?"

Sometimes people know friends or coworkers who have seen a helping professional. We often hear, "A friend recommended you to me." If your employer has an employee assistance program, you may want to talk with your supervisor or call your human relations office to see whether your employee benefits program can provide any assistance to you. The *Yellow Pages* of your telephone book can provide the names of licensed psychologists, mental health counselors, marriage and family therapists, and clinical social workers who have expertise in assisting people with loving relationship issues and problems. Today, a majority of professional assistants have web sites and are listed in most or all of the commonly used Internet search engines. Alternatively, if you have health insurance, you can call your primary care physician or insurance carrier and request a referral or the names of professionals in your area. Many individuals have received helpful assistance from their ministers, rabbis or priests. If you see someone who is from the secular community, however, even though he or she may have other professional credentials, we still would urge you to see someone who is licensed by the official professional regulatory body in your state.

3. "What are the costs involved?"

If you see someone via a community agency or a religious affiliation, costs may be nothing at all, a voluntary donation, or set on a sliding scale or a minimal rate. If you see someone through the auspices of your employer's employee assistance program, the first few visits may be free or at a very low cost. Private counseling and therapy, on the other hand, can be expensive, ranging from $75 to $150 per session. If you have health insurance and see someone who is "in network," your only costs may be a pre-established "co-pay" fee. It may be important to remember, however, that when you ask yourselves the question, "Can I afford to see a helping professional?" you also may want to ask yourselves, "Can I afford not to?"

4. "How confidential will all of this be?"

Licensed helping professionals in every state are required under federal law to maintain strict confidentiality (with only a few exceptions as discussed in the next paragraph). Title II of The Health Insurance Portability and Accountability Act (HIPAA), enacted by the U.S. Congress in 1996, includes a set of Administrative Simplification (AS) provisions that addresses, among other things, the security and privacy of health data. Even private helping professionals who do not accept insurance are subject to the HIPAA's security and privacy provisions. Very serious sanctions, including forfeiture of the license to practice and even imprisonment, can result.

Beyond requirements by law, moreover, helping professionals are very understanding of your desire and need to keep your information and situation confidential. The only times when a helping professional will breach confidentiality are: (a) if you are a clear and imminent danger to yourself ("If I know you are planning to jump off a bridge, I will make efforts to stop you."); (b) if you are a clear and imminent danger to society ("If I know you are planning to harm someone else, I will take measures to prevent it."); or (c) if subpoenaed to court by a judge. (In most states, the only three categories of individuals who have statutory confidentiality are attorneys, spouses, and ordained clergy.) In the latter case, however, because judges understand and respect the importance of confidentiality in the client-therapist relationship, very rarely will they require a helping professional to testify. As we tell our clients, "If your husband, wife, family member or best friend were to call me genuinely with your best interest at heart, without your permission, I would not even acknowledge that you have been in to see me." Furthermore, in all cases where confidentiality is breached for the above reasons, the helping professional is required to disclose this breach of confidentiality to the client (unless it is an emergency situation or involving abuse of a child).

5. "What do I need to do to schedule an appointment?"

When you call to schedule an appointment, be prepared to respond to the following questions from the helping professional or by a receptionist or intake specialist. For illustrative purposes, we have provided some examples of "typical kinds of answers" for each question:

- *"What is the problem or concern?"* (e.g., "My wife told me about two weeks ago that she wants a divorce. I've been very upset ever since. I don't know what to do. I need to talk to someone as soon as possible.")
- *"Who will be coming in for the appointment?"* (e.g., "Both my fiancé and I.")
- *"Are there any special considerations that you would like us to know about?"* (e.g., "My husband doesn't know that I will be coming to see a counselor. If he found out, I know he'd really get mad. He gets violent some times. It's important that he not know.")
- *"When will you be able to come in for an appointment?"* (e.g., "I get out of work at about four thirty and my husband is self-employed. I'd say that we could get to your office by five o'clock any night but Monday night, when he has to close the store by himself.")
- *"How can we contact you if we need to?"* (e.g., "My mother is living with me right now and I don't want her to know that I'm coming to see you. Please don't call me at home. If you need to contact me, please call me on my cell phone."
- *"Do you know where our office is?"* (e.g., "I'm pretty sure I know where your building is. Could you please confirm the address?")
- *"Will you be able to get here about thirty minutes before your first appointment to complete some paperwork?"* (e.g., "Yes, I will be able to do that. And my friend said that sometimes therapists may be running a little behind schedule. So just in case that happens, I'll tell my supervisor that I won't be back to work until around three o'clock.")

WHAT ARE YOUR GOALS

At some point during a first counseling or therapy session, most counselors or therapists will address with their client(s) what might be reasonable goals for them to work toward. Goal-setting is an integral part of counseling and therapy. "What do you hope that we will accomplish?" is a rather frequent question. In our work with individuals and couples, we have found four critical goal-setting issues:

1. *"Are you sick or are you sorry?"* What we mean by asking this question is, "Do you have a deep-seated personality or biological problem that is causing your problems or difficulties? If so, we may need to consider including some psychiatric interventions in our treatment plan." Or, is it because of situational issues such as, "It sounds as if your life is just messed up a little right now." If so, then our focus should possibly be on identifying ways to improve your life and your lifestyle. *Or*, is it a little of both?" There's a big difference, for example, between being depressed because you have a biochemical predisposition for endogenous depression and being depressed because your mother died last month and last week your husband (or wife) asked you for a divorce! Depending upon how we and our client(s) answer this overall question and whether the problems and difficulties are relationship-specific, we then may move toward the next question.
2. *"Is it you, the other person or the relationship?"* What we mean by this question is: "Are you having relationship problems or difficulties because of something within yourself (e.g., maybe you have a commitment-phobia?), something with the other person (e.g., maybe your partner has a commitment phobia?), or is it your relationship (e.g., the two of you have difficulties communicating with each other because you remind each other of your previous spouses?)

Usually, it is because of combinations of these three possibilities. Nonetheless, it is important to identify where we should focus our attention.

3. *"Do you want to end it, fix it, or just rest for a while?"* Another important question is, "If you have any outcome expectation, would it be: (1) to end your relationship; (b) to improve your relationship; or (3) to rest for a while and decide what you want to do at a later time?" In terms of this last alternative, sometimes people simply like to get away from each other for a while, stop the arguing and fighting (e.g., "Stop the bleeding and allow each other to heal a little."), and at a later time revisit this question and then try to decide what to do. Hopefully, your answer will be an honest one! It is not uncommon for people to come to see us with "hidden agendas." For example, one of us recently met with a couple, and although both of them said that they wanted to improve their marriage, there was a clear impression that she wanted a divorce but was going through the motions so that no one could ever say she didn't try.
4. "No, I will not help you get back to where you used to be." People will frequently say to us, "We would like to get our marriage back to where it used to be – when we were happy and not fighting all the time." It is a real shock to them, however, when we reply, "No, I will not help you do that." Then, after drawing a sketch for them similar to the one in Figure 16.1 (and while they stare at each other aghast at our statement), we point to the sketch and say, "If your relationship was all that 'good' in the past, you wouldn't be here now. No, I will not help you go back. But nonetheless, I would be most pleased to assist you in moving forward and in establishing a loving relationship like the one you would like to have." Usually when this happens, they look at each other and at us with a genuine appreciation for what we are saying to them and an agreement that "upward and onward" is ultimately where they want to go.

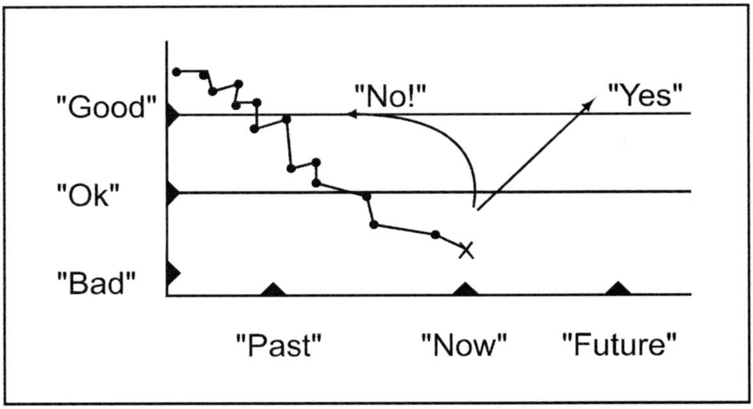

Figure 16.1. Going Ahead – Not Back to Where You Were.

It generally takes more than one session to identify specifically where an individual or a couple wants to go. We usually suggest, nonetheless, that it is important to have some general idea of where you would like to be heading before we start going anywhere.

ONE THERAPIST, ONE CLIENT

When a client asks Dr. Emener, "In addition to seeing me, would you also work with me and my husband (or wife)?" or when a couple asks him, "Would you see us individually as well as work with us as a couple?" he typically will respond with "No." He then proceeds to explain to them what he means when he says, "I can only have one client." When I first began working as a therapist, toward the end of my first session with a married couple they asked if I would see them separately. I said, "Yes." The following week I met with Richard. During my session with Richard, he said to me, "About a year ago my receptionist was on maternity leave for six weeks. I hired a replacement from an employment agency. She was very good and did an excellent job. On her last day at work, I took everyone in the office out for drinks to celebrate her good work and, in effect, to thank her. As the evening wore on, it eventually came down to the two of us in the lounge. And to make a long story short, we wound up back at her apartment and made love for the rest of the night. It was wonderful. But I have never seen her again." We briefly processed that experience and it was rather clear to me that it was not a significant issue for Richard nor was it particularly pertinent to his marital problems at the present time. The following week, however, when I was meeting with both Richard and his wife, Sally, she unsolicitedly said to me, "One of the things I have always admired about Ritchie is that he has never cheated on me." Richard immediately looked at me and inhaled for about four minutes! Needless to say, I also was extremely uncomfortable. If I had said anything to Sally about what Richard had told me, I would have betrayed Richard's trust and confidence. And by not saying anything to Sally, I felt that I was somehow betraying her trust and confidence. So, since that time, except for very rare occasions, I will only work with one client: him, her, or him and her.

Some professional counselors and therapists do not subscribe to Bill Emener's position on this and they are very effective. For example, when Bill Lambos is acting in the role of a court-certified family mediator, different rules apply and his clients are informed about this from the beginning. In addition, there are occasions in which Bill Lambos will agree to see a couple both separately and conjointly, *as long as the identified client remains the couple.* In such cases, rules for confidentiality are carefully discussed with his clients prior to seeing either person separately. Nevertheless, in our roles as psychologists, counselors and therapists, we will agree to treat *one client and only one client in a given family or relationship.*

Occasionally one of our clients will invite his or her spouse or loved one to a session or two, but on such occurrences it is very quickly established that: (1) he or she is our client; (2) there are specific reasons and goals for which the other person is being invited; and, (3) the other person is meeting with us by his or her (our client's) invitation. If we are working with one person and it is clear that he or she and their loved one or spouse need to see a marriage counselor or marital therapist, we recommend them to another helping professional specifically for that reason. The same applies if we are working with a couple and one of them needs to work on some individual, personal issues: we will recommend that he or she see a helping professional individually, specifically for that reason. Our experience has been that this approach works very well for us and for the people with whom we work. Thus, we would suggest that you try to understand the principles we are addressing here and not feel offended if your individual helping professional refuses to simultaneously see you *and* your spouse or loved one, and vice versa.

Wants and Willingnessess

It is not all that difficult for most people to identify what they want in or from their relationship with another person. Moreover, these relationship wants and needs most often can be obtained quickly if the other person would do what he or she is convinced the other person easily could do if he or she only wanted to. As Charlotte said to Henry, "You know, my dear, these things that you want in our marriage are also things I want in our marriage. However, every time I listen to you, I'm the one who has to change, work harder, or make sacrifices in order for us to have these things that we both want. What are you willing to do?"

As you have seen throughout this book, one of the techniques we occasionally employ is to ask both individuals to accept a homework assignment. With respect to wants and willingness, we ask each of them to individually, and without consulting the other, bring the following two lists to our next session:

1. *Things You Want In, or From, Your Relationship*; and
2. *What You Are Willing To Do To Get and Have Them.*

Then at our next session we review and discuss both lists and try to identify common Wants and Willingnesses. This process is designed not only to help people improve their relationship by getting more of what each wants and by sharing the responsibilities for getting them, but also to help them learn (1) how to work together cooperatively to identify their wants, and (2) how to cooperatively share responsibilities.

WILLINGNESS TO WORK

As suggested elsewhere in this book, there are differences between the *desire*, *capacity* and *willingness* to love. An example of the *desire* to love is in the simple statement, "I would like such things to happen." An example of *capacity* for such things is, "I would like such things if I am able to do what it may take to have them." An example of my *willingness* for such things, however, is, "I would like such things to happen and I am willing to work, sacrifice, and do whatever it takes for us to have them." As Karen once said to her fiancé, Ralph,

> *"You say that you love me with all your heart and that you love me with as much love as you have to offer. There are some things in our relationship that you and I both want, but you are not willing to do anything, make any changes or inconvenience yourself in any way in order for us to have them. And that, Ralph, is what I struggle with the most! I believe that if you really wanted some of these things you say you want, then you would be willing to do something or at least try to do something about them. You would like to have many things in our relationship, but you don't really want them. If you did, you'd do something about them, but those things would take time, effort and energy. You talk the talk, but you don't walk the walk!"*

If it is true that our willingness to work for things is an indication of how much we value them, then we would suggest that Karen is expressing an important aspect of a loving relationship worthy of your consideration as you (and your loved one) think about, analyze and attempt to improve your loving relationship. This is why we typically will ask people directly or indirectly, "Are you willing to invest some time, effort and energy into getting what you want?"

BE YOUR BEST TO GIVE YOUR BEST

"Are you willing to invest time, effort and energy into *being the best you can be*?" This is another important question helping professionals frequently ask. If you go to see a helping professional because you have problems and difficulties associated with a loving relationship, don't be surprised if you are asked, "What are you doing to take care of yourself?" Two philosophical assumptions underlie this query: (1) in a "good" loving relationship, I take care of me, you take care of you, both of us are attentive to and supportive of each other, and both of us are attentive to and supportive of our relationship; and (2) if I don't take care of me or you don't take care of you, then both of us and our relationship are in trouble. As is suggested throughout this book:

The most important thing you offer your loved one is yourself.

Thus, if one of your goals is to have a "good" loving relationship with someone you love (now or in the future), then it makes sense to offer your loved one something that's highly valuable and worthwhile – you at your best. "Be the best you can be for your own benefit, and I will also benefit from your being your best!"

REAL VERSUS SOCIAL RECOVERY

The summer season had finally come into full swing when Dr. Emener first met Gloria, a twenty-nine-year-old dental assistant, who said, "I love the beach. I used to go all the time, but I have yet to put a toe in the water." Approximately six months before seeing Bill, her husband had filed for divorce. He said to her, "I'm sorry, Gloria, but I have fallen in love with another woman." Gloria went into a severe depression. She became socially dysfunctional, missed many days of work, and "basically became a shut-in who never went out except to go to work, go to the store or take out the garbage." When Dr. Emener asked her why she came to see him, she said, "I am tired of just existing. I want to start living again."

As they were discussing some goals to consider working toward, they agreed to begin by focusing on some relatively "simple" things – such as going to a movie with her mother, to dinner with a girlfriend, and, possibly, a walk on the beach with a coworker. It is important to remember that when Bill first met Gloria, goals such as these were not "simple." Pointedly, she said, "I will have to work up to them. Remember, I've been a shut-in for the past six months!" We are pleased to report that over the next six months, Gloria increasingly became more and more successful in going out and doing things.

When Gloria came to a session six months later, about a week before Christmas, she entered Dr. Emener's office feeling really good about herself and said, "On Saturday afternoon I went shopping by myself and then met a girlfriend for dinner and a movie. I'm so proud of myself!"

During their first session that January, they began talking about her deep feelings of anger and rejection. Further along, they discussed the fears of abandonment that Gloria had lived with since she was a child who "went from foster home to foster home." That March, she began going out on some dates with men whom she had known and "felt safe with." When she came to their first session in June, she said, "Roy and I joined a sailing club together. He's really cool. We have been enjoying some great times together lately. It was a year ago yesterday, Dr. Emener, that I saw you for the first time. I sure have come a long way. I'm really proud of myself!" Gloria then pulled a piece of paper out of her purse. It had a diagram on it like the one in Figure 16.2. It was the diagram that Bill had sketched for her in March.

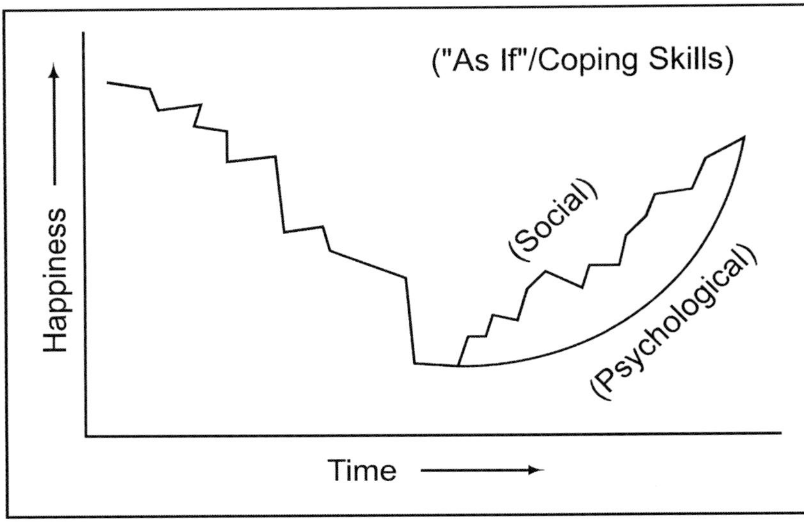

Figure 16.2. Real (Psychological) versus Social ("As If") Recovery.

As she developed better coping skills, slowly taking some risks, such as going out with her girlfriends and then occasionally going out with men, her coping skills continued to improve and her "As If - Social Recovery" was steadily improving. Her inner, personal, psychological improvement and recovery, however, lagged behind a little, and that certainly was understandable. The more she went out and acted as if she were adjusted, the better she felt about herself; and the better she felt about herself, the more she felt comfortable going out and acting as if she had adjusted. "In other words," she said to Dr. Emener, "as I continued to accomplish my social recovery goals, the easier it was for me to accomplish my psychological recovery goals." Interestingly, she had carried the sketch around in her purse, "Just as a reminder of my progress whenever I needed a pick-me-up."

If or when you go to see a helping professional about a difficulty or problem in a loving relationship, especially if you are down and out from a painful breakup of a relationship, don't be surprised if you begin by establishing "Social Recovery" goals and then focusing on your "Psychological Recovery" goals at a later, more comfortable time. For example, when Gloria and Dr. Emener discussed and processed her progress, she said, "The goals we started out with were reasonable and realistic. I was really down when I first came to see you! When we later worked on my heavier, psychological issues, I was ready. It's like the old cliché, 'It's hard to contemplate draining the lake when you're up to your ass in alligators'."

WHAT ARE MY/OUR OPTIONS?

In addition to discussing goals with you, such as "Social Recovery" goals and "Psychological Recovery" goals, a helping professional also may suggest that you discuss "Options" that may be available to you. During Dr. Emener's first session with Billie, a forty-one-year-old stockbroker, they discussed her sixteen-year marriage to Joe, a claims adjuster for an insurance company. They had two teenaged children. She added, however, that she had been feeling "totally unloved by Joe for the past eight years." Toward the end of their session, after telling Bill all of the things she had done to try to improve her relationship with Joe, she said, "Well, what are my options?"

Dr. Emener responded to her question with, "What options do you see?" After pondering that question for a few moments, she said, "Well, let's see. *One*, I could stay married to Joe and meet my needs for love and affection from my children and my relatives. *Two*, I could stay married to Joe and have affairs. *Three*, I could try to negotiate a separation. *Four*, I could file for divorce. Or *Five*, I could see if Joe would be willing to come in with me for marriage counseling."

Dr. Emener suggested to Billie that, as a homework assignment, it might be helpful to write out her five options and generate a list of the pros and cons for each option. She agreed that that would be a helpful thing for her to do and that she would bring her lists to their next session.

About two weeks later, Bill received a short note in the mail from Billie. It read, "I wrote out my lists. That was helpful for me.

However, I cancelled my next appointment with you – Joe and I are seeing a marriage counselor next week. I truly am hoping for the best. If it doesn't work out, I'll get back in touch with you. Thanks for your help, Billie." We do not know what happened with Billie and Joe. Dr. Emener never heard from her again.

Occasionally, there are times in our lives when we get caught up in our emotions and feelings, times when we cannot think clearly in terms of where we are, what our options are, and ultimately what we want. And as simple as it sounds, sometimes just verbalizing our feelings and thinking through our options can be extremely helpful. Thus, if you go to talk with a helping professional about a difficulty or problem you may be having with a loving relationship, don't be surprised if he or she asks, "What are your options?" We remain optimistic and truly believe that it was a good question for Billie to have addressed.

* * * * * *

Seeing a helping professional can be very scary.
He or she will probably be honest with me.
If my loved one goes with me, he or she also may be honest with me.
I may be honest with him or her.
I may even be honest... with myself.
Not only that, I may be sharing my truths with someone else.
I trust, however, that my counselor will help me deal
with the pain of my discovery.

Chapter Seventeen

How a Professional Counselor, Therapist or Family Mediator Can Be Helpful to You

As we learned in the previous chapter, there is a multitude of things that helping professionals can do to help with your relationship issues, difficulties and problems. Many of them are discussed throughout this book. Nonetheless, there are some specific things that we repeatedly have experienced to be helpful, both directly and indirectly, to many people Please do not assume, however, that because we discuss specific therapy techniques in this chapter (or anywhere else in this book) that they necessarily would be appropriate or requisite for you. Rather, they are illustrative examples of some of the things that professional assistants *can or may do* – not necessarily things that professional assistants *will or should do*. All people, all relationships and all helping professionals are different. Each professional assistant is unique, as is every client who seeks assistance. Fittingly, your experience with your professional of choice will be unique – unique for you and for him or her as well.

RESPONSIBILITY: CAUSE ⇔ CURE; PAST ⇔ FUTURE

If you have ever seen the (admittedly silly) film *The Cannonball Run* with Burt Reynolds, you may remember a scene in which the Italian contestant gets in his Ferrari and immediately rips the rear-view mirror off and throws it out the window. When his driving partner looks at him as if he is crazy, he smiles and in a thick Umbrian accent replies, "What's-a-behind us, does not-a-matter!"

Dr. Lambos often uses this scene in therapy sessions as a vehicle (pun intended) for demonstrating two very important and related points about solving relationship problems: First, focusing on the past instead of the future is often counterproductive; more often than not, it directs focus on perpetuating the problem rather than on finding a solution. Second and closely related to this, focusing on *who is responsible* for the problem instead of *what to do about it* typically contributes little towards finding a resolution. We suggest that when choosing how to deal with a relationship issue with your helping professional, you decide whether it is more important to feel self-righteous by laying blame at your partner's feet *or* to fix the problem and, in doing so, strengthen and/or save the relationship. Like it or not, it is often impossible to achieve both – one must make a choice. The vast majority of rational people in a meaningful relationship – one sufficiently important to them to warrant investing in professional assistance – will choose the latter, as long as they realize that is the choice before them.

Along these lines, Dr. Emener is readily reminded of his first therapy session with Rick and Susan. Rick was the floor supervisor at a large auto repair shop, and Susan was a regional account executive at a well-known firm in the community. They had been married for four years and had a two-year-old daughter. "We came to see you," Rick said, "because our marriage seems to be falling helplessly apart and we don't know what to do about it."

Susan quickly interjected, "For about two months I had an affair with a gentleman in another city. It is all my fault. If Rick would just be patient with me, we can fix it."

As their conversation continued, Dr. Emener drew a diagram for them similar to the diagram in Figure 17.1. When he completed the nine-cell diagram (called a "contingency table" in the social sciences), he put Susan's name in the upper left cell, the "me-me" cell, and said to her, "Susan, it sounds like you see yourself as having been the cause of your marital problems, and you also see yourself as being the source of the cure."

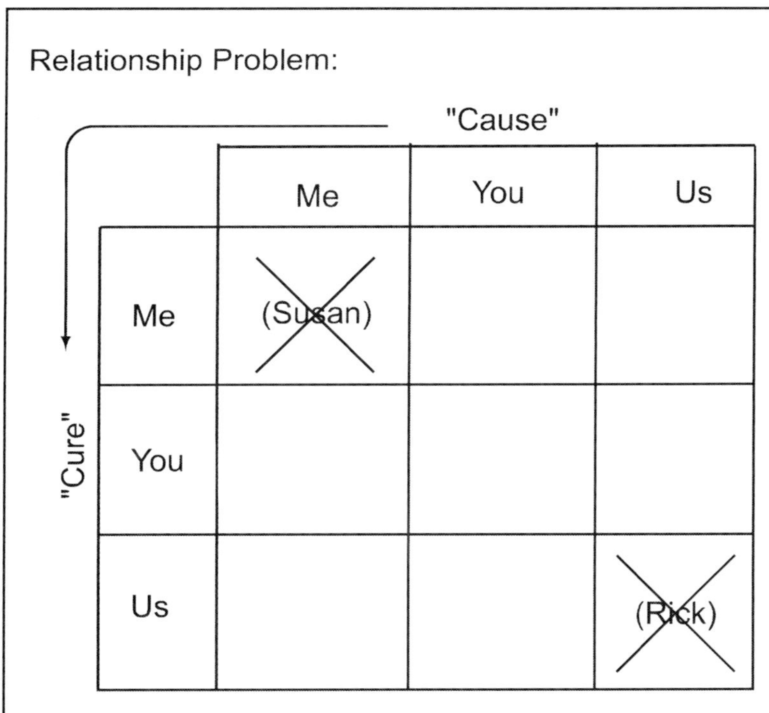

Figure 17.1. Who's Responsible for the Cause and the Cure.

Dr. Emener then put Rick's name in the bottom right cell, the "us-us" cell, and said, "Rick, you are suggesting that the two of you are the *cause* of your marital problems and, therefore, the two you should be the primary sources of the cure for your marital problems." Their facial expressions and nods indicated that they understood what Dr.

Emener was saying. At that point he put "X's" through Susan's and Rick's names on the diagram, drew an arrow from "cause" to "cure" and said to them, "I suggest that we redirect our attention away from identifying who was or is the cause of your marital problems and focus more of our attention on identifying ways by which you can improve your relationship. In my many years as a marital and relationship therapist, I repeatedly have discovered that attention to 'Whose fault is it?' has seldom resolved or fixed anything! Faulting, shaming and blaming very rarely will ever improve or fix a relationship."

To reiterate, attention on who was or is the cause of relationship problems, seldom helps people move toward resolution, repair or improvement. To wit, Rick said to Susan, "Okay, I agree. Let's quit blaming each other and ourselves. Let's focus our attention on what we can do to improve our relationship."

APPRECIATION AND UNDERSTANDING

A second issue that bears on the course of counseling, therapy or mediation, is isolating concerns that have what we refer to as "deal-breaker" status. Deal-breakers are things about one's partner or the relationship that *must* be addressed or the relationship will fail. When prioritizing issues on which to work, it helps greatly to isolate these deal-breakers and work on them first and foremost. Not to do so may be analogous to attending to a sprained finger while the patient is bleeding from the carotid artery! In addition, resolving the deal-breakers often lessens the importance of those other, merely irritating things that a couple can live with, helping the couple to see such smaller imperfections as less important. An example of this process from Bill Emener's practice illustrates these points nicely.

When Sam and Lisa came to see Dr. Emener, they told him that they had been living together for about two years, were engaged to be married the following spring, but were having some serious problems in their relationship. Sam had recently graduated from law school, which indeed had taken up much of his time, and Lisa had recently graduated from nursing school, which had taken up much of her time. "We have been living together for the last two years," Lisa said, "and now that we have finished school and have more time to spend with each other, we don't know each other! Sometimes it seems that the only thing we do is argue all the time."

In addition to recommending a self-help book, Dr. Emener invited them to participate in a homework assignment. Although he asked them to read the book together, as a joint experience, Dr. Emener also asked them each to do something alone without any consultation with each other: make three lists (if these lists seem familiar, it is because you have seen them before, specifically in Chapter 2 and Figure 2.5):

List I. "Things that I like, love and cherish about ______." Basically, what are those things that you like, love and cherish about each other? What are those things about each other that you hope will never change? These are the things about each other that significantly contribute to the fact that you love each other as much as you do.

List II. "Things that I wish were different about ______, but it's okay that they aren't." These are the things about each other that you wish were different, such as "She always leaves hair in the sink," "He never puts the cap back on the toothpaste," "She never puts gas in the car when she uses it," and "No matter how many times I tell him, he always leaves the toilet seat up." Although these are things about each other that you wish were different, they are things that you can live with. These can be thought of as annoyances.

List III. "Things that I wish were different about ______, and they need fixin'." These are things about each other that you not only wish were different, but that bother you so much that they could be relationship threatening.

For example, "I get annoyed when you leave the newspapers lying all over the house (list II.), but when you get angry at me and avoid me and don't talk to me for three days, I can't stand it (list III.). That is something I just cannot and will not tolerate."

When they left Dr. Emener's office, they assured him that they would purchase and read the self-help book he recommended and bring their three lists to the next session. Dr. Emener reminded Sam and Lisa that for a multitude of understandable reasons, they did not appreciate or understand each other, each other's perception of their relationship, and each other's frustrations with each other and with their relationship. This homework assignment was designed primarily to assist them in enhancing their appreciation and understanding of such things.

I Could Do – You Could Do

Three weeks later when Sam and Lisa came to their second session, they briefly discussed the self-help book and what they had learned from it. Dr. Emener then laid out copies of their three lists for all to see. Dr. Emener invited each of them to share and talk through with each other (not with him) their three lists. At the conclusion, they indeed had experienced an enhanced and enriched understanding of and appreciation for: some of the reasons why they loved each other as much as they did; some of the things that each of them had been doing that frustrated the other; and those things about each other and their relationship that definitely needed to be addressed. As Sam said, "I was not surprised to hear most of the things on Lisa's lists. Nonetheless, it was helpful to hear them. Importantly, however, there were some things on her list that I did not expect, and let me tell you, I truly believe I now understand and appreciate her much more than I did ever before."

Lisa tearfully replied, "Sam, I feel so loved by you. And I want our relationship to work. I want to spend the rest of my life with you. I only hope that now we will be willing to do whatever it may take to make it work." Sam held her in his arms and gave her the most tender yet forceful hug one could imagine. At the end of the session, Bill invited them to participate in another homework assignment, asking each of them to make two more lists:

List 1. "Things that *I could do* to improve and enhance our relationship."

and,

List 2. "Things that you could do to improve and enhance our relationship."

"In other words," Sam said, "my first list would be a list of those things that I could do to make our relationship better and my second list would be a list of things that I think Lisa could do to improve our relationship." Dr. Emener nodded. When they left the office, their arms around each other, they promised Dr. Emener, and more importantly, each other, that they would work on their two lists and bring them to their next session.

About one week later, Bill received a call from Lisa. She wanted to tell him that the two of them had completed their two lists, their impatience had gotten the better of them and they went out to dinner and shared their lists with each other, and were already starting to do some of the things they had put on their lists to improve their relationship. "Is that okay?" she asked.

With genuine joy in his heart, Dr. Emener replied, "Lisa, that's wonderful! You are improving your relationship; keep doing what you are doing!" She began to cry. By the end of the conversation, it was clear that Lisa and Sam had turned the corner.

The couple canceled their next scheduled appointment because they saw no need for them to come back. Lisa added, "I have, and Sam has, every reason to believe that things will continue to improve for us. If we need to come see you, we will call and schedule an appointment. If not, we will be sure to send you a wedding invitation."

Bill did not attend their wedding, but an invitation arrived about four months later. It is still on his bulletin board.

ANALYZE THE LOVE IN YOUR RELATIONSHIP

Time spent with a helping professional is of a dual nature. In one sense, it is often intense due to emotions that arise when defense mechanisms such as denial and avoidance are disabled, and therefore the time can be as frightening as it can be rewarding. Moreover, time in the office of a professional assistant is, for most people, necessarily limited. It is expensive if one goes on a self-pay basis and/or subject to insurance plan restrictions if paid for via a third party. (Clients and even insurers often forget the high costs that accrue over the many years of study and internship prior to becoming a licensed counselor, therapist or mediator.) The point of this is that to get the most "bang for your buck" from professional help, it is very important to prioritize things so that the serious issues are dealt with first. For example, Dr. Lambos typically approaches therapy with a new couple by addressing concerns in the following order:

1. Goals are set, rules are clarified and boundaries are established.
2. Sensitive or emotionally difficult areas are identified so that they can be approached with a minimum of discomfort to each partner.
3. Issues are listed in order, from most to least critical. The "deal-breakers" are at the top of the list.
4. The issues in (#3) are addressed in order, with appropriate heed to (#2), until the clients feel that no more sessions are necessary (at least for the time being).

On the other hand, some clients may be unable to identify their problems so readily. All they know is that *something* isn't working, and they leave the rest up to the helping professional. In our day and age of increasingly sophisticated clients, this is rarer than it used to be, yet it still occurs often enough that a good professional assistant will need to have a Plan B for such situations. Dr. Emener has found that for such couples, analyzing the love in the relationship can serve this purpose quite well.

During his first session with Tom and Mary, who had been married for a little over three years and were having "serious marital problems," Dr. Emener drew a triangle similar to the one in Figure 17.2. Dr. Emener then said to them, "Based primarily on my experiences as a therapist, I believe there are three important sides of love – *intimacy*, *passion*, and *commitment*. (The Love Triangle is discussed in detail in Chapter 1, "Love" in our companion book, *Our Loving Relationship*). After discussing these three aspects of love

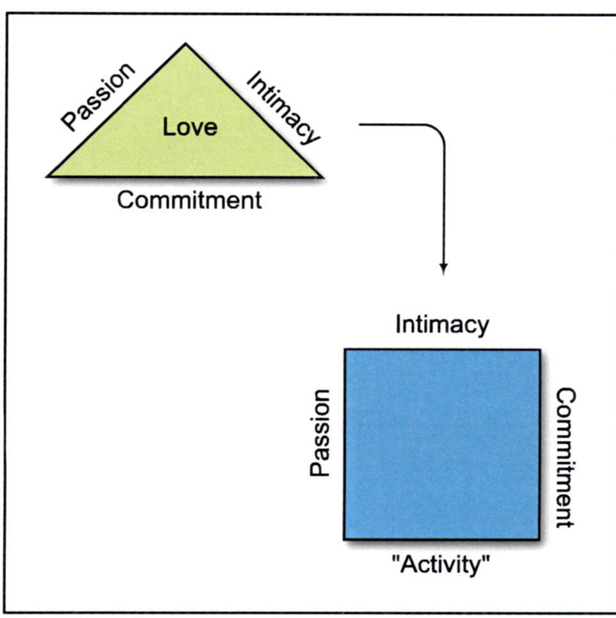

Figure 17.2. Analyze the Love in Your Relationship.

with them, Bill then asked them to use a ten-point scale to individually rate the extent to which they felt there was intimacy, passion and commitment in their relationship. A rating of "1" would represent "very little," and a rating of "10" would represent "very high." They both agreed to participate in the exercise. Tom, however, reached for a pad and pen and said, "If I may, Dr. Emener, I would like to suggest that there are four aspects of love – intimacy, passion, commitment, and activity. I believe that Mary and I understand what we are talking about in the areas of *intimacy*, *passion*, and *commitment*. However, *activity*, which I think of as 'how we spend our time?' is an equally important aspect of our relationship." Mary agreed and the two of them independently gave a rating from 1 to 10 on the four aspects.

Interestingly, both of them tended to give fairly high ratings to passion and commitment (7's and 8's), low to moderate ratings on intimacy (5's and 6's) and very low ratings to activity (2's and 3's). As the discussion unfolded, it became clear to Tom and Mary that "they were not spending enough time with each other." Mary, who had a full-time job as a school teacher and was very involved in local tennis tournaments, did not spend large blocks of quality time with Tom. Likewise, Tom, an insurance salesman who worked fifty to sixty hours per week and was very involved in his sailing club, "had very few blocks of quality time to spend with Mary."

Toward the end of their conversation, Tom said, "It seems to me, Mary, that we have a lot of love in our hearts for each other and we feel very committed to each other and our relationship. The problem seems to be that we do not spend enough quality time with each other and, as a result, our relationship is like a sand bar of intimacy!"

With tears streaming down her face, Mary said, "Tom, I am willing to give up some of my tennis tournaments. From now on I will devote two weekends a month exclusively to you and our relationship."

Tom, with his eyes also welling up, replied, "And I, Mary, simply will not enter so many sailing races. Or maybe I could accompany you to some of your tennis tournaments or you could be with me on the boat for some of my races?"

While holding Tom's hands next to her face, Mary said, "Tom, maybe those details don't matter – as long as we spend some quality time together."

As Tom and Mary experienced during their first session, it can be very helpful for individuals to identify what aspects of their love and relationship need to be focused on and attended to. Fittingly, it is not uncommon for a counselor or therapist to ask you and your loved one, "What aspects of your love and your relationship do we need to focus on? What is it that needs fixin'?"

Structure Your Schedule, Including Time for Psychological Vacations

Another recommendation we offer clients is to plan their daily, weekly, monthly and yearly activities, not only with their family, but with each other. For example, it might be helpful if the two partners could plan to have at least one meaningful heart-to-heart conversation per day, even if it's only for fifteen minutes before retiring for the night. Likewise, if a couple can plan to do at least one thing together per week, maybe spend a whole day or weekend together per month and annually take at least one week-long vacation together, just the two of them, it helps them to remain in touch with and connected with one another.

It is very easy for adults in loving relationships to be distracted from each other and from their relationship by family, occupational and other types of responsibilities and commitments. It also is easy to assume that because the couple is receiving professional assistance, they cannot enjoy the relationship until therapy has concluded. Neither of these assumptions is warranted and can only add to the strain of already fragile relationships. Many times when we have asked individuals in long-term, loving relationships, "When is the last time the two of you went away on a three or more day vacation together, just the two of you?" they have looked at each other, then looked at us and said, "We can't remember."

The love that two people feel for each other and from each other is many times invested in the time they spend with each other and the things they do with each other. In a nutshell, if your relationship is important to you, plan your daily, weekly, monthly and yearly activities so that the two of you don't accidentally drift apart and one day look at each other as if you were looking at a stranger. Likewise, don't assume that you can't enjoy one another while you are seeing a professional. If your loved one and your relationship with your loved one is important to you, don't look for time to spend with him or her – *make the time.*

A related issue with respect to structuring and scheduling time is the concept of time-out periods. When a couple is working with a helping professional, it also is important for them to remember that they cannot be "in therapy" or "in mediation" for the entire, 24/7 time period. Although much important work and change is accomplished in the space between sessions, a couple must also realize that for therapy to be successful, the partners must find or set aside time to be together, put the issues "on hold" and enjoy their relationship even as it is evolving. We like to call these time-out periods "psychological vacations." If you spend large amounts of time with your loved one, doing and enjoying things together, yet feel that neither of you can be yourself or have forgotten the "essence" of your partner, maybe it is time for the two of you to take a psychological break.

Mediation as an Alternative to Counseling and Therapy

Family or couples mediation was once reserved for the couple undergoing divorce, and of course, mediation remains a valuable alternative to the family court system. It is increasingly common, however, for couples to seek the help of a family mediator to strengthen a marriage or relationship rather than to help dissolve the relationship amicably. This is sometimes referred to as "therapeutic mediation." Your authors find this term confusing, however, and prefer to simply recognize that mediation is a technique for resolving disputes that can and do involve keeping a relationship intact and/or strengthening it, as opposed to only helping to dissolve it.

What is the difference between a family or couples *mediator* and a family or couples *therapist*? Less than one might think. In fact, many family mediators are also licensed therapists and vice versa (Bill Lambos is an example). A mediator is a specialist in *alternative dispute resolution*. The alternatives include attorneys, the family court system, nonprofessionals, and other helping professionals. The biggest difference between a family mediator and a family therapist is in focus: whereas a family therapist is more often than not focused on improving a relationship by helping individuals change their perceptions, feelings and behaviors related to the relationship, a mediator places the emphasis on the nature of a dispute. Think of a mediator as part King Solomon. She or he is a neutral and impartial third party whose job is to help find a solution to a problem. But unlike King Solomon, mediation is not binding unless the parties sign some type of agreement upon its conclusion – the mediator may never impose a solution. Mediation is an excellent alternative to counseling or therapy for situations when the couple's difficulties revolve around external factors as opposed to internal psychological ones.

What kinds of disputes can be mediated? In fact, there is almost nothing that cannot in principle be mediated. Within the context of existing relationships, Bill Lambos has mediated prenuptial agreements, disputes over how money is allocated, child-rearing guidelines, behavioral contracts for couples in recovery from substance and even Internet addiction, rules and boundaries regarding in-laws and blended family issues, and other disagreements too numerous to list. Understandably, some couples that don't feel they need therapy or counseling will readily agree to work with a mediator.

There is one important difference between mediation and therapy, however. By ethical and legal standards, one individual cannot be both a therapist and a mediator to the same individual or couple. The hallmarks of mediation are the mediator's impartiality and neutrality. The focus is always on the disputed issue and how to achieve a solution amenable to both parties. A therapist, on the other hand, may well advise one member of the couple that he or she is the person with the problem and needs to change. Simply put, therapists are trained to help people change, whereas mediators are trained to help people agree. This leads to a simple rule of thumb when deciding which type of helping professional might best serve the needs of you and your significant other:

> *If the two of you are seeking help to overcome personal issues that negatively impact the relationship, then it is usually best to seek counseling or therapy.*

However…

> *If you have a disagreement about a thing or a situation and both parties have dug in their heels, so to speak, then mediation is usually advised.*

In neither case, however, does seeking one type of assistant over the other necessarily depend on whether the goal is to dissolve or repair the relationship. Therapists can be vital resources for couples ending a relationship or undergoing divorce, and mediators can keep a couple together by helping resolve an ongoing intractable dispute.

Benefits of Support Groups

During her first visit to Dr. Emener, Elaine said, "After six years of marriage, Ed told me he wanted a divorce. I still believe that he was in love with another woman. I don't really know. I just think so. Our divorce was finalized about a month ago. I feel so lonely, scared and depressed."

In addition to talking at length about Elaine's feelings, lifestyle and future plans, Bill suggested a self-help book for her to read and also suggested that she join a support group at a women's center not far from where she lived. When she came for their next session, she told him that she had called the center and found out that there was a divorce-support group that met every Thursday evening for two hours. She went for an initial screening interview and then to two of the meetings. Later, she reported: "Going to those meetings was the best thing I could have done for myself!"

Not everyone needs or benefits from participation in a support group. On the other hand, however, support groups, especially those that are led and facilitated by a professional counselor or therapist, can be extremely beneficial and helpful to many people who are experiencing difficulties, problems and lifestyle adjustment concerns related to previous, current and/or future loving relationships. Thus, if your counselor or therapist suggests that you consider joining a support group, seriously consider participating – it indeed could be very helpful to you.

* * * * * *

It is important for us to think about and learn from
our past.
It is important for us to think and plan for
our future.
Professional assistants can help us do such things.
It is most important for us to be – in the present.
When you see a helping professional,
you will be – in the present.

Chapter Eighteen

SOME SUGGESTIONS ABOUT GETTING HELP FROM A PROFESSIONAL

The extent to which you, your loved one and your relationship may benefit from seeing a professional assistant is highly influenced by your viewpoints, attitudes, anticipations and opinions regarding helping professionals. We trust that the notions discussed in this chapter will help you get the most from your experience of seeking professional help.

WE HELP YOU HELP YOURSELF

It is not uncommon for an individual to come to one of us and say, "I would like you to tell me what to do about my relationship with my loved one." Nor is it uncommon for a couple to come to one of us and say, "We would like you to fix our relationship for us." For philosophical and professional reasons, our responses to these two statements tend to fall into the category of routine.

First of all, neither we nor other qualified and competent helping professionals tell people what to do in or with their lives. Rather, helping professionals offer analysis and the opportunity for exploration and reflection in order for you to determine where you want to go in, and what you want to do with, your life. Your life is your life; you must be the individual making the decision.

Secondly, we frequently remind people who come to see us that as professional assistants, we choose not to fix, nor could we fix, them or their relationship for them. An individual may be able to go to his or her dentist, lie down in the chair, be put to sleep, and with minimal cooperation allow the dentist to fix his or her teeth. But as helping professionals, we can no more help people than we can climb inside their heads or take their place in the relationship. *Our goal is to help individuals help themselves*. The somewhat familiar analogy that we may use is, "Give a person a fish, and you have taken care of their hunger today. Teach a person how to fish, and you have taken care of their hunger forever."

With regard to these two philosophical issues, we have been known to say to our clients things such as, "I will be your limo driver for this short period of your journey. But you will need to tell me where you want to go; remember, I'm only the driver," and "I prefer to think of myself as the coach and cheerleader on the sidelines; you are the player who will go out onto the field and do the work to win the game." Thus, do not be surprised if you go to see a counselor or therapist and he or she does not agree to tell you what to do, or does not agree to solve your problems for you. Counselors and therapists are there to help you help yourself.

AVOID QUICK-FIX TEMPTATIONS

Professional help entails doing hard work, and more often than not it results in experiencing temporary discomfort as you learn to accept your own need to grow and change. On the other hand, it often results in substantial rewards in terms of relief from suffering and improvements in happiness. For example, Dr. Emener recalls a particular occasion when a couple came to see him because they had been having serious marital problems. About one month prior to seeing him, they had taken a one-week cruise together through the

Mediterranean, believing that the cruise would fix their relationship. It didn't work. It is interesting to note, moreover, that they said, "Only three things happened as a result of our cruise: we came back with good tans; we both gained weight; and we added $3500 to our credit card balance. But the truth of the matter is that the basic nature of our relationship didn't change one bit."

Enriching, enhancing, improving and fixing a troubled loving relationship is not accomplished by one event or one purchase. *Improving a loving relationship involves a process over time, which can be fraught with much emotional upheaval.* Moreover, it typically also involves your commitment, work and change. As Dr. Lambos recently said to a couple, "In therapy, the reward is usually commensurate with, or equal to, the effort expended. It is therefore important that if you want a large return on your investment in therapy, you must try to avoid looking for simple solutions to complex problems." Thus, as enticing as it may be, try to be careful and not get caught up in the temptation to look for quick fixes.

AVOID SUBCONSCIOUS SABOTAGE

Change can sometimes be very difficult to maintain. Repetition, routine and continuing to do what we have always done, can be comforting and much less threatening than doing something different. And if you, or you and your loved one, start trying to do things differently for your individual and collective benefits, be sensitive to the possibility that either or both of you might subconsciously sabotage your progress in order to go back to doing what for years was familiar and therefore relatively comfortable. A skilled helping professional will assist you in recognizing when you are slipping back into old patterns, and do his or her best to put you or the relationship back on the track toward change and improvement.

THE PARALYSIS OF ANALYSIS

Toward the end of Dr. Emener's third session with Ken and Tina, he said to them, "I have the feeling that sometimes the two of you are almost afraid to do anything with or for each other for fear that it might be wrong." They looked at each other, smiled with light laughter and said, "That is interesting. We were just talking about that last night!"

Ken then added, "Just this morning I was saying to Tina that I am coming to believe that some of the true joy people have in life comes from living life, not analyzing it."

When we are attempting to enrich, enhance, improve and strengthen a loving relationship, it is important that we are analytical and try to understand what is going on. Nonetheless, it is equally important for us to be sensitive to the possibility that our penchant for analyzing things can be psychologically paralyzing and render us less spontaneous, less authentic and less natural than we would want or prefer to be.

This is an important point, and raises another closely related issue that we looked at in Chapter Seventeen: one cannot be in therapy 24/7 and still have a relationship or a life worth continuing. Although many of the positive results of professional help occur as a result of changes people undergo between (rather than during) sessions, there must be substantial time-out periods from the work of therapy. Again, we refer the reader to the previous chapter, as well as to the next section of this chapter, for a more detailed look at this issue.

STAY FOCUSED ON THE PRESENT

In his book *The Art of Happiness*, the Dalai Lama continually emphasizes that the past is gone forever and the future has not yet occurred. Therefore, happiness can be found only in the present. Regardless of your personal opinion about Buddhist philosophy, we believe he makes an excellent point.

For example, when Angela was telling Dr. Emener about the difficulties in her relationship with Troy, he followed up their discussion regarding her possible "paralysis of analysis" issues by saying, "Angela, I suggest that when you are on a date or doing something with Troy that you try to stay focused on what is going on with *you* and what is going on with *the two of you*. Try to stay attuned to how you are feeling *at the moment*. Try to remain focused on yourself, Troy and your relationship with Troy."

Smiling in agreement, Angela said, "In other words, Dr. Emener, you are suggesting that I save my reflections and forecasts for when I get home."

"Yes," Bill replied, "and the reason why I am suggesting this to you, Angela, is that you had indicated to me that Troy was beginning to get frustrated with your increasing desire to talk about what the two of you had done or experienced in the past, or about what you plan to do in the future. I believe it is important for us to reflect on our past experiences and learn from them, to think about our future experiences and plan for them, but also to stay focused primarily on the present – on what we are doing at the moment."

The next day Bill received a telephone call from Angela in which she said to him, "Last night Troy and I went for a long walk after dinner. I tried what we talked about yesterday and it was wonderful. We had more fun together than ever before."

STAGES OF CHANGE EFFORTS

A well-known psychologist named James O. Prochaska and his colleagues have developed a widely accepted and much studied model of the stages of individual change called the transtheoretical model of change. Although this model is now applied and taught in many areas of health psychology (in particular, in substance abuse recovery programs), few remember that it was originally developed to address the stages of change a couple undergoes when seeking to improve their relationship. Prochaska's model posits the following six stages of change:

1. *Precontemplation* – lack of awareness that life (in particular, one's relationship) can be improved by a change in behavior;
2. *Contemplation* – recognition of the problem, initial consideration of behavior change and information gathering about possible solutions and actions;
3. *Preparation* – introspection about the decision, reaffirmation of the need and desire to change behavior, and completion of final pre-action steps;
4. *Action* – implementation of the practices needed for successful behavior change (e.g., regular sessions with a helping professional);
5. *Maintenance* – consolidation of the behaviors initiated during the action stage; and,
6. *Termination* – former problem behaviors are no longer perceived as desirable (e.g., when skipping a planned walk on the beach in order to have time to watch football results in frustration rather than pleasure).

When working with couples, it is not uncommon for us to identify some of these stages in their efforts toward improving their relationship. Depending on the sophistication and background of our client, we may simplify the six stages down to four and draw a diagram similar to the one in Figure 18.1. Since the couple is already in our office seeking change, we skip the pre-contemplation phase and note that the first stage involves *awareness* – when we are trying to heighten our understanding of, and appreciation for, what is going on within ourselves, the other person, and within our relationship. The second stage is *agreement* – when we tend to agree on what our problem areas are and what aspects of our relationship on which we need to focus our attention. Then, in stage three, we individually and collectively make *commitments* – when individuals begin to say

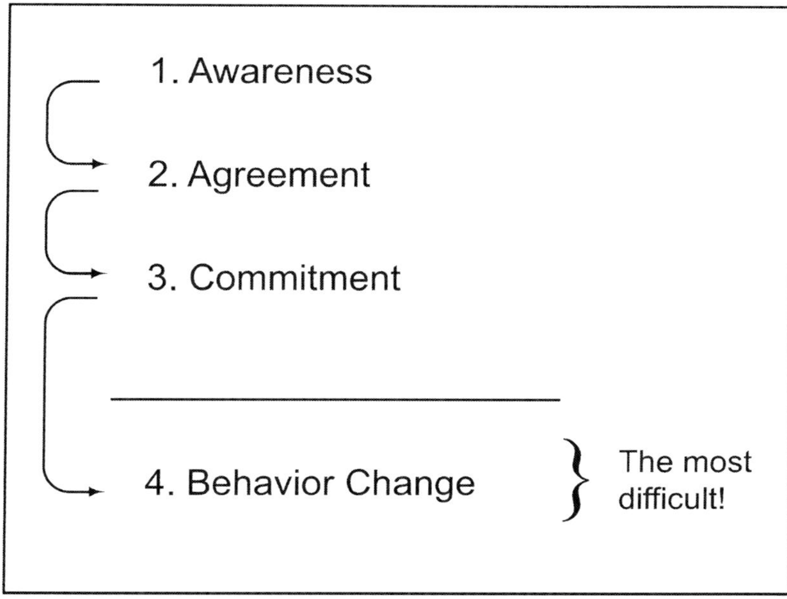

Figure 18.1. Stages of Change Efforts.

things like, "From now on I will… and from now on we will…" The most difficult stage, however, is stage four when our awarenesses, agreements and commitments are translated into behavior change. As a client once astutely said, "Stages one, two and three are when we talk the talk. That's easy. The fourth stage, however, is when we have to walk the walk. In this stage, we focus on changing behavior. Indeed, this is the most difficult stage." And as another person recently noted, "Stage four is where the rubber meets the road."

Regardless of how many stages one wishes to identify, the point remains that achieving the lasting and positive changes associated with increased happiness and/or decreased suffering involve a process of change that evolves through stages. This is true whether or not a couple seeks professional assistance or is able to achieve such change on their own. Moreover, the progression through stages implies the passage of time – a topic we address next.

Progress May Be Slow and Gradual

As our society has adjusted to life on "Internet time," with rapid change and constant motion being the norm rather than the exception, some people have also grown more used to immediate (if not instant) gratification. We would like to warn our readers that there is no such thing in therapy. Achieving personal change or improvement in loving relationships involves adjusting long-held perceptions and beliefs, and changing long-established behaviors. This in turn involves, as we have seen, a progression through stages that takes both time and effort. When clients ask us, "How long will it take to fix this?" we respond with, "I can't say, but my bet is – longer than you were hoping. You had better ask yourselves right up front, is fixing this relationship worth the investment it will require?" Most of our clients, having made it as far as getting to their first appointment, will respond in the affirmative.

Rita, for example, an account executive with a large corporation, had recently been was transferred from Dallas to the Tampa Bay area when she first came to see Dr. Emener. She told him that she had been seeing a therapist in Dallas for over a year and had been making excellent progress. "I do not want to slide or fall back just because I moved to Tampa, and I hope and trust you will be able to assist me in continuing to improve my life." The process of trying to understand what Rita had experienced prior to coming to see him culminated in Dr. Emener's sketching a diagram similar to one in Figure 18.2. They had identified three changing states of her life: *happy*, *uncomfortable* and *troubled*. In a nutshell, this is how she described her experience: "Up until the end of 1991, I was relatively happy with my life and happily married to Walter. We had just celebrated our fifth wedding anniversary. But for reasons I do not understand, he started being absent from the house more and more, and I believe began seeing other women. By 1992, my life was very uncomfortable, and by October of 1993 I knew that I was in trouble. By the time our divorce had been finalized, my life was simply a wreck. That is when I began

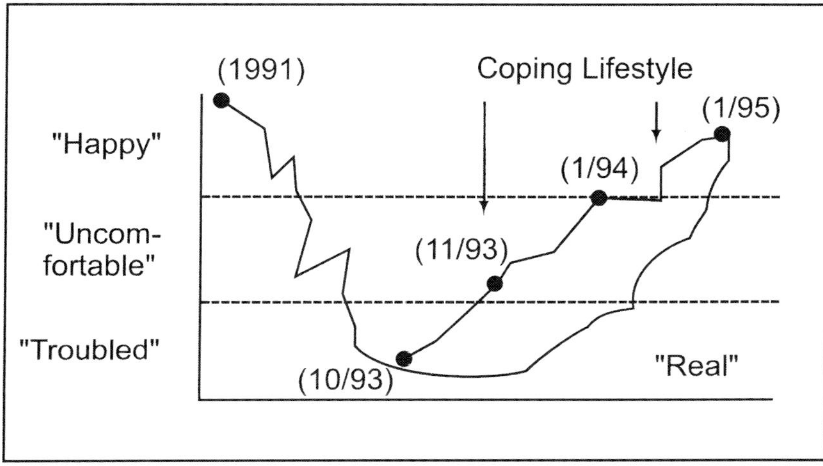

Figure 18.2. Progress May Be Slow and Gradual.

to see Dr. Johnson in Dallas. By November of 1993, with the help of some short-term medication, I was able to cope and go back to work. I had a relatively comfortable Christmas and started to enjoy life a little bit when I was transferred to the Tampa Bay area. Dr. Johnson suggested that I continue with my antidepressant medication until you and I feel that I no longer need to take it. But I know it is going to take some time before I can get my life back together and start to go out with men again. All I want to do is live a happy life."

Basically what Rita was saying was that with the help of some short-term medication and the psychotherapy she had been receiving from Dr. Johnson, she had developed some effective coping skills and was able to live a relatively meaningful and enjoyable life. At the same time, however, her psychological and spiritual, or "real" happiness in life was still below what her "coping," "as if," or "socially appealing" lifestyle would have suggested. At the end of that first session with Dr. Emener, they agreed that she would continue to work with him with the goal of continuing to have a "coping lifestyle" so that she could continue to function occupationally and socially, and that eventually her "real happiness" would catch up with her every day, "real" lifestyle behaviors.

Dr. Emener saw Rita for a total of six sessions, and as she was leaving his office after their last session she told him that she was enjoying her dates with Fred and was probably going to continue to see him on a regular basis. She also said to him, "I was a little nervous when I discontinued taking my medication and later started going out with Fred. But every day, every week, my life seems to be getting easier and much better. My happiness in life, indeed, seems to be coming around. When you and Dr. Johnson told me that my progress may be slow and gradual, I was not sure what you were trying to say to me. Now I do."

With some "good self-help work" on your behalf and the assistance of a professional assistant, your issues, difficulties and problems with your individual life and the loving relationships in your life can be resolved. But just because your progress may be slow and gradual, it might not mean that you are not making progress. As Rita said, "Recovering from and bouncing back from a dirty deal in life sometimes simply takes time. I've done a lot of hard work over the last year and a half to help myself get to where I am today, and it surely has been worth it!"

REALISTIC EXPECTATIONS: BEHAVIOR AND EMOTIONS

As noted above, the stages of change experienced by those seeking to improve a relationship are similar in some ways to the stages of recovery from dependence on a substance such as alcohol. One of the ways in which the two processes overlap is as follows: *each and every additional day of experiencing and working on the change process, results in an incremental (and sometimes small) movement towards positive change.* Of course, there are often temporary setbacks, and most assuredly some days are better than others, but overall, the longer the behavioral changes are maintained (e.g., sobriety or being more considerate of ones partner), the more such change feels comfortable and natural.

When Matt and Rosa came to see Dr. Emener, they told him that they had been married for five years and that for the past two years they had been having some serious problems in their relationship. For example, Rosa said, "I just don't feel special anymore. I feel more like one of Matt's possessions."

Dr. Emener believed Matt and Rosa when they told him that they loved each other very much and wanted to improve their relationship. "One of my problems," Matt said, "is that I am from a very large family in which the men 'owned their women.' I do not want to be a chauvinistic person, but without a doubt I am from a chauvinistic background." Bill believed Matt when he said, "I want to be a loving man and I want to be loving toward Rosa with all my heart. But sometimes I just don't know how."

A related difficulty was that when Matt would do something to try to be loving toward Rosa, she would have difficulty believing his authenticity. For example, she said, "Sometimes I don't know if he really means what he does."

Dr. Emener sketched a diagram for them similar to the one in Figure 18.3. As the couple looked at the diagram, Bill said to them, "One potential difficulty that you might try to avoid is the way in which each of you struggles with accepting each other's loving actions and behaviors. For example, Rosa, when you explained to me what happened when Matt brought some roses home from work, you had difficulty being excited about the flowers because some of your long-term, angry feelings had caught hold of you. And when you did not respond to Matt with the level of appreciation and joy that he was expecting, he also was disappointed. The end result was that both of you felt bad about a very nice thing."

Matt looked at Rosa and said, "Sometimes when I try to do loving things for you and with you, Rosa, you still become upset and angry with me. It would be helpful if sometimes you could just appreciate what I do for you. If I bring you flowers, enjoy the flowers. If I take you to a movie, enjoy the movie."

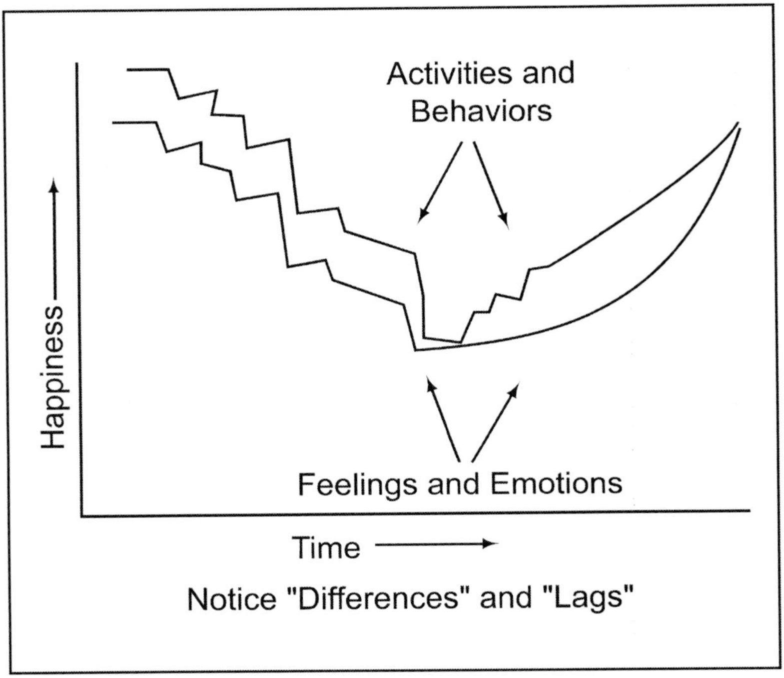

Figure 18.3. Realistic Expectations: Behavior and Emotions

Okay, Matt," Rosa replied, "I will try to do that. I will try to respond to what you do for me, and maybe as time goes on some of my deeper feelings and emotions will change and I will genuinely feel happier about my life and being married to you." As Matt held her in his arms, the two of them began to cry.

In loving relationships, changes in long-term *feelings* will sometimes follow changes in long-term *behaviors*. Just because we change our behavior toward each other today, doesn't mean that our feelings and emotions will immediately change. But if we continue to act lovingly toward each other, chances are that as time goes on we may (again) begin to feel loved by each other.

Don't Expect Immediate Results

As Matt and Rosa experienced, when two individuals have been experiencing long-term relationship difficulties, their feelings about themselves, each other and their relationship tend to be very deep and entrenched. For example, Rosa said to Matt, "You have been shitting on me for the past two years, and just because you have begun to be nice and loving towards me for the past two weeks doesn't mean that I can quickly overcome all of the hurt I have been experiencing for the past two years." If you begin to engage in "new behaviors and activities" with, for, and on behalf of your loved one, don't expect his or her feelings toward themselves, you and your relationship to change over night. Likewise, if your loved one begins to do loving things for you and you appreciate what they are doing yet continue to have less than positive feelings about yourself, them and your relationship, try to be patient with yourself. *Behavior change does not necessarily guarantee emotional change* (thus, for example, the term "dry drunk"). Nonetheless, if you engage in long-term behavior change, feelings and emotions will gradually and slowly come around.

The Downside of an Upswing

Putting things into perspective and looking at your progress over a long period of time can help you (1) appreciate the progress you are making and (2) avoid overreacting to what you may be experiencing in the last day or two. Like the stock market, long-term trends include up and down days. One thing we ask our clients to keep in mind when they reach a plateau or feel stuck in their progress is to consider that they may be in a slump that is part of an overall pattern of progress – the downside of an upswing.

Valerie, a thirty-four-year-old high school Spanish teacher, had been living with Ricardo for over two years and had been talking about getting married, "When suddenly he up and left me!" Over the next five months, Valerie and Dr. Emener had six therapy sessions together. At their last session, when discussing her progress during that five-month period, Bill sketched a diagram similar to the one in Figure 18.4. "Yes, that's it, Dr. Emener. That's what my recovery from Ricardo's leaving me looks like a saw- toothed line that continues to go up."

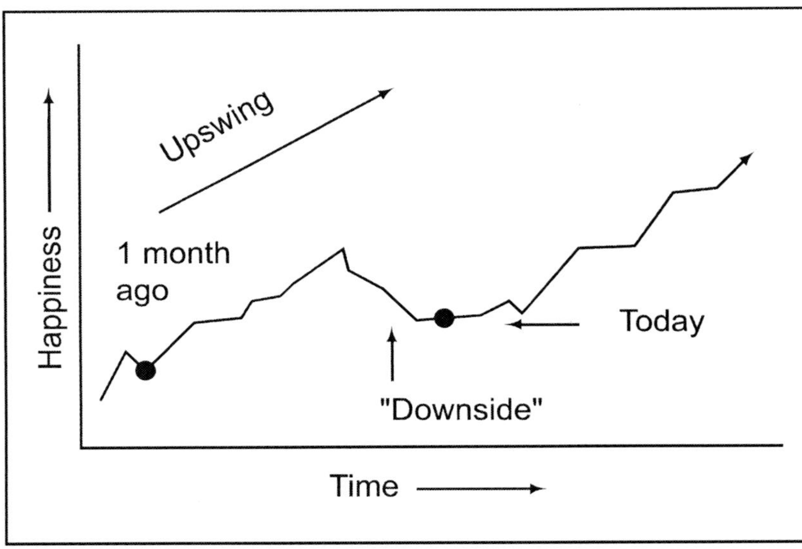

Figure 18.4. The Downside of an Upswing.

As they looked at the diagram, however, Bill said to her, "I suggest that you try to continue to remind yourself, Val, that as long as the line continues going up, you know that you are making progress."

Valerie looked up, smiled and said, "Yes, it has been that way and it is continuing to be that way. As time continues to march onward, my happiness continues to improve, and even though sometimes it appears to be gradual, it is definitely improving. My mother asked me how I was doing and I told her that I have been a little down for the past two days. She instantly began to worry. But I immediately told her not to worry because I was simply on *the downside of an upswing.* I told her that my worst day of this week, today, is still better than my best day a month ago. And as far as I am concerned, that's progress!" Doing what Valerie was doing can be very helpful.

In general, we repeatedly find that it helps clients to focus on the overall trend rather than on the short-term. When you and your loved one are trying to improve your relationship, don't dwell on bad things from your past, focus on the good things in your present.

When to Come Back

Clients with whom we are working frequently ask us, "We have agreed that there is no need for us to schedule another session. But how will I know if or when I need to come back to see you?"

In response, it is not uncommon for us to sketch a diagram similar to the one in Figure 18.5 and say, "We have met for enough sessions

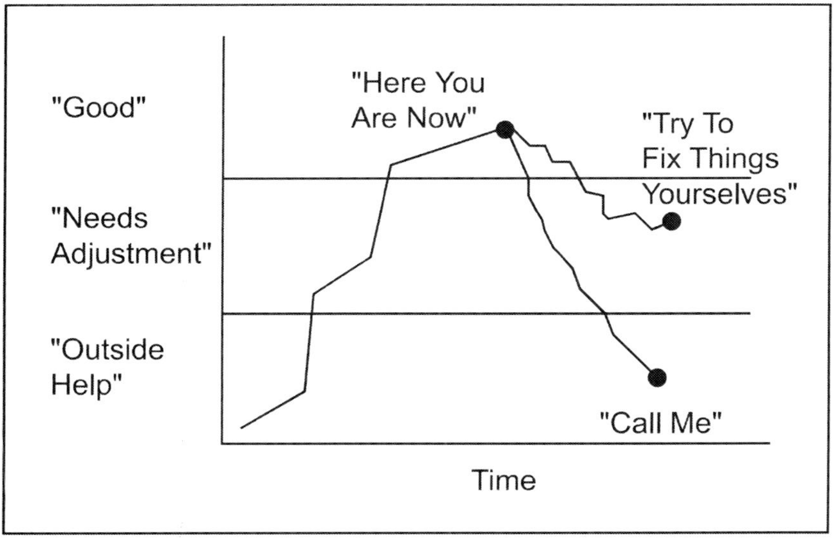

Figure 18.5. When to Come Back.

and I think you will agree that when you first came, you definitely needed some outside help. Over the last several sessions, you were working on your relationship-lifestyle on a daily basis. Nonetheless, it continued to need adjustments and improvements. From what you have been saying today, however, your life has been improving and is now up into the 'good' level and you are deriving much pleasure and joy from your lifestyle and your relationships. Here is where you are now. Therefore, the first recommendation is that you continue doing what you are doing – it indeed appears to be good for you. Keep doing it! If in the future, however, you find your life or your relationships starting to 'need some fixin', try to improve things yourself. As a result of our sessions together you not only improved your lifestyle and your relationships, but you also learned how to improve or fix yourself. Thus, try to help yourselves first! But should your attempts to help yourself not meet with success, then we'll schedule an appointment to get together."

As therapists, we attempt to do two things when working with an individual or a couple: (1) we try to help them improve their individual lives and their relationship; and, (2) we try to help them learn to help themselves so that as time goes on, if they run into a difficulty, they do not have to call us right away. (Again, we want to teach them to fish, not just give them a fish.) We try to help them learn self-help strategies and skills that will help them carry on and continue to improve their lives on their own. "So in other words, Bill," Todd recently to Dr. Emener, "if we start to run into some troubles, we can go back through some of our notes from our sessions, go back through some of the self-help books that you have recommended to us and try to fix things ourselves. However, I also hear you saying that we shouldn't wait to come back to see you as we are on our way to divorce court!" On that note, Dr. Emener, Todd and his wife, all enjoyed a hearty laugh.

* * * * * *

If your car is not running well, it needs fixin', you don't know how to fix it, and you're unhappy with it, driving it and complaining about it won't make it run any better – and it may even get worse.

The only way to make it run better and enjoy it is to get someone who really knows what they're doing to help you fix it.

This also tends to be true for loving relationships.

Epilogue
Reflections and Doorknob Issues

At the end of a counseling, therapy or mediation session, it is not uncommon for two things to occur: (1) the helping professional may reflect on what was discussed and experienced in the session and offer a "last minute thought" or "it may be important for you to remember" kind of statement; and/or (2) the client(s) may offer what we like to think of as a "doorknob issue." These typically are phrased as "One last thing I thought I should mention to you..." or "Oh by the way, I thought you also should know that..." and "Something that I wanted to tell you but forgot was..." After reading the previous eighteen chapters of this book – our own book – we found ourselves reflecting on the book's content in a similar way! We were reminded of some general issues that we felt were important for our readers to remember as you finish this book. Thus, in the first part of this chapter we share with you our reflections. Following this, we offer some brief comments regarding doorknob issues and a request for you to share your doorknob issues with us.

Reflections

The establishment, development and maintenance of a loving relationship are exciting yet intriguing mysteries. In addition to many other considerations, a relationship involves constant attention to competing, juxtaposed values. For example:

1. *Now vs. forever.* A person can look at his or her loving relationship from a perspective of temporality versus a value of eternity: "The most important issue is how we feel about each other at this moment" versus "It is critical for me to feel that this relationship will last forever."
2. *Love vs. friendship (with sex).* One person may decide that unless he or she can experience a deep feeling of love for a significant other, the relationship is not worth having. A different person may take the perspective that "what really matters is that my significant other is my best friend; romance and sex, when they happen, are added rewards."
3. *All or none vs. good enough.* An individual can look at his or her personal happiness, as it interfaces with his or her loving relationship, from a perspective of "Having what you want" versus "Wanting what you have." One individual may say, "I will never stay in a relationship with another person unless he or she is the kind of person I want, and we have the kind of relationship that I want." While another person may say, "The person I am with and my relationship with him/her may not be what I want, but I am willing to do whatever I can do to learn to want what I have."
4. *It's about me vs. it's about us.* A person may look at his or her being in a loving relationship from a position of "wanting my own individual autonomy and freedom" versus a position of "wanting a connected, interdependent and committed loving relationship with another person."
5. *Pain vs. emotional investment.* One person may see relationship struggles or failure as sources of intolerable pain that seem impossible to overcome. A different person may have a "no regrets" perspective that every relationship carries with it the risk of failure, but as long as the majority of experiences are good, it is worth the ride.

Of course with each of these juxtaposed value sets, a person can hold an *either/or* attitude or a *both* attitude. And as one uncovers the delicate and intricate root system beneath most loving relationships, the mystery becomes more mysterious. "Sally and I are very successful *workmates* as well as wonderful and fun loving *playmates*, but I wonder if we ever could be *soulmates*?" Greg once asked Dr. Emener.

"I don't know," Dr. Emener replied. "Do you have to be good workmates and good playmates in order to be soulmates? Or put another way, could two people be good soulmates yet not be good workmates or good playmates?"

After pondering his retort, Greg said, "I don't know. Those are intriguing questions. It would be interesting and helpful for us to discuss them." Dr. Emener responded, "That indeed would be interesting, Greg, but in terms of helpfulness it may be more important for you and Sally to discuss them."

You may have noticed that throughout this book, on numerous occasions when individuals came to see one of us about a relationship issues, we eventually talked at length about them – the person himself or herself. Many of our clients realize this. When you think about it, it makes sense. In many ways, a loving relationship is like a reflecting pool or a mirror. It vividly reveals to us many aspects about ourselves. Intuitively, it is reasonable to believe constructs such as:

My ability to trust another individual is an indication of the extent to which I can trust myself.

If I am not comfortable with myself, then I probably will have difficulties

feeling and being comfortable with another person and my relationship with that person, and

My ability to love another person is an indication of the extent to which I can love myself.

As a rule of thumb, whenever we sense a difficulty with a significant other in our own lives, the first question we ask ourselves is: "What is going on within me?"

Every human being is unique in a myriad of ways – different from anyone else. Moreover, every human being is constantly changing. Thus, every loving relationship is unique and constantly changing. What may appear "right" or "good" for another couple may not be "right" or "good" for you. What may be working for you and your loved one today may not work tomorrow. Understanding and appreciating your uniqueness and differences, and remaining flexible, postured for and attentive to constant change, are critical aspects of "good" loving relationships.

In view of these latter considerations, commitment – a critical consideration of any loving relationship – thus entails numerous, important and finer distinctions. Let's remember: change is inevitable. To wit, the following are some illustrations of commitment statements people make to each other: some are functionally consistent and some are functionally inconsistent:

Functionally Inconsistent	**Functionally Consistent**
"I love you just the way you are. I hope you will never change. Promise me you will never change."	*"I love you the way you are today and am committed to being with you as each of us changes over time."*
"We have such a beautiful relationship. I don't want it to ever change."	*"I am committed to working with you so we can enjoy our ever-changing relationship."*
"I want to marry you because I know our relationship, just the way it is, will last forever."	*"I am committed to doing whatever I can to keep our relationship alive, vibrant, meaningful and loving for as long as possible."*

As one of Dr. Emener's clients suggested to his wife, "I'm not worried about our marriage lasting forever. If we can continue to enjoy a meaningful and fulfilling relationship, which is what I'm committed to, our marriage will take care of itself."

Being committed to a relationship and being committed to a particular form of a relationship are two different things. For example, when two individuals first meet and begin seeing each other seriously their relationship has a particular form. In the early stages of their marriage, their relationship takes on a different form. When two married individuals have demanding careers, three or four children, two cars and a big house, their relationship again takes on another form. In the autumn of their years when their children are grown and out on their own and it is just the two of them at the dinner table each evening, their relationship again reveals another form. As one of our mothers, Mrs. Emener, experienced when she became a widow and the other's mother, Mrs. Lambos, is experiencing now, even though their husbands had died, their relationships with them from a spiritual perspective remain very much alive. The only things that changed were the forms.

True loving relationships never end, they just change their form.

An issue of *The St. Petersburg Times* many years ago carried a syndicated column written by Regina Brett entitled, "The Former Lover You Never Forget." Ms. Brett beautifully described the experiences many of us never seem to forget – the former husband or wife, boyfriend or girlfriend, or lover "who has never left us." After detailing her "Corvette summer" with him twenty years prior, she concluded:

> *Even though a decade has passed, on some level I never stopped loving him. I knew we would always feel something for each other, something beyond chemistry and contempt.*
>
> *For better, for worse, he reached inside of me and rearranged the workings of my heart so I could love someone else.*
>
> *It turns out he didn't really break my heart after all. He only made it stronger.*

Being committed to a relationship indeed appears to be much more important than being committed to a particular form of a relationship.

What is a relationship? Good question. And just when we think we are in a position to answer that question definitively, we read another book, talk to another person or experience something new, and our conceptualization changes. In many ways, we then feel like we have to start all over again. It is often said, "The journey is as important as or even more important than the destination." Maybe discovering what a loving relationship is, constitutes the goal of our journey. Similarly, there is no perfect relationship. Just when things appear to be going great, something happens. A "good" relationship is something that needs constant attention. It is akin to heating a house in the wintertime. No house is perfectly insulated from the elements. A good thermostat monitors the temperature and signals the heater when it needs to kick in to heat the house. When the house is warm again, the heater shuts off. But eventually the temperature will drop and the cycle continues. When something goes awry or something interferes with a relationship, the two individuals hopefully become aware of it and attend to the problem in order to return their relationship to the level of comfort and meaningfulness they both want and enjoy. Fittingly, as in the analogy of the house, the cycle continues. As we have said many times throughout this book, it is the process of the relationship that is important, not just the outcome. Like happiness, a good loving relationship is not a station you arrive at, it is a manner of traveling.

In the process of developing a good loving relationship, "you and I" also becomes "us." And typically, that does not happen until "You" and "I" are no longer exclusive, independent realities. In a meaningful relationship, we find the comingling of intertwined lives, the genuine sharing of fears, wants and desires, the simultaneous struggling for togetherness and oneness, the preservation of two unique, individual lives in the presence of a shared relationship lifestyle, and the simultaneous awareness of, appreciation of, and respect for our relationship's beginning, temporal existence and never-ending essence. We do not "have" a relationship. Rather, a relationship is an interdependent process of being – a process that translates into, or "becomes," a relationship. In this sense, the term "relationship" is not just a noun or an adjective – it is also a verb.

A relationship involves many risks. And sometimes the biggest risk is our risk of freedom. When given further thought, nonetheless, it is only the free person who can take risks in the first place. If you are free, then you can risk freedom. But if you truly are free, then you may not actually be risking anything. *Freedom is not a place in life – it is a manner of being.* And from a spiritual or philosophical perspective, one can be free no matter where one is. Thus, it is no wonder that some people will say, "I am free *and* I am in a wonderful, enjoyable and meaningful loving relationship."

Doorknob Issues

We assume that now that you have finished reading this book and bounced its ideas, principles and considerations off of your life and experiences, you have some ideas, principles and considerations of your own that the book has not addressed. We would greatly appreciate knowing what your doorknob issues are for us. Thus, please take a few moments of your time to share them with us. You probably have some good suggestions and criticisms that we would all benefit from knowing.

Please write to us and share:

William G. Emener, Ph.D., CRC
Distinguished Research Professor
Department of Rehabilitation Counseling
College of Arts and Sciences
University of South Florida
Tampa, Florida 33620
Email: emener@cas.usf.edu

William A. Lambos, Ph.D.
Licensed Clinical Neuropsychologist
Cognitive Neuro Sciences, Inc.
5201 W. Kennedy Blvd.
Suite 615
Tampa, Florida 33609
Email: walambos@eegscience.com

Thank-you!
Bill and Bill

* * * * * *

If all of our yesterdays are dreams of happiness,
and if all of our tomorrows are visions of hope,
then our today is not a preparation for our life together,
it is our life together.

ABOUT THE AUTHORS

WILLIAM G. EMENER, Ph.D., CRC, is a Distinguished Research Professor in, and the former Chair of, the Department of Rehabilitation and Mental Health Counseling, and a former Associate Dean, at the University of South Florida, Tampa. Additionally, he has worked as a rehabilitation counselor and supervisor as well as a rehabilitation counselor educator and program director at Murray State University, Florida State University and the University of Kentucky. Dr. Emener's publications and writings include seven research monographs, twenty-three books, numerous book chapters in twenty-two different books, over fifty nonpublished professional papers, over 100 authored/coauthored articles in seventeen different professional refereed journals, and over a hundred professional papers presented at professional association meetings. He also has been an editor/coeditor of over twenty special publications (including the *American Rehabilitation Counseling Association Newsletter*) and was Coeditor of the *Journal of Applied Rehabilitation Counseling* from 1978-1982. While many of his books have been textbooks and professional readings, his more recent books are pop-psych books, self-help books, and contemporary romance novels.

Dr. Emener's recognitions include being a recipient of the 1980 *American Rehabilitation Counseling Association Research Award*, a recipient of the National Rehabilitation Administration Association's 1982 *The Advancement of Research in Rehabilitation Administration Award*, and in 1988 was honored with the title of *Fellow* by the

American Psychological Association. He was the 1983-1984 President of the National Rehabilitation Administration Association and the 1989-1990 President of the National Council on Rehabilitation Education.

For 33 years, Dr. Emener also had a part-time private practice as a licensed psychologist in Florida and Kentucky, with specializations in employee assistance programs, marriage/couples counseling and addictions/substance abuse counseling. A former college basketball player, Bill's hobbies and interests now include playing his guitar and piano, fishing, boating, scuba diving, motorcycle riding, slow pitch softball, reading contemporary novels, playing golf, and occasionally walking a sandy beach with a six pack.

WILLIAM A. LAMBOS, Ph.D., is Executive Partner and President of Cognitive Neuro Sciences, Inc., (CNS), a multi-site integrated healthcare practice with headquarters in Tampa, Florida. CNS's approach to health care is based on a combined philosophy of wellness, self-efficacy and self-regulation, and healthy interpersonal dynamics. Dr. Lambos possesses a post-doctoral certification in Neuropsychology from Fielding Graduate University, master's and doctoral degrees in Experimental Psychology from McMaster University, a master's degree in Rehabilitation and Mental Health Counseling, and has satisfied the coursework requirements for a post-masters certificate in Marriage and Family Therapy, both of the latter from the University of South Florida. In addition, he is certified as a family mediator by the Supreme Court of the State of Florida and provides dispute resolution services in divorce, childcare and healthcare quality assurance cases.

Dr. Lambos' recognitions include certifications in EEG-biofeedback and QEEG analysis by both the Biofeedback Certification Institute of America (BCIA) and The Society for the Advancement of Brain Analysis (SABA), on whose Board he sits.

While Dr. Lambos' B.A. degree from Vassar, with honors, and membership in Phi Beta Kappa and his publications in scientific journals clearly reveal his revered acumen and scholarly prowess, his quick wit, hearty laugh and overall enjoyment of life are among the reasons he enjoys a reputation of "a life of the party" kind of person.

SUBJECT INDEX

D

E

F

G

H

I

Y